THE
CASE
FOR
MODERN
MAN

BOOKS BY CHARLES FRANKEL:

The Faith of Reason

The Bear and the Beaver

BOOKS EDITED BY CHARLES FRANKEL:

Rousseau's Social Contract

The Uses of Philosophy: An Irwin Edman Reader

THE
CASE
FOR
MODERN
MAN.

BY CHARLES FRANKEL

 HARPER & BROTHERS, NEW YORK

THE CASE FOR MODERN MAN

Library of Congress catalog card number: 55-10693

TO CARL

CONTENTS

I. A PORTION OF REASON   1

II. IN SEARCH OF A PHILOSOPHY OF HISTORY   9

III. LIBERALISM AND THE IMAGINATION OF DISASTER   23

IV. THE ANXIETY TO BELIEVE   45

V. LIBERAL SOCIETY AND ULTIMATE VALUES   74

VI. THE REDISCOVERY OF SIN   85

VII. CAN HISTORY TELL THE TRUTH?   117

VIII. THE PROGRESS OF THE HUMAN MIND   146

IX. MR. TOYNBEE'S TRANSFIGURATION OF HISTORY   164

X. THE REVOLUTION OF MODERNITY   196

ACKNOWLEDGMENTS   211

NOTES   213

INDEX   237

AUTHOR'S NOTE

A word should be said about the use of footnotes in this book. Where a footnote seemed not to interrupt the exposition, but to carry it along, I have placed it at the bottom of the page. But for the most part, I have preferred to keep the main theme before the reader and to put side issues at the back of the book. For similar reasons, I have chosen not to use the small, but distracting, numbers that warn (or tempt) a reader to turn to the back of the book for more information. The reader who wishes to see what support, amplification, or qualification I have to add to what I say in the body of the book should turn, after reading a chapter, to the section in the footnotes which is devoted to it. He will find the passages to which the notes refer identified by page number and key phrase.

C. F.

THE
CASE
FOR
MODERN
MAN

I.

A PORTION OF REASON

> Listen to the sad story of mankind, who like
> children lived until I gave them understanding
> and a portion of reason.
> —*Prometheus Bound*

PROMETHEUS, so the myth goes, stole the secret of fire from the gods and gave it to the human race. From this act of defiance men received understanding, reason, and all the arts of human civilization—the use of metals, knowledge of the seasons and the stars, mathematics and music, history and poetry. This book is concerned with the contemporary effort to renounce the gift of Prometheus—to belittle the portion of reason man has.

It is an episode which is as yet unfinished, and its outcome cannot be predicted. It depends on the estimate we ourselves make of our powers, and on our decisions as to the goals we wish to seek. Most of all, it depends on what we think of the hopes with which the modern era began. For three hundred years or more the Western world has been the scene of a revolution which has become a world revolution. It is the revolution which made the present era aware that it is modern—impatient

1

of received dispensations, proud of its enlightenment and powers, and convinced that the world is not the scene for the chastisement of man but the raw material for his arts and his intelligence. The prophets who tell us that this revolution of modernity has been a failure are many. They say that the disasters of recent history have demonstrated that the human reason is the prey of darker forces or higher mysteries, that men cannot be trusted to choose their values for themselves, that history follows a pattern which human beings cannot understand or master. When Prometheus gave us a portion of reason, they say, he was not our benefactor but our tempter.

This book is a defense of the revolution of modernity. It is an attempt to show that these doom-filled prophecies are unwarranted, and that the hopes with which the modern era began are still the hopes by which we may steer our course. It is a project with a twofold purpose. Its first purpose is to see what a sober man can still believe about human history and destiny, what ideas he can reasonably employ, and what hopes he can reasonably permit himself in his political faiths and public actions. Its second purpose is to break a path toward a concrete social philosophy—toward an image of a better society, and a strategy for attaining it, which will recommend itself to the imaginations of liberal men.

If I wished to follow the present fashion I might say, therefore, that this book is offered as an antidote to anxiety. But I have no new nostrums to propose, and no paths to peace of mind or contentment of spirit. Most of these, it seems to me, do not bring peace to the mind but only sleep. They confuse morals with morale, and self-control with self-hypnosis. It seems to me perfectly plain that most of our personal anxieties and individual uncertainties are rooted in quite objective social disorders; and if we do not know what to believe, or what to believe in, the reason is not the turmoil within but the fog outside. To see our

2

way through this fog we need social ideas, not personal therapy.

But if we do not know how to diagnose our social ailments or how to proceed to deal with them, if we do not know where to turn to get a grip on our affairs or what dimly humane outcome might possibly be seen in them, it is in part because the ideas we have inherited for interpreting the historical period in which we live are discredited. We are confused not simply about what is going on around us but about the intellectual equipment we have at our disposal. Old models and old ideals do not apply; we are being told, indeed, that they never applied.

At least some of this confusion, it seems to me, is unnecessary and avoidable. It is a manufactured confusion, the result of conscious distortion and of unconscious bad thinking. It is the result to a very great extent of a systematic and massive assault by intellectuals, by philosophers, historians, sociologists, and literary men, on the intellectual tradition which has stood behind the most splendid achievements of modern man. This book is written in the hope of clearing up some of this confusion. It is an effort to get greater clarity about the ideas we can use for interpreting the present moment in history and for turning it from a fatality with which we must live into an opportunity we can exploit. In the process of considering these ideas it is quite possible that certain persons will find some greater serenity of spirit. But this will be a fortunate by-product of our inquiry. For I am interested in these ideas not as means of personal salvation but as instruments of social action.

This book is necessarily an effort to take stock of that body of ideas and ideals which has been known, with some looseness, as "Liberalism." Most of us grew up in an intellectual climate in which the prevailing winds blew favorably for a number of beliefs. We thought, for example, that the existence of a variety of social interests and values was legitimate; more than legitimate, we thought it desirable. Fixed distinctions of class or

3

status were looked upon as gratuitous. When there were conflicts of social interest, or disagreements between social classes, something like a rational compromise was considered possible. To aid in this the existence of a kind of general solvent of prejudice and selfishness—call it good will, or social conscience, or public spirit—was taken for granted. Scientific methods were considered applicable to human affairs, and the best means for bringing these affairs closer to human desires. Most of all, the likelihood of human progress within the durable framework of parliamentary government, civil liberty, and enlightened public opinion was assumed.

These beliefs were never universally shared. But they set the standards of public discussion, took some of the bitterness out of political debate, and sustained the hopes of most of those who permitted themselves to have any hopes. They were celebrated in our public ceremonies and implicit in our public manners. If they did not always provide clear-cut answers to all our problems, they provided the first questions that controlled our social thinking and the first impulses that went into our social action. And behind them was a set of half-articulated attitudes and expectations about man's nature and history, about the durable factors in himself and his environment on which he might depend, and on the ideals it was reasonable and most important for him to pursue in his effort to control his destiny.

This outlook on history and these ideas, we are told now, are the main cause of our present unhappy situation. They are responsible for modern man's most disastrous failures, it is said, and even for the contemporary panic of illiberalism. All our present uncertainties come to a focus in the decline of these ideas and of the vision of human history which stood behind them; and the general validity of these ideas and this vision, their relevance to our present trials, their usefulness and their prospects, are the first things with which we must come

4

to terms in any assessment of the intellectual materials, or of the store of tradition and aspiration, which we have at our present disposal. On its intellectual side, the crisis of our time is a crisis in our interpretation of history; in particular, it is a crisis in the attitude we ought to take toward the liberal interpretation of modern history.

In this book we shall examine what has been said about this interpretation of history by its most serious and representative critics. The men whose philosophies we shall consider—Jacques Maritain, Reinhold Niebuhr, Karl Mannheim, and Arnold Toynbee—speak not only for themselves, but for a host of others. I have chosen them because their criticisms of the liberal view of history are peculiarly thoroughgoing and peculiarly typical. They speak not only for those who have been able to articulate their suspicions and discontents with the liberal interpretation of history, but for the inarticulate, but massive, feeling that we are at the end of the liberal era, and that our future lies along a radically different path from the one that we have been following. Each of these men attacks the liberal interpretation of history at one of its key points. Professor Maritain condemns it for its espousal of an experimental attitude in morals; Mr. Niebuhr rejects its faith in human perfectibility; Mannheim denies its belief in the objectivity of human reason; Mr. Toynbee holds that the entire modern era, with its attempt to build a civilization on secular and humanistic grounds, has broken the fundamental laws of history, and has been guilty of the sin of pride. All of them are convinced that the liberal interpretation of history is itself a major reason for our present troubles; and when we put their criticisms together, they constitute a rejection of the liberal vision of human history almost in its entirety. In examining these philosophies we are subjecting to a full-dress reappraisal the fundamental ideas with which liberal men entered on their present trials.

5

I believe that these liberal ideas, notwithstanding all the criticisms that are being made of them, are essentially right—right in their logic, right in their estimate of what is possible, and right in their estimate of what is desirable. At the present moment, with its emphasis upon ideological correctness, it is probably necessary to say, however, that I do not regard the view I shall develop in this book as anything like an official canon of liberalism. I am not trying to lay down an exclusive definition of what it means to be "liberal" or "modern," or to draw up a party line for liberals. A liberal society or a liberal social movement cannot impose any world view or any interpretation of human history on its members. My effort is more modest, and, I hope, more useful. It is an attempt to formulate an outlook which, I believe, expresses the working principles of practical liberalism, and which will help those with liberal inclinations to see farther, to move with less lost effort, and to take command of their problems in a systematic way. I do not insist that every man or every liberal share my point of view, and I am willing to grant that more than one road leads to Rome. But the road I describe, I cannot help but believe, leads there most quickly and most efficiently.

This book, therefore, is a book—to put it somewhat ominously —about "the philosophy of history." It is a book about the theories of human nature and social organization we ought to adopt, the ideals it is legitimate and possible to seek, and the social strategies we should employ in trying to deal with our present difficulties. No doubt, "the philosophy of history" has an arrogant sound about it. It can be, as it has been, an excuse for banalities dressed up as higher truths, for doubtful and irresponsible speculations, for plain falsehoods and for fancy nonsense. There has been much that is a transparent dodge in the effort to descry "the meaning of history"—much whistling in the dark, much effort to cushion the shock of disaster by showing that parochial values have a cosmic guarantee behind them, much attempt to soften the blows of fate

6

by the promise that, despite all appearances, history, even the blood bath of history, is in the process of washing everything clean. Much philosophy of history has only been a way of saying dishonestly what Willie says to Joe honestly in one of Bill Mauldin's battlefield cartoons: "What do y'mean this ain't the most important hole in the world? I'm in it!"

But there is another side too. In looking for enduring values, a philosophy of history offers a larger context for the measurement of current problems and temporary solutions. It gives us a chance deliberately to erect safeguards so that basic values will not be lost in dealing with emergencies, so that we will not needlessly complicate other problems in our preoccupation with just one problem, urgent as it may be. A philosophy of history offers us a long view and a hard view. It gives us a chance to keep first things first, and lifts political action above the level of expediency and opportunism. For the attempt to develop a philosophy of history has been a way in which men have tried to make a sober and circumspect appraisal of the historical resources available to them, the limits upon their powers, and the alternatives open to them. It has been an attempt to deal with problems, not in isolation from one another but in some systematic way, to take account of long-range considerations, to safeguard primary ideals, to pick out the most important variables in the social process. A philosophy of history can be a way, at once, of making the social imagination more responsible by pinning it down to what is immovable, and of making it freer and more flexible by giving it a larger vision of human possibilities. It is a theory of how things get done in history, and of what men can make of their history. As such, it is an implicit strategy of social action, and it can be a sober prelude to the development of a coherent social program.

Such a philosophy of history stood behind the liberal ideas that once sustained us. The great names that are attached to it are those of Voltaire, Condorcet, and John Stuart Mill; its greatest

7

achievement in the writing of history is probably Gibbon's *Decline and Fall of the Roman Empire*. But it was a philosophy of history which had no single canonical statement, which was sometimes fuzzy around the edges, and ambiguous about some of its most fundamental conceptions. If we look at the whole array of philosophies of history which have adorned (or littered) the history of the West, this liberal philosophy occupies only a very small corner. It is singularly uncharacteristic of philosophies of history in general, and it never had the field even partly to itself. But it is nevertheless the philosophy of history which has differentiated modern Western society most completely from other societies, a belief in certain social techniques and ideals which has most clearly set off the modern world from its predecessors, and Western Europe and America from Eastern Europe and the Orient. It sustained the most characteristic hopes of modern man, and helped him to his most splendid triumphs.

It is my purpose in this book to re-examine the credentials of this philosophy, and to do so by considering the most representative and influential indictments which have been drawn up against it. Liberal men now look out on the world, their imaginations jaundiced and dispirited, doubtful about the fundamental categories in which to view their past, uncertain about the way to implement their hopes for the future, even uncertain about what hopes to have. I hope that this book can do something to revive that jaundiced imagination, and to restore, in a criticized form, the ideas and ideals which once nourished it.

II.

IN SEARCH OF
A PHILOSOPHY OF HISTORY

IT IS HARD to know the reasons for the American suspicion of philosophy. It may be that it is only a passing incident in the history of a society that has been on the move, a society that has had plenty of room for error and waste, and so has not had to be finicky about its methods or its moral economy. It may be that it shows only good sense, considering how irrelevant, pedantic, and solemn much philosophizing has been. Or it may be, as Hegel suggested, that the owl of Minerva appears only at dusk, and that it is only recently that Americans have had reason to believe that the dusk of their civilization is at hand.

It may even be that the whole notion that Americans have been more suspicious of philosophy than others is an exaggeration. Bertrand Russell has observed that the British are noted for their scorn of philosophy and for the distinction of their philosophers. If Americans distrust philosophy, they share this distrust with the rest of the human race, and are members of an ancient and honorable company which has included a good many philosophers themselves.

Nevertheless, when all accounts are drawn up, it is plain that Americans have had some peculiarly American reasons for fighting a running battle with philosophy. Living in an open society, they have been suspicious of attempts to find unchanging conditions in nature or fixed goals for man. Living in a democratic society, they have resented the effort to make wisdom into a professional specialty. And living in a practical society based on a successful technology, they have been inclined to feel that the ultimate problems solve themselves—or dissolve themselves— when men concentrate on the penultimate ones.

If philosophy in general has met with difficulties, however, the philosophy of history has had an even harder row to hoe. The philosophy of history has met with indifference and worse in America because the American attitude toward philosophy has here been reinforced by the ambivalent American attitude toward history. At one extreme, Americans have been very interested in history, trying to recapture between the covers of novels or the walls of museums images of the past which they have been just as busily erasing in their daily lives. At the other extreme, Americans have been convinced that they are bound by no inherited precedents, and that they can make the past roll over and do tricks. Henry Ford, who also built a museum at Dearborn to preserve the record of his own past, once shocked us by expressing this attitude straight out. "History is bunk," he said, or is alleged to have said. And whether he said it or not, the words speak for something deep in him and deep in American experience. For American history began symbolically with a Declaration of Independence, and it was, among other things, a declaration of independence from the past, from hereditary authority and his-torically enshrined privilege. And American history has been made by successive generations of immigrants and children of immigrants, whose main drive has been to escape the past, and whose style in life has been defined by the desire to break away

10

from the old country, the old folks, and the old ways. American suspicion of history has reflected an indifference to what has gone before. It has been a response to the mobility and opportunities of American life, an expression of the conviction that nothing in the past could serve as a model for what America was doing or was capable of doing.

When we look back on this record, and when we consider how deep its roots go in the American soil, the sudden upsurge of interest which is now taking place in America in philosophical reflections on history must be put down as one of the more striking aspects of the present intellectual scene. It suggests that something fundamentally new is emerging in the pattern of American life. Philosophy is reviving in America, and it is reviving mainly in the shape of philosophies of history. Our phrases are the phrases of philosophers of history, old and new—"Crossroads of History," "The End of an Era," "A Time of Troubles," "The Illusion of Progress." They resound from the pulpit, echo in editorials, and whisper between the lines of sober estimates of the business cycle. The novels of contemporary experience, with their parade of bare, uninterpreted events, of actions that are meaningful, at best, only as elements in a struggle for personal integrity, suggest how bitterly men are reacting to a world from which a sense of direction seems to have vanished. The revived quest for supernatural absolutes, the search for "new frontiers" in society and morals, the wistful turning to the wisdom of the Orient, the vogue of seers and prophets—all suggest how deeply the need is felt for a sense that we are on the move in a definite direction, and that there is a purpose and objective behind the flux of events. Even our fear of Marxism, one cannot help but suspect, reflects our interest in it, our nagging feeling that it is one step ahead of us in providing what we all need—some sense of where we are going and how we are to get there.

Even professional philosophers and historians, who are not

11

always the most finely tuned instruments for registering each tremor in the popular mind, have been affected. There is a long tradition in modern philosophy which has looked on history as a low-grade intellectual discipline. There is an equally powerful tradition among modern historians which has looked on philosophy as the lazy man's substitute for digging for the facts. To bring philosophy and history together in a philosophy of history has seemed to both philosophers and historians like trying to mix oil with water. But American philosophers are now treating the philosophy of history as if it were a serious subject. And American historians are increasingly engaged in ruminative re-examinations of their methods and purposes in writing history, and are looking with cautious interest at philosophies of history like Mr. Toynbee's. Self-consciously and diffidently, but insistently, philosophers and historians are asking the questions that philosophers of history have traditionally asked: What is most important in history? Is it ideas or faith, technology or great men, property systems or geography? Can man control his destiny? If so, by what means? And for what purpose? Does history have a meaning? What is the place of our own besetting dilemmas and tenderest aspirations in the grand sequence of human affairs? And these are the questions also being asked by men who are neither professional philosophers nor historians.

What does all this mean? Why has a pragmatic and prosperous people, enamored of technology and quick results, suddenly shown such a softness for speculation about the distant destination of mankind? When we consider the deep social and psychological currents which have run against such speculation in America, how can we explain our present disturbance of spirit about the meaning of human history or the laws that govern its movements? Why the urgency with which we are trying to locate our present situation in the design of history, and human history itself in a larger design?

The simple and encompassing reason, plainly, is that we have lost our historical bearings. The most obvious purpose of a philosophy of history is to provide a map of events. It lays down the boundaries by which we mark off one epoch from another, estimate the direction of events, and measure their pace and importance. It picks out the crucial landmarks by which we can chart our course and tells us something about the lay of the land so that we can choose our destinations. It was a philosophy of history, for example, which told the men of the Middle Ages that they lived in a true middle age between the revelation of God's plan for man and the final execution of His judgment; it was another philosophy of history which taught modern men to mark off historic eras from one another in terms of their modes of production and property systems. And when new philosophies of history emerge in any considerable number, it is a sign that old paths have been blocked and old destinations foreclosed. The old distinctions—say between "capitalism" and "socialism"—no longer clarify the alternatives before men. The old variables which were considered decisive—say the economic system—no longer seem to make the important difference—say between having civil liberty and not having it—in which men are interested. And the old estimate of the "meaning" of history no longer indicates the old values that are threatened or the new possibilities that have emerged.

To ask about the sources of this historical disorientation is, of course, to ask about the sources of our deepest discontents. The first and most obvious reason is that America has emerged from its historic isolation from world affairs and into that international diplomacy which is only a continuation of war by other means. We are historically disoriented because, for what is really the first time in our history, we have the daily sensation of living in a world full of enemies. A habit which is second nature to members of other cultures is still a new experience to us—the habit

13

of looking out on a world in which peace, security, and the permanence of our civilization are by no means among the assured things of life. And so, worried as we are about the threats to our culture, we have become aware that all cultures are mortal, and are turning to questions about the broad conditions that govern the rise and fall of civilization in general. This is the classic context in which philosophies of history have been born: doubts about the permanence of a given culture lead to questions about the permanence of any of man's achievements.

Furthermore, in emerging from its historic isolationism, America has emerged from its sense of being isolated from history, of not having to share the burdens of the past. Americans have been getting their noses rubbed in the past. They have had to recognize the past as a reality persisting in the present, a limit upon the things they can do abroad and even at home. And they have had not simply to take history more seriously, but to look for a new point of view toward history. For as the American sphere of action has become world-wide, it has become apparent that a merely American, or even Western, view of the issues that are at stake simply will not do. The philosophies of history which have been speaking for "the meeting of East and West" have been responses to this situation. They have been attempts to provide us with what might be called a metaphysics of global diplomacy, a sort of philosophic Esperanto, which might enable us to speak intelligibly to the rest of the human race.

There are those among us who have been looking too, it should be plain, for something more than just an intelligible universal language. They have been looking for a persuasive language, for an instrument of world propaganda as well as an instrument of world understanding. They point out that our enemies confront us with something peculiarly new and frightening—a fully developed and highly explicit philosophy of history which represents one of the strongest weapons in their arsenal; and they argue that

14

we need a philosophy of history of our own if we are to compete with our enemies in what has been called with such remarkable imprecision "the battle for men's minds." Philosophies of history have traditionally served purposes of this kind. They have been, among other things, rhetorics of persuasion, ways of backing up old social systems or new social programs, of converting men to new allegiances or making them firmer in old ones. Philosophies of history, like Saint Augustine's, or Herbert Spencer's, or Karl Marx's, have informed men that they have no other alternative but to select the specific program offered to them; they have made men feel that in seeking their interests they were also doing their duty; they have shown men that their individual actions serve an historic purpose and that their personal ambitions are inadvertently part of a larger design. Philosophies of history have made men feel that their cherished values are backed up by the full push and pressure of historical laws. They have indicated that certain selected groups of men—a race, or a nation, or an economic class, or an occupational group—are the peculiar carriers of these values. And so they have given men the psychological assurance necessary to permit them to make decisive or dangerous choices, and to commit themselves to social movements with a minimum of reservations.

And they have provided, besides, a group of evocative symbols—words and phrases, great events in the past, great men, great decisions—around which collective feelings are generated and focused, and which give a social movement a degree of cohesiveness and internal morale for which the rational recognition of common interests is a poor substitute. Such symbols are triggers for the memory and imagination: they evoke images of what men are striving for, and set off memories of the effort and suffering already invested in the cause. Whatever its intellectual ingredients may or may not be, a philosophy of history can provide a sense of continuity and of an adventure shared: it converts

15

a social program into a mission and turns co-operation for a common purpose into comradeship. Perhaps no other products of the human mind have had such large and immediate consequences in history. And it is plain that a large part of our present interest in finding a philosophy of history is not so much intellectual as rhetorical, not so much an effort to diagnose our problems as it is to sell ourselves to others.

But one cannot help but suspect that there is something more than just an ordinary propagandistic purpose behind our present attempts to see history large. If we are trying to convince others, we are also trying to reassure ourselves. There is a new note, a peculiar combination of malaise and audacity, of ultimate doubts and ultimate dogmatizing, in the reflections on history of men like Mr. Niebuhr and Mr. Toynbee, or Professor Northrop and Professor Sorokin. They are responding to a major revolution in the balance of world cultures—the emergence of East European and Oriental civilizations to a level of parity with the West. Western culture is no longer clearly in the driver's seat; and our habitual perspectives on history have been shaken at their base as a result.

It has not been possible for a long time, of course, for informed men to regard their own culture as the only model of civilization, or as the heir to all mankind's hopes. But it is easy to forget that the cultural relativism of past generations was itself a relative thing—the attitude of men who never really doubted for a moment that their own society had an assured future. The idea of the relativity of Western culture, of its limited validity for others, was an instrument mainly for teaching the West tolerance of others. But we can now only hope that others will be tolerant of us, and the relativism with which our present reflections on history seem to begin is something quite different, and much more radical. It is an attempt not simply to look at history equitably or to recognize the legitimate differences between men; it is an attempt to

16

repair our own limitations, to stabilize our own culture, by rising to a higher synthesis—a truly universal culture—which will absorb and transcend the differences between men. And it begins by rejecting principles which have been fundamental in our intellectual tradition since at least the time of Voltaire.

In this respect, our present concern with philosophies of history is not unlike that with which "the philosophy of history" as a subject bearing a distinctive name first arose. The term "philosophy of history" seems first to have been used by Voltaire, who wished to distinguish his own version of the history of man from that of Bishop Bossuet, whose seventeenth-century *Discourse on Universal History* had provided the regnant theological interpretation of the nature and meaning of human history. Voltaire's criticism of Bossuet was that this putative "universal history" was in fact and at best the history of a small segment of the human race, living on a corner of the European peninsula jutting out from the Asian land mass; and it was, moreover, an interpretation of the history of all mankind written from the point of view of a special religious revelation vouchsafed only to this small portion of mankind, and unintelligible to any who did not share in it. In place of this sectarian interpretation, Voltaire proposed a *philosophic* view of history, based on principles of universal reason and applicable on a basis of equality to all civilizations, East and West. To see history without provincialism, to see all men and all societies under the same unchanging laws, responding to the same universal passions, beset by the same problems and searching in different ways for the same goals, and to understand all this without the help of a sectarian revelation and without benefit of clergy—this was to have a philosophy of history. Voltaire's philosophy of history was a reaction to the first great shock of impact on the European mind of the new science and of expanded contacts with the rest of the world. And our current concern with philosophies of history is in part a response to the second

17

great shock which the Western mind has suffered, when the rest of the world has risen to equality with the West.

It is easy now to see, or at any rate to say, that eighteenth-century historians like Voltaire talked a better game than they played, that they responded to the shock of contact with other cultures by absorbing other men and other ways of life into their own habitual categories. There can be no doubt that in their histories and travelers' tales Chinese sages sound like French *bons vivants,* Polynesian natives like readers of Erasmus, and old Romans like latter-day Whigs. But in principle they were trying to do something better; and if their principles now seem so clearly better than their practice, it is because their principles were clear —to get beyond a parochial point of view, to find standards of truth and morality that were objective and universal, and to measure all societies by the same principles.

Our present search for a universal point of view toward history, then, is nothing new. Western historians and students of society have been trying, deliberately and for a long time, to look at history and human behavior from such a point of view. But they have thought this universal, neutral point of view was supplied by the categories and canons of scientific methods; and it is these very methods which are now being rejected by current philosophers of history as parochial and "merely Western." The most sympathetic anthropologist, arguing for the right of a "native" culture to be different, would never have imagined that the members of this culture could study *him* or *his* culture and arrive at reliable conclusions without using his methods. We may not have believed that we were the masters of all wisdom; but we did at least think that Western society was the school at which all men could learn rational methods of inquiry. We did not think that our fundamental intellectual methods were culturally limited in their validity. But this is precisely what we are asked to believe now. Our most fundamental conceptions of sound reasoning and

18

sound argument are under suspicion. This turning away from traditional intellectual standards represents a loss of confidence for which it is difficult to find a parallel since the time of Saint Augustine—also a time, it will be remembered, when the long-established frontiers of the Western world were crumbling. And it is out of this profoundly unsettled frame of mind that has been engendered by the displacement of Western society from its control over mankind's affairs that the present search for a philosophy of history has emerged.

There is more behind this radical loss of confidence, however, than just the changed status of Western society in the world at large. It is a consequence of something that has happened within that society. No science can argue a man into having good will, and it is frightening when intelligence is applied in a moral void. The faith in objectivity and intelligence which has characterized liberal societies has been based on the assumption that there existed in society a fund of good manners, good sense, and common decency which made it possible for men to understand one another and to negotiate their differences peacefully. In its larger aspect, the present resurgence of interest in philosophies of history is an attempt to find a fund of public values, or an element of shared purpose or common destiny, which might give men a basis for understanding and voluntary co-operation. As an example, a striking number of arguments have taken place since the war among professional historians concerning the standards and values that should govern the writing of history. These debates have been treated by historians as a mainly academic occurrence, a sort of self-enclosed professional quarrel. Historians, of all people, should know better. They write in ordinary language, and their values and judgments are usually those of enlightened common sense. The emergence of differences about the standards and values that should govern the writing of history is the emergence of differences about moral values, intellectual methods, and the

19

meanings of words which once seemed to be clear, simple, and unambiguous. The first sign of a social revolution, Thucydides observed long ago, is when old words lose old meanings. The restoration of our broken lines of communication is one of the purposes behind the present search for a philosophy of history.

And connected with this there is an even larger purpose—to shore up our crumbling moral boundaries, and to restore our sense that there are regular patterns in human nature and society which will allow us to understand what is going on. A plain and recognizable feature of the everyday lives of the most ordinary men and women is our sense of drift, and of drift without limits or direction. We are unable to predict not simply what will happen; much worse, we cannot even be sure what will not happen. We have witnessed the emergence of aboriginal drives and passions, of extremities of cruelty and unreason, of unprecedented patterns of individual conduct and organized social depravity, which make it hard to believe that there are any generalizations that apply or any limits that really hold. Our deepest conceptions of what is possible in human affairs have been shaken. Fifty years ago, even thirty years ago, when a man said that anything was possible, it was an expression of hope; it is now a shrug of despair.

We have come to see, in short, that for all our sense of living in a dynamic world we had been counting on the facts of orderly society and orderly change; and we have come to see that orderly society and orderly change are neither natural nor normal, but rare and precarious achievements. And it is the sharp edge of our anxiety which has driven us, as men have been driven before, to look for something permanent, in human nature or human society or in some higher order of things, which will allow us to take a firm and steady view of what is happening to us.

There is, therefore, something peculiarly radical and acute about our present need for a philosophy of history—as we can see by looking back upon the nineteenth century, a period in which philosophies of history flowered luxuriantly. The nineteenth century was not a calm century. It had its revolutions, its riots in the streets, its outbreaks of unreason, its dissolute ruling classes and its disoriented masses. It had its hard creeds and its insipid skepticisms. Intellectually, technologically, sociologically, it was the period of speediest and profoundest change that the West had seen up to that time: everything from the relation of man to God to the relations between the sexes was altered. Old classes were disinherited, old skills displaced, old beliefs discredited; new classes emerged, a new public sensibility, a new education, a new kind of reading and writing, a new kind of town and a new kind of countryside. And out of this, new philosophies of history arose which were attempts to pick out some stabilizing element—the growth of science, perhaps, or the emergence of a new social class—which would allow men to get on top of events and turn the drift of the times to their advantage.

But when we compare the nineteenth century to our own the analogy halts. The philosophers of history of the nineteenth century—Marx, or Herbert Spencer, or Auguste Comte, or John Stuart Mill—could take something for granted. Even Marx, who did not take much for granted, and who saw more deeply into the radical character of the nineteenth-century revolution than anybody else, was less disturbed and more serene than we can now be. As any unbiased reader of his works will testify, he at least took for granted the persistence of the traditional humanist morality of the West. For all his impatience with "bourgeois morality," and for all his temperamental and philosophical dogmatism, Marx was not a Stalin. If he was unconcerned about the prospect of revolution, if he could welcome it, it was partly because he assumed without question that certain ethical principles would prevail, no matter what.

On the whole, he was right. For all its stumbles and fumbles, the nineteenth century managed to absorb the changes it saw within the framework of accepted standards. Its revolutions were limited in scope and duration, its hereditary ruling classes lost their power without losing their heads. The one great exception was the American Civil War. But with that one exception, even wars were fought by men who knew where to begin and where to stop. Where to begin and where to stop, a sense of limits—this is what is most obviously and acutely missing now. Everything —the simplest joys of ordinary men, the highest refinements of our moral tradition—has a doubtful future: even the survival of the race seems to be an open question. And to find those limits again, to find some firm structure in the process of History itself which is immune to the vicissitudes of time and circumstance—this is what, in the last analysis, has driven men back to the philosophy of history. The large and unharnessed reflections on the nature and destiny of man, the statements of faith, the calls to hope, the pronouncements of doom, which now bemuse us are not idle—at any rate, they are not artificial—intellectual exercises. They are one face, the better face, of the same phenomenon which has produced the present obsession with subversion and disloyalty. They are responses to our sense of the total flux and evanescence of all things, attempts to fix some point of reference, to find an element of order and permanence to which we might cling as all else dissolves. In the past men have looked for a philosophy of history when they could no longer take orderly society and orderly change for granted, when they could no longer count on existing arrangements to set limits within which plans could be rationally made. In looking for a philosophy of history today we are trying to get our historical bearings again, to find the terms in which we can understand what is happening to us, and control —or if that is impossible, surmount—our destinies.

III.

LIBERALISM AND THE
IMAGINATION OF DISASTER

An INTELLECTUAL revolution, however we may define it, is at least a revolution among intellectuals. Sometimes it may consist in a sweeping change in the theories they hold about the nature of the universe—the sort of thing that has happened, for example, in modern physics. Sometimes, however, it may cut deeper morally and intellectually. It may involve a change in the intellectual's beliefs about the intellectual life itself —its conditions and prospects, the objectives it serves, and the standards which should govern it. It represents a shift in prevalent conceptions of intellectual method, and of the relation of reason to other human interests and to society at large.

We are all nervous now, and it is easy to mistake the tick of fashion for the crack of doom. But the evidence is growing that we are living in the incipient stages of such a revolution. The signs are all about us—in the search for faith, or orthodoxy, or peace of mind, in the growing appeal of new philosophies of Anguish and the resurgence of old philosophies of Sin, in the confidence with which large historical prophecies are pronounced,

23

and in the fear or apathy with which concrete proposals for doing something about our problems are greeted. In the sense that it contemplates a change in the methods and values that govern the life of reason, this nascent revolution is like the revolution which took place in the sixteenth and seventeenth centuries, when intellectuals emerged from the cloister, when their values became secular, and when they took the new sciences of nature as the models of proper intellectual method. It resembles, again, the sort of large uneasiness of mind which came over the intellectuals of the newly industrialized nineteenth century, facing, on one side, the social challenge of the emergence of new and apparently rootless classes, and on the other, the intellectual challenge of Darwin's new theory of natural selection.

Like these other revolutions among intellectuals, the present revolution is a response to larger disturbances in the minds and bodies of men who are not professionally concerned with words or ideas. But it is quite unlike these other intellectual revolutions of the modern era in one fundamental respect. It rests upon a conscious rejection of what, until very recently, most educated men in the modern world have regarded as the tested methods for gaining reliable knowledge. It is an intellectual revolution whose main note seems to be the limitations of intellect, a revolution which, with only a few important exceptions, is quite frankly and directly an attempt to get back to things more fundamental than reason, or to conceptions of reason and argument that antedate the rise of modern science. It does not, in a word, accept the idea which the eighteenth century hammered out with such difficulty, and which has been a central, regulating ideal in the perspective and aspirations of modern men—the idea that reason stands above sect and party, and that it can be an independent agency in the organization of a culture. To say that this revolution contemplates a reversal of the liberal and humanist trends which have been the hopes of modern culture is not an overstatement; it is a sober paraphrase of what its leading spokesmen say.

For the historical analogue of the intellectual revolution which now seems to be taking shape, we must go back, not to Mill or Marx or Thomas Hobbes, but to Saint Augustine, or to that "failure of nerve" which overtook the Mediterranean world when the Greek city-states collapsed. It represents a deliberate shift in the focus of intellectual attention. It is an attempt to restore sobriety and humility in human affairs by the remarkable technique of fixing men's minds on transcendent and unattainable ideals. In place of confidence in what man can achieve, it emphasizes the limits of his possible achievement. Where there was a sense of the independence and neutrality of intelligence, it would substitute a sense of the dependence of intelligence on other things—on the heart within or the Mystery above—and its rightful subordination to these things. It speaks of the "treason of the clerks," but it does not mean the intellectual's betrayal of intellectual standards (which is what Julien Benda, who coined the phrase, meant), but his treason to what is outside or above intelligence. It no longer would conceive of reason primarily as an instrument of understanding and control, but as an instrument of therapy and consolation. It proposes a new orientation for the inquiring mind —where once it started with limited doubts and ended with probable beliefs, it is now to move between the poles of ultimate skepticism and absolute dogma. It seems, in short, to contemplate one of those polar shifts in perspective which have periodically overtaken the Western mind in its career.

This intellectual revolution speaks with a peculiar relevance and poignancy to the present mood—to the sense, so endemic to our times, that the old assurances have disappeared and the old limits of life have vanished. Anxiety, the feeling that one must wait impotently for some nameless doom, could at one time be taken as the sign of individual neurosis. It is now a pervasive

25

state of mind, supported by impersonal institutions, the invisibility and anonymity of social power as we experience it, the tremendous pace of events, and the failure of our intellectual defenses. Yeats' lines, written forty years ago, express the contemporary mood almost perfectly:

> . . . Somewhere in sands of the desert,
> A shape with a lion body and the head of a man,
> A gaze blank and pitiless as the sun,
> Is moving its slow thighs, while all about it
> Reel shadows of the indignant desert birds. . . .
> And what rough beast, its hour come round at last,
> Slouches towards Bethlehem to be born?

This mood, and the intellectual revolution it supports, are embodied in the new philosophies of history. Like illiberal minds, the liberal mind in the contemporary world has been subjected to a series of mounting shocks; and, unlike illiberal minds, its hopes were large. It is natural, therefore, that it should be something known as "the liberal outlook" which should be the main object of our current disenchantment; and it is explicable, too, that it should be sensitive and liberal minds that have turned most articulately against this outlook. If there is now a new assurance on the part of the illiberal, and a failure of assurance on the part of the liberal, the source of these feelings is the increasingly widespread conviction that the liberal outlook on human affairs and the liberal vision of history have demonstrated their incapacity to guide us. To believe in human progress, to measure that progress by secular values, to believe that it is mainly implemented by scientific techniques—these have become the shibboleths that tell us who has failed to learn anything from recent history.

For it is a philosophy of history, philosophers of history are telling us, which is responsible for most of our present troubles. For a period ranging from two hundred to six hundred

26

years, it is being said, Western society has been laboring under a fundamental misconception of the nature and possibilities of human history. It has been pathetically trying to understand events in terms of categories that do not fit them, and indeed could not fit any possible world in which human beings might live; it has been blindly seeking to achieve ideals which no human beings could achieve, or which are deeply corrupting when they are achieved. In Fascism and Communism, in the broken hopes of modern men, in the sheer darkness and terror of our times, the emptiness and mischievousness of this view of history has been brought home to us.

This theme has become the standard point of departure for our present thinking about politics and society. It has brought together theologians, historians, and social scientists, has created new schools of literary criticism, and has established an unspoken understanding between the anxious man of affairs and the *avant-garde* intellectual. It has been taken up, not only in conservative and ecclesiastical circles where it has always been popular, but in liberal and secular circles as well. It is a liberal historian who writes that the belief in human perfectibility left liberalism unprepared for Hitler. It is liberal literary critics who tell us that liberalism has a dangerous penchant for abstractions, for oversimplifying, for denying the indelible mystery and ambiguities of human experience. The source and center of the intellectual revolution which seems now to be taking shape is the conviction that liberalism's approach to human affairs is empty, moribund, and responsible for most of our troubles. And it is this idea which constitutes the central theme of nearly all the new philosophies of history. The weaknesses of the liberal view of history are their point of departure; its replacement is their common objective. The essence of their message is that we cannot make headway against our present problems unless we get rid of the liberal philosophy of history and put a better one in its place.

27

"Liberalism" is a troublesome word, and men have used it to hide their views as well as to define them. One of Ibsen's characters remarks: "He has neither character nor convictions nor social position. So liberalism is the most natural position in the world for him." I had better say something to characterize the movement which is now so much under attack, and to indicate how I will use the term.

"Liberalism," as I intend to use the term, stands for a distinctive social movement in the modern world. For approximately two-thirds of the nineteenth century, liberalism in the United States and Great Britain stood for the espousal of the economic doctrine of *laissez faire,* and this doctrine is sometimes said to be its essence. However, this was in fact only a passing phase. Between 1905 and 1915, for example, a Liberal party in Great Britain introduced social security and labor legislation and gave the final blow to the power of the House of Lords; between 1933 and 1939 a liberal government in the United States made large-scale government action in economic affairs a permanent part of the American system. As the experience of the last seventy-five years suggests, liberalism has had certain guiding principles and attitudes which were much more fundamental than *laissez faire.*

One of them, quite simply, is what might be called an engineering approach to social action. The Eighteenth Proposition of Oxford Liberalism announced to the Victorian age: "Virtue is the child of Knowledge: Vice of Ignorance: therefore education, periodical literature, railroad travelling, ventilation, and the arts of life, when fully carried out, serve to make a population moral and happy." "The objects of this Society," declared the prospectus of the Rochdale pioneers, "are the moral and intellectual advancement of its members. It provides them with groceries, butcher's meat, drapery goods, clothes and clogs." Liberalism has regularly proceeded on the assumption, in short, that while increase in material well-being may not guarantee virtue, it removes the prin-

28

cipal source of vice. Long before Marx's economic interpretation of history, liberalism was the social movement that spoke most distinctively for modern man's sense of the new powers which technology and science had brought him. It is a movement associated with the industrial classes and industrial outlook engendered by modern society, a movement that expresses the experience of the restless, mobile inhabitants of cities rather than of the settled, stratified country dweller. It goes with the sense that men tend to have in cities—that man makes his environment; and it expresses the peculiarly modern conviction that man can remake his life more effectively by the material reconstruction of his environment than by changing the philosophy he verbally professes. The vision behind liberalism is the vision of a world progressively redeemed by human power from its classic ailments of poverty, disease, and ignorance.

Again, liberalism has consistently taken a secular approach to political and social affairs. Except in countries where there has been a long tradition of clerical control, liberalism has not been antireligious or anticlerical as such. But it has usually stood for the doctrine of the separation of Church and State, and for antipathy to ecclesiastical control of key social activities like education or politics. From Locke and Voltaire on, liberals have argued that it is sufficient to consult human interests in this world when evaluating a social proposal or a political order. It has treated religious and philosophical beliefs as private affairs, of ultimate moment, perhaps, to the individual's salvation and to his sense of the meaning of life, but without political significance as such. In discussing the foundations of political authority it has confined itself to purely secular and naturalistic considerations—the minimizing of violence, the protection of property, the maximizing of pleasure—which might have equal cogency for men of any denomination, or of none.

This suggests, very briefly, the general perspective of liberalism,

29

the social experience and moral climate that sustain it. But within this general perspective, which is not unlike the perspective that has animated other social movements in the modern world, liberalism has been distinguished by certain persistent principles of social action. On its political side, liberalism has stood first and foremost for parliamentary institutions and civil liberties. And behind this insistence on a permanent legal framework for disagreement and negotiation has stood a fundamental conviction about the nature of social power. Liberalism inherited from Thomas Hobbes the belief that the struggle for power is the persisting fact about political life, and it is a belief which has remained a fundamental assumption for the long line of liberal writers on politics, from John Locke to James Mill to Bertrand Russell to so recent an exponent of the philosophy of American liberalism as Professor J. K. Galbraith. Competition for power cannot be eliminated from human affairs; there is no perfect society which can guarantee that one man's interest will never collide with the interest of another man. The pursuit of a just society, therefore, is not the pursuit of an absolute which, when attained, will allow a liberal social movement to close up shop. The business of liberalism is a recurrent one—to correct imbalances of power, and to organize social institutions in such a way that no one has too much power. For the major source of social injustice is the monopoly of power by any group, political, economic, or ecclesiastical; and the only way to prevent social injustice is to counter power with power. Only by diffusing power in the community does one expand the area in which men act by free choice and not by coercion.

This concern for expanding the area of voluntary behavior is exemplified in another principle which has characterized liberalism. This has to do with the conditions which surround membership by individuals in groups. The liberal social philosophers of the seventeenth and eighteenth centuries characteristically argued

30

that civil society rested on a "social contract"—an agreement on the part of individuals to come together and observe common rules for the sake of certain definite advantages such as the preservation of life and the protection of property. This conception of a "social contract" has been criticized on a number of counts, legitimate and illegitimate, and it has now been dropped from the liberal lexicon. But the idea of a "social contract" was at bottom a metaphor, and a peculiarly apt one. It expressed a social ideal, and the ideal persists. From the point of view of liberalism, membership in any association should never be absolutely irrevocable. The individual should always have a choice about his social affiliations.

What does this mean in concrete terms? It has meant, in the first place, a remarkable change in the relationship between the individual and the social groups to which he belongs. List a series of reforms which have contributed to the making of the modern world: the struggle against the medieval guild; the campaign to make it possible for men to be legally born, educated, and married outside the Church; the relaxation of laws governing divorce; the encouragement of secular charity; the lifting of restrictions on emigration and immigration; the progressive adoption of the policy that full employment and minimum economic security are obligations of the State to its citizens: in all of these men of liberal principles have been predominantly on the side that would release men from being tied down immovably by any social affiliation. This is the heart of what is meant, I think, when liberalism is spoken of as "individualistic."

In the second place, this drive to release the individual from unalterable dependence on any particular social group has changed the nature of most of the social groups that characterize modern society, and changed men's style of thought about society. Such liberal reforms as those mentioned above have had an effect on the structure of Western society, and on the

31

fundamental social attitudes of Western man, which surpasses the more obvious and dramatic political upheavals in terms of which the history and progress of liberalism are usually told. A single individual now belongs to many social groups—a family, a labor union, a business, a church, a parent-teachers' association, a professional society, a political club. No one of these groups protects all his interests. Many of them overlap in the interests they protect, and compete for the individual's loyalty. A man can turn to the Church or to the State, for example, for the education of his children, to the local political clubhouse, to a veterans' society, or to a social service agency when he needs the doctor's bills paid in an emergency. And most important, each of these groups functions with a considerable degree of independence from the others. As a result, it is more difficult for any of these groups to exercise really final power over the individual. And as a further result, each of these groups tends to take on a definitely functional character. Men come to take a business-like attitude toward their membership in a group, to approach it with certain clear and definite purposes in mind, and to appraise it in terms of how it serves these purposes.

The consequences for the shape of modern society, and for men's everyday experience within it, have been profound. Groups ranging from families to churches have come to be regarded as having restricted purposes, their existence is looked upon as contingent and provisional, and the loyalty men feel toward them is limited. Piety in social attitudes has come progressively to be displaced by the habit of asking for results; fixed patterns of authority have been loosened. It is by no means accidental, indeed, that the first objective of totalitarian movements has been to break up these independent groups, to make them all appendages of a single party, and to subject them all to the influence of a single, encompassing myth. Nor is it accidental that the path to totalitarianism has been prepared by the gradual disintegration and

32

devitalization of these independent groups under the impact of uncontrolled urbanization and industrial developments. For the sort of social group which liberalism once fostered has been the real support for individual liberty, the effective base from which it could operate; and it created a kind of social experience which made a "show-me" attitude normal.

We come, therefore, to a certain characteristic bias or emphasis that goes with liberalism and "the liberal outlook." It is something which is suggested by our ordinary usage of the term "liberal." Liberalism stands for a general predisposition in favor of reform. When men suffer, it is the defenders of the *status quo* who must bear the burden of proof, and not those who propose to see how this suffering can be avoided. Indeed, the great and distinctive contribution of modern liberal philosophers, from Voltaire to Bertrand Russell, was to domesticate the idea of reform in Western society, to make social reform an established habit for which deliberate provision has been made in Western institutions. To put it starkly, but I think exactly, liberalism invented the idea that there are such things as "social problems."

More generally, liberalism has characteristically stood for the principle that the actions of the State are subject to a higher moral standard. To take a liberal view of politics has meant to see that political values are not final values, and that politics is not an end in itself. And although the language liberalism has employed to make this point has changed, it has been the well-being of individuals, the advantages which they immediately enjoy, to which liberals have recurrently turned for the final estimate of the worth of a social policy. Neither early liberals nor later liberals have recognized any justification for social policies that do not in the end make a difference which the individual who is at the receiving end can feel and approve.

This brings us, finally, to the more purely intellectual aspects of liberalism. Political and social liberalism have been practical

33

movements of reform. They have been carried on by working alliances composed of diverse social elements. Far from requiring an official ideology, these alliances have done better without one. But if there has been no official liberal ideology, liberal thinkers have nevertheless tended to focus on certain themes, to emphasize certain methods, and to aim at certain broad intellectual and cultural objectives.

The belief in a society composed of a variety of groups struggling for power obviously presupposes that there will also be present certain widely shared interests, and certain attitudes that favor negotiation, mutual concession, and the nonpartisan solution of social conflicts. Among the social movements that have appeared on the stage of human history, liberalism stands distinctively for the view that it is possible to take something like an objective view of human problems, and that such an objective view is the major instrument for keeping a society at once fluid and cohesive. The development of the intellectual tools that are necessary for engendering and disseminating an objective intelligence has been a major concern of the modern liberal intellectual.

This has generally taken a distinctive turn. Empirical science, depending finally on public observation for the verification of its conclusions, has been taken as the model of objectivity in all fields. With the triumphs of modern science, intellectual liberals have distinctively emphasized, men can finally hope with some realism to remake their society by objective and nonpartisan methods of inquiry. The notion that science can be the central organizing agency for modern society is thus a distinctive feature of intellectual liberalism. Conversely, the story of intellectual liberalism is the story of a progressively more emphatic denial that scientific methods can be limited in what they study or in what they disturb. In its largest terms, intellectual liberalism has been the outlook of men who have felt that, with the emergence of science, modern society has a fox in its bosom—a dynamic institution which will allow nothing else to remain unchanged; and intellectual liberalism has been the outlook of men who have been prepared to live with science, and who have felt that its consequences can be turned to human advantage.

This relation between the social objectives of practical liberalism and intellectual liberalism's attachment to the empirical methods of science is a peculiarly intimate one. For liberalism has been a reform movement, and empirical methods are natural weapons for the reformer. "The practical reformer," as John Stuart Mill remarked,

> has continually to demand that changes be made in things which are supported by powerful and widely-spread feelings, or to question the apparent necessity and indefeasibleness of established facts; and it is often an indispensable part of his argument to show, how those powerful feelings had their origin, and how those facts came to seem necessary and indefeasible. There is therefore a natural hostility between him and a philosophy which discourages the explanation of feelings and moral facts by circumstances and association, and prefers to treat them as ultimate elements of human nature; a philosophy which is addicted to holding up favorite doctrines as intuitive truths, and deems intuition to be the voice of Nature and of God, speaking with an authority higher than that of our reason.

The belief that science represented the triumphant consolidation of empirical methods was the great spur to the liberal outlook on history and liberal confidence in the future. Philosophical liberals believed until recently that they had a peculiarly powerful instrument on their side, and that reform could finally be said to be in the saddle. Mill's dictum is central to the liberal theory of history: "The state of the speculative faculties, the character of the propositions assented to by the intellect, essentially determines the moral and political state of the community. . . ." And since empirical science, with its built-in methods for correcting and enlarging its own findings, was bound to bring progress in knowledge, the moral and political progress of mankind could reason-

35

ably be expected to follow: the indefinite improvement of mankind had become a plausible ideal. In the emergence of science mankind had come upon the turning point in its career—the point at which it could finally take control of its destiny, and free itself from a slavish dependence on its past.

These liberal attitudes and ideals came together, and were supported by, a general view of human destiny. It was a view of history which was occasionally expressed in systematic form— most notably in Condorcet's classic *Outline of the Progress of the Human Mind,* written at the end of the eighteenth century. More often, however, it was something which stood behind the spoken words and explicit arguments of liberals, and has to be inferred from what they say. In its main lines, however, it is continuous from Voltaire, Gibbon, and Condorcet in the eighteenth century to Bertrand Russell and John Dewey in the twentieth. It provided a coherent framework for liberal social thinking and an impelling vision to liberal social action. The details of this view will emerge as we proceed. But its main outlines are clear.

To hold the liberal view of history meant to believe in "progress." It meant to believe that man could better his condition indefinitely by the application of his intelligence to his affairs; it meant, further, to measure the improvement of man in secular terms, in terms of his growth in knowledge, the diminution of pain and suffering, the increase of joy, the diffusion and refinement of the civilized arts; and it meant that such improvement in the condition—and, indeed, in the nature—of man could be brought about by deliberately adopted legislative and judicial techniques which would gradually change the institutions that framed men's lives. The liberal view of history was associated with the doctrine—sometimes couched in terms of "natural rights," sometimes in terms of the utilitarian principles of pleasure and pain—that in matters of morals every man might be his own priest, judging the final worth of things for himself. It looked to public education and to the developing techniques of communication to spread intelligence in the community; and it looked for the steady elimination of socially inherited inequalities, which prevented men from defending themselves against exploitation, and were responsible for most of the crimes and follies that had dominated the record of human history. It expected, therefore, to see political authority dispersed in the community at large, and to see a steady movement away from government by coercion and toward government by rational consent. And at the basis of all this, supporting and propelling it, it saw the fact of intellectual progress, now assured by the advent of science—an intellectual progress which would move the human mind away from animistic and mythological modes of thought toward definite, positive knowledge of fact, and which would substitute this knowledge of fact for tradition or revelation as the new foundation for moral and political behavior.* "This picture of the human race, advancing with firm steps towards the attainment of truth, virtue, and happiness," wrote Condorcet, "presents the philosopher with a spectacle that consoles him for the errors, the crimes, the injustice, with which the earth is still polluted." The liberal vision of history did this for generations of liberals; and it brought illumination and warmth to liberal politics.

The liberal approach to the problems of the modern world has never, of course, been universally shared. But the power and appeal it exercised until recently, particularly in the United States, can hardly be questioned. For more than a century, something like this view of history provided most Americans with roughly consistent attitudes toward the past, with a conception of the over-all direction in which history was—or ought to be—moving, and

---

* If anyone thinks I am unduly adorning the liberal outlook, he should go back and consider what its subtlest critic had to say about it. In this characterization of the central features of that outlook, I take my cue from Edmund Burke.

with ideas about the nature and conditions of human betterment. And no other view of history has been more peculiarly appropriate to American experience, or better able to provide Americans with an image of the place of their most modern, technological, and democratic of countries in the total design of world history. We have had fewer fixed traditions than other countries, and more room to make decisions on the grounds of efficiency and individual happiness. Applying human skill to the mastery of nature has been our principal occupation for a century and a half. Social engineering and applied social science, as exemplified in our advertising, our organization of factories, our military institutions, and our schools, have flourished here as nowhere else. "No author, without a trial," Hawthorne once wrote, "can conceive the difficulty of writing a romance about a country where there is no shadow, no antiquity, no mystery, no picturesque and gloomy wrong, nor anything but a commonplace prosperity, in broad and simple daylight, as is happily the case with my native land." It may be bad for the novelist. But it is good for a belief in free-ranging intelligence, good will, and the idea of progress.

Indeed, if many Americans have been suspicious of history and unconcerned with the past, it is perhaps because they have had a rough philosophy of history all along without quite knowing it. Because they believed in progress, the past, they knew, was, if not gone, at any rate best forgotten. The inherent superiority of the new over the old, the right of each generation to make its own way without being limited by what had gone before, its capacity in fact to do so—these have been the unspoken assumptions of ordinary men, their way of initially approaching experience and of acting and reacting upon it. It was these unexpressed assumptions that made America in particular a natural habitat for the more articulate views of liberal philosophers on the nature and meaning of history, the perfectibility of man, and the role of emancipated scientific intelligence in human affairs. The liberal outlook on history was backed up until recently by a sort of check which Americans regularly cashed at the bank of experience. And if Americans have now lost their bearings, and are in search of a philosophy of history, it is because an attitude toward history which was so much a part of the national life has obviously collapsed.

For the bank now seems to have returned the check, marked "no funds." Writing after the outbreak of World War I, Leonard Hobhouse, the British liberal, observed: "It turned out to be in sober truth a different world from that which we knew, a world in which force had a greater part to play than we had allowed, a world in which the ultimate securities were gone, in which we seemed to see of a sudden through a thin crust of civilisation the seething forces of barbaric lust for power and indifference to life." A long depression and a second war, followed by anxieties about another depression and another war, have brought this mood to this country.

There is much to support it, and to support the feeling that the liberal outlook on history was a piece of pathetic foolishness. One by one, on every crucial point it seems to have been refuted. The disasters already accomplished by technology, and the greater disasters that are threatened, have undermined the genial assumption that there is a simple connection between engineering and happiness. The belief that there is a necessary connection between progress in knowledge and progress in morality has been shattered by the spectacle which the Fascists and Communists have placed before us of bestiality joined with technical efficiency. We see that disinterested science is not necessarily beneficent. And the idea that progress in science means the gradual elimination of mythological modes of thought has been challenged by the emergence, in this most "scientific" of ages, of mythologies whose

39

intellectual quotients are in inverse proportion to the primitive character of the passions they evoke.

Further, the belief that the growth of democratic equality would cause moral intelligence to be generally diffused in the community at large has been challenged by the vulgarization and standardization of culture, and by the heightened susceptibility of masses of men to intellectual manipulation. A sort of Gresham's law of culture has come to be exemplified—a situation in which bad ideas drive out good ones, and in which social passions have an epidemic character while social information moves sluggishly and distortedly through the social structure. The hope that political power would be diffused has been dampened by the growth of tight bureacratic structures in business, politics, and government which concentrate decision-making authority at the top. And the ideal of an enlightened and spirited public has been obscured by the image of the mob on one side and the anonymous, powerless individual on the other. An urban and technological civilization has progressively isolated individuals from one another, making their relations more formal and impersonal, their experience more private and lonely.

Most immediately, the naïvely or shrewdly misnamed "Russian experiment" has been a traumatic experience, chilling the sensitive minds of two generations. In countries where liberal traditions are strong, Communist parties have been ineffective as practical political movements, and have stood as half-amusing, half-shocking monuments to organized foolishness and fanaticism. But they have nevertheless usurped and perverted the traditional vocabulary of liberalism, and their calculated double-talk has left no clear and unambiguous language for stating the liberal case—a contribution to semantic corruption in which our advertising men and patrioteers have joined. Even more important, Soviet imperialism has done something which no other modern imperialism has been able to do: it has moved to power

40

by exploiting the generous impulses and large hopes that have gone with the liberal tradition. The Nazis showed us the depths of which human beings are capable; the Communists have shown us the same depths while manipulating a social vision. The faith in science, the belief in progress, the ideals of liberty, equality, and fraternity, have all been paraded before us in a murderers' masquerade. "I have the imagination of disaster," Henry James wrote in 1896, "and see life as ferocious and sinister." In the sixty years since he wrote the imagination of disaster has overwhelmed the liberal vision.

But we had better see whether we are being reasonable and prudent in being overwhelmed, or merely scared out of our wits —the only wits we have. Can we, amidst the collapse of our hopes, still maintain the essential elements of the liberal outlook on history? I think we can. And it is important to see if we can. For the liberal outlook on history was bound up with, and gave idiomatic expression to, the most distinctive features of modern history—its secularism, its dependence on science and technology, its attempt to organize society without appeal to any moral or political orthodoxy, and its faith in social mobility and free communication as the dissolvents of prejudice and error. It is possible that these things will be preserved with some other outlook on human affairs. But it is not at all certain that it will be easier.

In fact, the disasters of recent history are not enough to explain the present decline of the liberal outlook. It is not these disasters alone, but the *imagination* of disaster, and the attempt to convert that imagination from an historical circumstance into a metaphysical necessity. For there have always been reasons, after all, why liberals should feel surrounded by hostile forces, and alienated from the main drift of their times. Stupidity, fanaticism, the impatience of starving or desperate men, the

41

inertia of old habits, and the stubbornness of vested power are not modern inventions. They are merely things which we are now able to organize more efficiently. But if we have new techniques for organizing stupidity or for exploiting fear and ignorance, then, at least in principle, we also have techniques for controlling or mitigating these things.

What is peculiar about the present situation is not simply the pressure upon liberalism, but the peculiar sort of response which liberals are making to this pressure. Instead of having a program, practical, working liberalism now seems to be reduced to a series of defensive holding actions, to containment abroad and complaint at home. Strangely, the liberal now seems to be the man who has his head turned backward, and who is anxious to see things merely kept as they were. He can work himself up to fighting for what he has, but he listens skeptically to any suggestions that he might have something more. He has courage, but it is dogged courage. He has intelligence, but it merely holds the line. The last folly of which he wishes to appear guilty is the folly of hope.

The reason, I think, is the curiously split attitude which now prevails in liberal circles toward the liberal heritage. On the level of fundamental principles, everything in liberalism seems to be in solution; on the level of practical program everything is fixed. On one side, none of the old answers is accepted; on the other, no new questions are being asked. No coherent framework pulls problems together; no exciting vision suggests new goals that might be sought. Liberalism is riding with events. It does not convert them into opportunities, as a movement which knew where it was going, and had a comprehensive program for getting there, might do. It is meeting the issues as they come up, but it exercises very little influence over what these issues are.

It is not surprising, to be sure, that liberalism should now be under reconsideration by liberals; it has been reconsidered and

42

revised by successive generations of liberals, from Jeremy Bentham's criticisms of Locke's "natural rights," through John Stuart Mill's criticisms of Bentham, to John Dewey's criticisms of Mill. And liberalism, it need hardly be said, has never needed criticism more than now. But what is unprecedented is that liberal voices should be speaking, as they now are, in such strange accents, in the accents of Burke and Kierkegaard and Dostoevsky and Heidegger. It is what gives substance to the feeling that something like an intellectual revolution is taking place. A current of criticism that runs back to the reaction against the French Revolution has touched the American shore and the liberal mind, and is being taken seriously for perhaps the first time in our history.

The contemporary liberal, in short, is negative and defensive in his attitudes not only because he is under pressure from without, but because he has no push from within. What has gone out of practical liberalism is the liberal imagination, once so affirmative and flexible, now so nostalgic and rigid. A quality which was once the great distinction of liberalism is no longer discernible in it—the capacity to project programs that were more than merely stopgap devices, and less than utopian dreams. For, despite everything that is now being said about the classic liberals —the "doctrinaire" *philosophes* of the Enlightenment, the "narrow" and "mechanistic" Bentham, the "cold" and "intellectual" Mill—their great quality as social thinkers was a quality of imagination. They had the ability to create a fairly determinate image of what a better society would contain, to make that image large and exciting, and to think seriously and responsibly of programs for attaining it.

Why did they have this ability? At least part of the answer is plain. It is because of the view of history which they held, and because they believed in the meaning and possibility of progress. They were not just fools who believed that everything

43

was bound to go well: it was Voltaire, after all, who wrote *Candide,* and Mill who discovered that not even the achievement of all his social projects was enough to define or to bring happiness. But neither did they believe that intellectual obscurity was a form of higher wisdom, or that suffering must be accepted for its alleged educational advantages. The present cosmic hypochondria, the creation of a metaphysics which makes anguish and sin, mystery and frustration, the plan of the universe and the keys to history, has, it seems to me, chilled the liberal imagination. And it is to help take it out of cold storage that it is worth examining what the new philosophies of history have to say, and worth considering whether there is anything left that is desirable or defensible in that liberal view of history which, when the record is examined, will be seen to have stood behind the most viable and permanent social programs instituted in the West in the past two hundred years. Certainly, it would be a grisly impertinence to try to revive the old complacent faith in the automatic progress of mankind through the steady advance of the free market, technological invention, and enlightened public opinion. But clearly it is one thing to deny that the language of reason and progress, the ideals of liberty and equality, the ethic of the questioning mind and the emancipated spirit, have the special benediction of nature; and it is quite another thing to deny that they have at least a fighting chance.

IV.

THE ANXIETY TO BELIEVE

OUR problems today come at us in bunches. Any thoughtful taxi driver, stalled in New York traffic, will see that the problem will not be solved simply by putting his finger on the horn and driving ahead. And since he is likely to have plenty of time to think as he waits for traffic to get moving, he may find himself ruminating on population movements, the relocation of industry, city planning, and real-estate interests. Similarly, the man who is worrying about the education of his children finds himself thinking, not only about schools, teachers' salaries, and the division of the tax dollar, but about television, the newspapers, the mass media of communication, the divorce rate, the mobility of our population, and the state of the family. Stopgap and "practical" measures which deal with such problems by treating them in isolation generally manage to alleviate some pain, including the pain of thought; but they frequently solve these problems merely by putting them in the next man's lap.

It is plain, in other words, that we need to have some sense of the crucial variables in our present situation, the handles that will allow us to deal with clusters of problems together; and it is

45

equally plain that we need to have some sense of what our ends are if we are to make ends meet. Alice and the Cheshire Cat say it very neatly. " 'Cheshire-Puss,' she began, rather timidly . . . 'would you tell me please, which way I ought to go from here?' 'That depends a good deal on where you want to get to,' said the Cat. 'I don't much care where—' said Alice. 'Then it doesn't matter which way you go,' said the Cat."

We need, in short, what used to be called social philosophy— some thinking about the major paths open to us, and where we would like to get. And as a first step toward such thinking, we need some fairly coherent organizing picture of what has been happening to us—a philosophy of modern history. Alice's difficulty is that no one would give her a map of Wonderland. And our difficulty is much the same. The decline of the liberal philosophy of history has left us disoriented. And while it is too much to hope that we can find some map that will lay out the whole of the Wonderland in which we live, it would obviously be helpful if we could discover at least a few fixed points by which we could chart our course part of the way.

Clearly, the way to begin is to try to find out just where the outlook on history with which most of us grew up has misled us. And the emergent philosophies of history are attempts to do just this. Their point of departure is the failure of the liberal philosophy of human history; their account of modern history is an account of the disastrous consequences of liberalism; and the new maps they offer us are offered as corrections of liberalism at its weakest points. It is in these terms that they trace the course we have followed, mark the spot where we stand (which is usually the edge of the abyss), and indicate the new paths we must take. In sum, they offer themselves as alternatives to the liberal approach to human affairs. Let us therefore try to find out where we stand by examining what has been said about the liberal philosophy of history by its most reflective and radical

46

critics, and by seeing what substance there is in the alternatives they propose.

There are four central theses on which the liberal conception of history turns. The first is the belief that human progress can be measured in secular terms, and that a secular morality, which does not go beyond the sphere of temporal human interests, is sufficient for interpreting human history and for organizing human affairs. The second is the doctrine of "the indefinite perfectibility of man." The third is the belief that it is meaningful to speak of such a thing as objective truth in the study of history and human society, and that intelligence and good will can rise to a level of impartiality that is not wholly limited by personal idiosyncrasy, social status, or historical position; it is therefore meaningful, this thesis holds, to regard progress in social science as an objective possibility, and to expect that such progress might give man increasing power to control his destiny. Finally, there is the belief that a society can be approached in terms of its parts, and that it does not have to be understood or remade all of a piece and all at once. It is a belief that social progress proceeds by deliberately instituted legislative, judicial, and administrative techniques, and by the piecemeal reconstruction of human institutions—and not by spiritual conversions, moral appeals for a change of heart, or the sudden intervention of external powers. On the denial of each of these theses a new philosophy of history has been raised. We turn now to consider the first of these.

"What we suffer from today," Chesterton once wrote, "is humility in the wrong place. . . . A man was meant to be doubtful about himself, but undoubting about the truth; this has been exactly reversed. . . . The old humility made a man doubtful about his efforts, which might make him work harder. But the new humility makes a man doubtful about his aims, which will make him stop working altogether." This diagnosis has been raised to the level of a systematic theory of modern history. It holds that the history of modern society is the history of the inexorable development of a deadly disease—the denial of eternal truths. In modern culture everything is relative and nothing is absolute. We have no first principles, no ultimate values, no unshakable commitments, no conviction that there is any final meaning to life. In the end, on any moral issue, we have no alternative but merely to shrug our shoulders and express a preference—for freedom or toleration if we happen to feel that way, or for tyranny and the persecution of minorities if we happen to feel differently. As a result, our homes are without discipline, our schools without clear purposes, our foreign policy weak and spineless. There is cynicism in our personal moralities, opportunism in our politics, and a general sense of aimlessness and drift in our daily lives. And worst of all, we have succumbed to this case of galloping skepticism as a matter of principle. For we live under the spell of a philosophy which has turned disrespect for authority into a virtue, and made us all fearful about believing in anything.

In vague form, this point of view is expressed every day by judges, generals, editorial writers, police commissioners, college presidents, and politicians, as well as by historians and philosophers. In more explicit form, it has been expressed in new approaches to literature and society, and has been developed into influential philosophies of education, law, and politics. But probably the most eloquent and circumspect spokesman for this position, and certainly its most influential and representative, is the distinguished French philosopher, Jacques Maritain, who has spent a number of years teaching and writing in this country. Professor Maritain has developed his analysis of modern culture in a number of books, but most specifically in his full-dress study in the philosophy of history, *True Humanism,* and in his briefer

48

volume, *Scholasticism and Politics*. In practical politics, Professor Maritain, despite his drastic criticisms of the philosophical foundations of liberalism, has himself usually been on what would be called the "liberal" side. He stands unequivocally for a pluralistic culture and the civil liberties, and he has been one of the staunchest defenders of the Republican tradition in France. He writes from the point of view of a Catholic; but he believes that the logic of his arguments should be convincing to everyone, and his views have in fact been adopted by a great many non-Catholic and secular thinkers.

Professor Maritain's theory of history has a clear and plausible shape, and it recommends itself to some of our deepest intellectual habits. It begins with the obvious point that any human society is a structure of "authority." It contains, that is to say, a certain hierarchical structure. Some people command, others obey; or, if it is a completely egalitarian society, there are, at any rate, certain general rules to which everyone is expected to submit. However, submission to these rules, as Professor Maritain points out, can obviously take place for different reasons. It can be coerced or it can be something to which people consent. A society can be tyrannical or it can rest on the willing and voluntary agreement of its members. But if it is the latter, then those who submit have to believe that it is for some good purpose. And so they have to have values, and they have to believe in these values.

It is at this point that Professor Maritain's essential thesis emerges. If men have to believe in values, he argues, then they have to be convinced that it is not just their own individual interests, or the temporary fashions of their community, that are involved. They have to be convinced that the values which justify the exercise of social authority, and their own submission to it, rest on something outside themselves, something that is eternal and unchanging. It has to be something higher than their

49

own wills or the wills of their rulers, something which they discover and do not merely choose for themselves.

And so, in any sound culture, Professor Maritain urges, men find themselves face to face with what is beyond human life, with what transcends the human scene. A sound culture needs a philosophy which asserts that there are fixed absolutes, truths that belong to no historical period in particular but apply to all of them in general. It needs an outlook on its own history which sees it as an element in the larger history of man, and an outlook on that larger history which sees it as an element in the design of the universe. History has to be seen as a series of achievements and failures which are meaningful because they serve some purpose and exhibit some truth that lies beyond history itself. For history cannot be an end in itself. The career of mankind is meaningless unless we see it against the backdrop of what is timeless.

But this, Professor Maritain is convinced, is precisely what modern culture has forgotten. And it has forgotten it because it has been under the spell of a philosophy of history which denies that there are any such things as eternal truths. For what, after all, does it mean to assert the indefinite perfectibility of man? If men progress in all spheres, or even if such indefinite progress is considered to be possible, then the picture of human history that results is that of men ceaselessly throwing off old beliefs and values as false, and constantly adopting new beliefs and values which will be rejected in turn. A culture that holds such a conception of history is simply stating that it is built on sand, that nothing to which men commit themselves—no moral principle, no political system, no cause, no belief—has anything solid to support it. It holds a philosophy of history, to put it briefly, which is unlivable, and which erodes the convictions that make human decency, and, indeed, elementary social order, possible. And this is what modern liberal culture has done.

The downward drift of modern civilization is nothing but the lengthening shadow of the liberal philosophy of history.

Nor can liberalism easily minimize or mitigate the difficulty. For this melancholy picture of history follows from fundamental premises of the liberal position, and cannot be altered without discarding the essentials of that philosophy. No viable society, for example, can rest its authority on anything short of eternal truths; but the philosophy of liberalism is empirical, and argues that all beliefs must be brought to the test of ordinary human observation. This is simply to condemn man in perpetuity to the sphere of the merely probable: for all beliefs that rest on human experience alone are limited, and are subject to reversal by future experience. Again, liberalism proposes purely secular values as the basis for its moral and political arrangements. It makes a systematic effort to keep theological and other such considerations out of the picture. But this means that the basis of morals and politics, for liberal culture, is only the notoriously transitory and capricious human will.

In short, Professor Maritain believes that we are getting exactly what we asked for, even if unknowingly. If we complain about the aimlessness of our lives, the decline of firm standards, the cynical flouting of moral principles, the increasing part that violence and terror play in modern society, we have nothing to blame but liberalism itself. Rarely, if ever, has a social movement which aimed at spreading the gospel of peace succeeded so completely in spreading the gospel of force. The liberal outlook was an effort to consolidate classic humanist standards in the modern world; it hoped to introduce government by toleration, mutual concession, and rational consent; it believed it represented reason. But, in fact, its deepest logic entailed just the reverse. The motives of liberalism were good; but it acted on these motives with a blind disregard of the conditions under which human life has to be lived, and of the larger truths that

51

transcend human life but to which human beings must be subject. "The modern world has sought good things in bad ways," says Professor Maritain; "it has compromised the search for authentic human values, which men must save now by an intellectual grasp of a profounder truth. . . . We have to deal today with a considerable liquidation—a liquidation of five centuries of classical culture."

The key to the difficulties of modern society, to employ Professor Maritain's own terms, is the fact that it has been humanistic, but in the wrong way and on the wrong basis. It has hoped, as all humanistic cultures do, to develop man's powers to the utmost and to subject the physical world progressively to the human will. But modern culture, quite simply, has had no clear conception of what it means to be human, of what the idea of man includes and leaves out. To define man means to set his limits, to contrast him with what he is not. A true humanism recognizes that human goals cannot be achieved unless external standards and limits are introduced by which man's development can be guided, and unless man's dependence on forces greater than himself is taken into account. This is what modern liberal humanism has failed to do. Its humanism has been "anthropocentric"; it has conceived human nature "as self-enclosed and self-sufficient." It has denied, on one side, that there are any limits to human power and aspiration, and, on the other, that there are any agencies outside man which might lift him above his limitations.

This view of human nature and destiny has shown itself in a false theory of knowledge, a false moral theory, and an impossible philosophy of history. In its theory of knowledge, it has denied that men can know any absolute truths; and so it has chosen to define the whole realm of truth in terms of what man, with his puny nature, can discover by himself. In its moral theory, as a result, it leaves human moral codes without any external standard by which they can be judged. Human nature—with all its individual idiosyncrasies, its fleeting passions, its tendency to arrogant self-assertion—this human nature is elevated into its own judge. "Anthropocentric" humanism is simply the revival of the ancient and discredited view of the Sophist Protagoras that man is the measure of all things.

The results, as Professor Maritain tells the story, cover the whole spectrum of modern disasters. From the doctrine that man is the measure of all things, it follows, for example, that moral disagreements are merely matters of taste—a belief that is now epidemic in modern society; and from this it follows, in turn, that social authority rests on nothing but force—a belief which the Fascists and Communists have simply taken over from the "tolerant" liberals and shorn of its trimmings. Again, if there is no moral design to the universe higher than human interests, it follows that "man alone, and through himself alone, works out his salvation." So liberal culture lets itself in for an unguarded rationalism. It takes no account of the forces above reason that alone can lift men out of themselves; it offers men the help of no powers greater than their own; it does not tell them how the "supra-rational" can flow into them, inspiring them and illuminating their lives. And by the same token, it leaves men powerless to deal with the unreason in themselves. For human reason is weak and cold, and is regularly overcome by irrational drives. Unless men can find some light and warmth above reason with which to combat the power of what is below reason, reason itself is condemned to defeat. There is, in short, something essentially self-defeating about a simple rationalistic dependence on the powers of human reason to affect human destiny: rationalism cannot even save the life of reason.

Finally, an "anthropocentric" philosophy of history has made meaningless the entire spectacle of human history. For if there

53

is no eternal point of view outside history from which we can judge it as a whole, then there is no purpose or meaning to history in any of its parts. Nothing in history has any meaning at all. It is the simple logic of this belief, says Professor Maritain, that has driven modern man to nihilism, and made it impossible for him to commit himself with conviction to any deal or to any social cause unless he deliberately and cynically decides to think with his blood. The lost, rootless masses of modern society; the restless, unhappy deification of earthly things that besets and distracts the modern world; the hysterical nationalisms; the idolizing of leaders; the fanatic ideologies; the piddling love of gadgetry; the cults of violence—these are all the work of a philosophy of history which denies the existence of eternal truths. What liberalism has done has been to undermine the foundations of moral authority in the modern world.

What is it about the liberal approach to human affairs that has led to this belief—now so widespread—that liberalism cannot give men the strength of conviction they need to live in this world, and that it undermines the very foundations of social authority? A moment's attention to some recent intellectual history will help us to understand.

Since the early part of the nineteenth century, it is unquestionable that most philosophies of a liberal bent have been, to use the current expression, "relativistic" in their approach to all moral codes and social systems. They have denied, that is to say, that there are any eternal moral principles which are unquestionable, or any immutable standards by which all men and all societies can be judged. In any system of values, for a philosophical "relativist," there is an element of simple preference or interest which cannot be eliminated by argument; and so in any moral system there is always something accidental or personal or limited, something wholly a-rational, which is "relative" to a man's tastes or to the

54

special historical circumstances of a specific place or time. So there cannot be any single system of morals or politics which holds good for everyone; and there cannot be any special group of experts who can lay down the infallible last word on questions of value.

The primary social motive behind this liberal relativism is plain—it is a highly useful tool for unseating the fixed absolutes by which defenders of the *status quo* perennially try to discredit proposals for reform. It has been encouraged as well by the peculiar heterogeneity of modern society and by its mobility—by the welter of different classes, creeds, and occupations that now come together in our cities, by the rapidity with which traditions are replaced, manners changed, and styles put on and off, and by the unprecedented degree to which individuals have been able to move around in space and up and down on the social ladder. But behind the rise of this philosophy there have also been a number of impressive and radical intellectual developments. The first of these stems largely from the philosophy of the eighteenth-century Scottish thinker, David Hume. Hume pointed out that moral statements—statements which tell us how men *should* behave—cannot possibly be proved by pure logic or by an appeal to facts alone. It is also necessary to appeal to human emotions, and particularly to the sentiment of fellow-feeling and sympathy. Moral principles, therefore, cannot be "true" in the way that arithmetic can be true or physics can be true.

The relativistic approach to human values thus stimulated was further encouraged by influences emanating from an independent quarter—the development, in the nineteenth century, of the biological sciences, and of an evolutionary and historical approach to human affairs. These influences, culminating in Marx and Freud, led men to stress the role of ideas and moral values as the selective, practical responses of a vital creature to its environment, and as agencies for adapting human life

55

to changing circumstances. While these new doctrines argued a point which is logically quite different from Hume's, they nevertheless served greatly to reinforce the notion of the relativity of moral codes and social systems. Finally, the *coup de grâce* to the belief in absolutes was given by developments in mathematics and logic which showed that even the so-called "self-evident axioms," cherished for centuries as models of the irrefutable, were in fact matters of human choice and, to a certain extent, of human convenience.

The relativistic philosophy which has resulted from these developments, it is unarguable, has dominated liberal intellectual circles for at least a century. Values have not been regarded as eternal verities about which human beings have no choice. They are the expressions of human preferences, and have a psychological and social setting and an historical career. If there are any moral standards, according to this philosophy, it is human beings who make them. If there is any meaning to history, it is human beings who put it there. To the extent that liberalism has been allied with an empirical outlook in philosophy, it has adopted this view; and to the extent that it has attempted to organize modern society on the basis of purely secular considerations, it has put this view increasingly into practice.

Philosophical relativism is thus the product of significant and serious ideas, and in its foundations is something quite different from the popular attitude of indifference to proof and to truth expressed by the phrase, "Everything is a matter of opinion." And yet, in its general shape and temper this philosophical relativism seems so close to the popular relativism around us, to the confusions and doubts about moral standards and to the simple indifference to morality, that it is easy to see why it should be regarded as the systematic expression of moral skepticism or moral apathy. And this impression has been encouraged by a great many persons who, at some remove from the actual argu-

56

ments on which philosophical relativism is based, have heard the words of this philosophy without understanding its music.*

Professor Maritain, however, is acquainted with the actual arguments on which this philosophy is based. And his belief that philosophical liberalism is the fundamental cause of the decline of moral authority in the modern world raises questions of the gravest moment, and merits the most serious consideration. What is there to the belief that a purely secular, humanist, and relativistic philosophy cannot provide human beings with the guidance they need in their affairs? Must we go beyond the sphere of probable knowledge and temporal human interests to find an adequate philosophy of human history?

Basically, there are four arguments behind the view which Professor Maritain and many others hold concerning the inadequacy of any philosophy that denies that there are absolutes. The first is that such a philosophy cannot give us any help in determining our moral goals and purposes. If we desire a certain end, it can tell us what the best means to this end is; but it cannot tell us what our ends should be. For example, if you happen to like a society full of idiosyncratic individuals, then you can see that you ought to have a school system that encourages the child to work by himself; but whether or not you ought to like a society that is full of idiosyncratic individuals is something a relativistic philosophy cannot tell you. So long as you stick to a relativistic point of view, there are no final ends which you absolutely *ought* to adopt; and so how you act becomes completely a matter of taste, limited only by your prudence in adopting the proper means for reaching whatever ends you happen to

* Mussolini, or his philosophical ghost writer, used to say, for example, that Fascism was philosophical relativism in action. Many who do not think highly of Mussolini's politics apparently think highly enough of his philosophical talents to take this statement at face value.

have. Thus, in the view of its critics, the provisional, flexible attitude which modern liberalism has taken toward the question of ultimate values has only been a way of encouraging opportunism and self-assertion at one extreme, and irresolution and cowardice at the other.

The argument seems plausible. And it seems plausible because the premises with which it begins have a modicum of truth in them. To begin with, it is of course true that if you do not hold any firm ideals you cannot come to a moral decision; and if you deny that the purposes you have are guaranteed by one-hundred-per-cent-certain eternal principles, you have to admit, of course, that at some point you have made some assumptions, or introduced certain ideals, about which you have, for the moment, simply decided to ask no questions. Thus it looks as though a relativistic philosophy is forced by its own logic to admit that it places the choice of human ideals on an arbitrary basis.

And yet, as a moment's reflection will indicate, no such conclusion really follows. There are two fallacies in the argument that a philosophy which denies moral absolutes cannot give us any guidance in our choice of ends or ideals. The first of these fallacies is a too rigid separation of means and ends. In fact, when we think about means, we also redetermine our ends. Consider the simple example we mentioned above. If you think that you want to encourage individual idiosyncrasies, you may decide it is necessary to let each schoolchild work by himself. However, when you think about this for a moment, you realize that this would probably mean that a large number of children would not learn the three R's or other skills which have to be maintained in a going community; and idiosyncrasy, if it costs that much, does not seem worth it. So you drop this as one of your ends, or subordinate it to other things. This sort of process of deliberation is a simple everyday affair. It invokes no higher logic and appeals to no eternal absolutes. And yet two things have happened in the process: you have revised the original end you had in mind, and you have discovered that, in fact, you had other ends which you consider more important. You have, in short, critically reorganized your goals or objectives. And you have done so simply by thinking about the means requisite for achieving these goals, and about the consequences that flow from achieving them. In sum, when you wish to evaluate a given end, you ordinarily do so by considering it as a means or condition that affects still other ends.

But how, it will be asked, can we avoid going on in this relativistic way forever, selecting one value which we treat as a means to something else, and then taking this something else and treating it as a means to something still further along the line, and so on? How do we know when to stop? If everything is open to question, how can we ever come to any conclusions?

These questions bring us to the second fallacy in the idea that a philosophy which rejects absolutes makes it impossible for us to decide on our aims and goals. This fallacy rests, quite simply, on an equivocation in the meanings of terms like "doubt" and "uncertainty." When a philosophical relativist says that all his beliefs are "provisional" or "logically uncertain," he does not mean that he is actually doubtful about all his beliefs. He merely means that they are *dubitable*—that they are logically subject to doubt, since they rest on limited observations, and therefore *might* be upset in the future. He does not mean that he expects them to be upset, or can hardly wait to see them overthrown. On the contrary, the only reason, he believes, for *actually* doubting any belief here and now is that there is specific factual evidence against it. And so long as there is no such evidence, the idea that it might turn up in the future is no reason for doubting what all the evidence now supports. For the notion that all beliefs or values are subject to reversal by future experience merely ex-

59

presses an abstract logical possibility; and an abstract logical possibility is no reason for plunging into a frenzy of doubt. It is abstractly possible that, beginning tomorrow, it will never rain again. But this is not a reason for throwing away our umbrellas.

In short, to deny that there are absolutes is merely to say that we will keep our beliefs responsive to experience; it is not to say that all truths or moral principles are doubtful. Moral values like good faith, charity, honesty, and self-respect are in no way subverted by the proposition that they are all relative; they are just as firm as they have always been, no more and no less. And so, when we are deliberating about means and ends, we normally stop, and we have a perfect right to stop, when we come to values that are giving us no trouble, and which we see no good reason to question. Such values are not absolutes: we have no advance guarantee that they will always be the final principles on which we lean. But until trouble does turn up, we leave well enough alone. A man who holds a liberal or relativistic philosophy can thus be just as assured about any given value as the man who believes in absolute truths. There is nothing in the liberal approach to human values which suggests that the choice of our goals is necessarily capricious, or that we must all live constantly in a state of uncertainty.

This brings us, however, to the second argument which underlies Professor Maritain's analysis of the liberal outlook. It is that a relativistic philosophy cannot give us a justification for a moral code or a social system as a whole. It can examine specific ideals in the light of others; it can criticize specific aspects of a social system in the name of certain selected interests; but all this will merely yield a relativistic philosopher a partial and piecemeal justification of his values. He cannot stand outside all particular systems of morality and tell us which one among them is right or just or worthy of being adopted. According to Professor Maritain,

60

if a relativistic philosopher holds the assumptions and preferences of a liberal democrat, he can say that concentration camps are an atrocity; if he holds the assumptions and preferences of a Nazi, he can say that concentration camps are a justifiable device for getting rid of socially undesirable elements. But he cannot show that the liberal democrat's entire system of values is right; and he cannot show the Nazi that he is wrong. Liberalism, says Professor Maritain, pretends to introduce the rule of reason into human affairs; but in fact it reduces human life to a scramble, to a competition of conflicting wills, and that is all.

This is an argument which carries a special appeal. In an era of total war, it seems very widely to be believed, we need a total justification of our values. A philosophy like liberalism, it is said, does not give men the support they need to face the tensions of modern society, and cannot stand up against the fanatical devotion which competing ideologies evoke.

And yet this argument is in fact a wholly artificial one. In the first place, it is simply not true that disagreements between partisans of one social order and partisans of another are usually disagreements between men who have absolutely no moral principles in common. These disagreements are much more usually disagreements about facts, and certain common values are presupposed. The Nazis, who claimed to stand above soft, civilized prejudices like arguing for their beliefs, nevertheless spent a good deal of time doing just that. And the arguments they offered were usually statements about facts—wholly imaginary facts, like the inherent differences between races or the need for *Lebensraum*. Similarly, the Communist does not say that blood purges are an intrinsically good thing; he says that they are unavoidable during a revolution, or that they are necessary for reaching desirable ends like the abolition of poverty. And what the partisan of democracy asserts in return are the purely factual

61

propositions that blood purges were in fact avoidable, and that, far from being necessary instruments in the abolition of poverty, they were actually ways of keeping an unsuccessful and tyrannical bureaucracy in power. If the arguments offered on one side are almost totally false, and the arguments on the other much more usually true, I find it hard to know what more anyone would want to fortify his faith.

In other words, it is not usually our general moral principles that become subjects of doubt or controversy; it is the application of these principles to specific cases. Indeed, when the demand is made for some ultimate justification of our system of values "as a whole," it is hard to know what could possibly be meant. This demand for a total justification of a moral system is a central theme in Professor Maritain's philosophy, but his discussion only suggests the classic story about the philosopher and the theologian strolling in the gardens of one of the colleges at Oxford. "A philosopher," said the theologian, "is a blind man in a dark room looking for a black cat that isn't there." "Yes," said the philosopher, "and if he were a theologian, he'd find it." Professor Maritain asserts that a relativistic philosophy, while it may be appropriate for examining particular uses of social authority, cannot justify the principle of Authority itself. It can tell us what particular social ideals are served or disserved by a particular social arrangement; but that there should be social arrangements at all, that men should have definite obligations and occupy specific positions in a social hierarchy, and that these social arrangements should have purposes we are obligated to fulfill—that there should be Authority in general—this is what requires justification. And this a relativistic philosophy cannot provide.

This is true; but I am afraid the cat simply isn't there to be found. Asking for a justification of Authority in general is like asking for a justification of eating in general. The most one can do, when one is asked why this irritable necessity for eating exists,

62

is to indicate the physiological laws which give eating a fairly influential role in keeping body and soul together. And if the questioner persists, and asks why there must be these physiological laws and not others, the best one can do is to refer to more embracing laws, like those in chemistry and biology, from which these physiological laws follow. The problem is not whether we should eat, but what and how much. Similarly, just as there are options about diet and opportunities for creative imagination in connection with cooking, so we have options and opportunities about the kind of social authority that should be exercised under given circumstances. There are all sorts of problems that arise in connection with the existence of authority, but there is no general problem of Authority as such. Most complex social activities obviously have, and need, definite structures in which men are obligated to perform definite roles; but we cannot show that "Authority" is good or bad, necessary or unnecessary, unless we choose some definite purpose and see whether that purpose is served by the particular instance of authority in question. A categorical justification of "Authority in general" is both impossible in principle and superfluous in practice.

The basic logical point is a simple one. How can one arrive at conclusions that contain moral values unless one has some moral values in his premises? Professor Maritain condemns relativism and liberalism because they cannot stand outside some particular set of moral assumptions, and tell us, among all possible systems of morality, which is the correct one to follow. But this is something which no philosophy, including an absolutistic one, can do. It cannot do so by going beyond the sphere of human affairs, or invoking a special revelation, or any other means. Putting our moral values down as the commands of God or the dictates of nature does not solve the difficulty: it merely puts it off one step farther. "Piety," says the young Euthyphro, in one of Plato's dialogues, "is doing what the gods command."

63

"Yes," says Socrates, "but is it pious because the gods command it or do the gods command it because it is pious?" When we justify our moral beliefs "as a whole" by showing that they rest on the commands of something outside the human scene, we still have to assume that it is moral to obey such commands; and this implies that the commands emanate from a source that is good, and therefore presupposes a conception of the good.

There is, in short, no way around the fact that it is human beings who write their own moral tickets, and that we act on our own responsibility when we choose the values on which we stake our lives. The demand for a total justification of our values is only an expression of the human desire, as insistent as it is pathetic, to have the benefits of free choice with none of its troubles and risks. "It was the woman who made me," said Adam. "It was the serpent," said the woman. "I am one of God's creatures," whispers the serpent.

Indeed, to put it bluntly, there is something disingenuous in the argument that a return to absolutes will eliminate skepticism. For it is not the philosophical relativist, but Professor Maritain, who says that moral values lie beyond our ordinary human capacities for proof. As he is the first to point out, when we seek a total justification of our moral principles, as he believes we must, we are forced back to first principles which human beings are incapable of proving by ordinary methods of reason and observation. This is a perfectly orthodox position, and if there are any infallible first principles, I have no doubt that Professor Maritain is right when he says that they cannot be proved by reason alone. But whatever the merits of this doctrine may be, it is certainly an extraordinary solution of the problem of moral skepticism. It begins with a premise that is false—namely, that we have no good reasons for holding the moral values we do unless we can trace them back to incontestable first principles; and it goes on from this invitation to skepticism

64

to assert that these first principles are incontestable because human beings do not have the wit or the evidence to discuss them. In a word, it begins by inventing an insoluble problem, and then proposes a Mystery as an answer.

But if the liberal attitude toward human history holds that man adopts his own moral ultimates, does this not confirm, it may be asked, what Professor Maritain has said about the "anthropocentric" character of liberalism? Does it not make morality "subjective," and man the measure of all things? And may not anyone then choose any system of values he pleases?

These questions constitute the third main argument against the liberal approach to the problem of human values. Like the other arguments we have considered, they start with a premise that is true, but draw incorrect conclusions from it. It is undeniable, according to any relativistic philosophy, that an element of choice, of simple human preference, is uneliminable from moral judgments. If it is this that partisans of the Absolute deplore, a liberal outlook can offer neither consolation nor a remedy. It can only point out that no one who seriously believes in human freedom would want anything different.

But the fact that an element of choice or preference is present in any moral system or social order in no way implies that human values are just a matter of choice, or that a man is not limited by anything outside himself when he makes the choices he does. He can choose to fly to the moon; he cannot choose to get there. He can choose, like Paolo and Francesca in the *Divine Comedy,* to live only for his beloved, and to cut himself off from everything else to which he has been committed; he cannot choose not to be bored with his beloved when she is the only thing in the world he has left. He can prefer a tyranny to a free society; he cannot choose not to pay tribute to tyrants when he gets the tyranny he wants. In a word, men are responsible for their

65

choices; but no relativistic philosophy argues that these choices are limited by nothing but the will of those who make them. On the contrary, they are relative to the stubborn, objective conditions of the world in which they take place. Choices are events in nature; they take place under definite conditions, psychological and social and physical, which human beings do not create; and they have unavoidable consequences which do not depend on the hopes and desires of those who make them. We cannot make a choice without paying a price; and in the end, it is not we, but a larger order of things, that sets that price.

It is such considerations that guide sober men when they make their choices. And it has been such considerations which have stood behind the continuing effort of liberal and empirical philosophies to employ scientific information and a dispassionate intelligence in the guidance of human choices. Philosophical relativism is the attempt to build a propaedeutic against man's recurrent desire to see the universe as his own private oyster, and to believe that his fondest hopes are guaranteed by the eternal nature of things. It is not relativism which is "anthropocentric" and "subjective"; it is a philosophy which tells us that we can make absolutes out of our desires, and which, even worse, sanctifies such willfulness by calling it divine. The man who truly loves God, wrote Spinoza, cannot expect that God will love him in return.

And so we come to the final argument that stands behind the idea that the *fons et origo* of our troubles is a philosophy of history that denies eternal truths. Liberalism, it is said by Professor Maritain and others, has an absolute of its own, a dogma just as fixed and arbitrary as any of those it so smugly condemns. It is the dogma that elevates human interests into their own judge, the dogma that the satisfaction of human desires is the entire substance of morality and the purpose of all history.

Why, it is asked, should the interests of a temporal creature, bounded by time and circumstance and an inevitable death, why should such interests be made the final test of the worth of everything? Liberalism, it is said, is a "materialistic" and "worldly" philosophy which arbitrarily rules out any transcendent goals for man.

But this is a curious argument. If it is not the interests of man that are ultimate for man, what is? Pigs do not write history. But if they did, it is doubtful that they would regard the crown and summit of all porcine history as man's discovery of sugar-cured ham. And it would be impertinent if men told the pigs to rewrite their history from a "higher" point of view. Similarly, if there is a higher standpoint from which all human interests can be judged, surely this point of view is relevant only insofar as men are interested in taking it. A transcendent absolute would be idle if men did not choose to adopt it; but they can only choose to adopt it if it moves their wills and excites their interest.

The mistake in the notion that a relativistic philosophy is narrowly this-worldly or materialistic is a simple one. It assumes that a philosophy which says that an appeal to human interests is the indispensable feature of moral or political thinking is espousing a particular set of moral values. But it is not. It is merely trying to put the discussion of morals and politics on an objective and public basis. It points out that if men are going to negotiate their disagreements over values rationally, they have to appeal to evidence that is equally available to all; it suggests that the impact of our values on human interests provide just such a publicly observable kind of test; and it points out, on the other side, that the appeal to absolutes is intellectually stultifying and socially disruptive because it introduces considerations for which there is no common evidence.

But none of this rules out in advance any particular set of moral ideals. Philosophical relativism does not say that all values

67

are "material values," or that it is illegitimate for anyone to seek other-worldly interests if he chooses. If a man wishes to turn from the imperfections and vanities of this poor world, if he wishes a life untouched by "the contagion of the world's slow stain," this *is* a human interest, felt here and now, and by a creature in this world. And on relativistic grounds, it must be entertained as a possible human ideal. If such an ideal is ruled out, it is not an abstract philosophy which does so; it can only be the objective facts of man's condition.

By itself, in other words, the liberal denial of absolutes neither implies nor denies any moral values. It does not presuppose that any one way of life is absolutely and forever better than other ways of life. It says that "it all depends": it depends on what human beings want, and on the objective conditions that determine what they can get. And it says that we cannot find these things out without looking into the facts. But it does not tell us in advance what these facts are going to be. In short, the relativistic philosophy which has prevailed in contemporary intellectual liberalism leaves room for all sorts of moral values, and rests on no dogmatic moral preference except, perhaps, a preference for the reasonable, nonviolent, resolution of the clashes of interests and ideals that arise among men.

But there is no point in gilding the lily. The relativistic approach to human values which modern liberalism has traditionally followed does rule out one kind of moral philosophy; and it is a moral philosophy for which the human race, it cannot be denied, has had a peculiar addiction. It is the philosophy which sees nothing necessarily bad in human suffering and pain, and something inevitably tainted and evil in human desires or their satisfaction. The popularity which this philosophy has enjoyed in human affairs does no credit to the human sympathies of human beings, and it is the best reason I know for taking a pessimistic view of the future of the human race. Those who wish to support this philosophy of sin and suffering are choosing the right target when they say that the relativistic philosophy of modern liberalism has tended to undermine it.

I think it is plain that if we are plagued by doubts and uncertainties, they are not the logical consequences of liberal philosophy. Our trouble is not the denial of absolutes; our cure is not a return to the eternal verities. A view of human history which makes man the carrier and ultimate standard of whatever values are found in history neither poisons the springs of the moral life nor undermines the foundations of social authority. But we are faced, then, with the question of how the notion has arisen—and why it is so widely believed—that the modern liberal outlook has corrosive effects on our moral and political convictions. The answer to this question suggests the essential issue that is at stake between those who take a point of view toward modern history like Professor Maritain's and those who share the liberal outlook.

There can be no doubt that a philosophy which holds that all human values are fallible will promote inquiry into existing social arrangements in a way in which an absolutistic philosophy will not. And it is obvious as well that when such inquiry takes place, it may yield the conclusion that some of these social arrangements, or even most of them, do not have the value it is alleged they have. So men's belief in the legitimacy of the existing order is undoubtedly weakened. They no longer believe that it has in all respects a rightful or unqualified claim to be obeyed, or, in other words, that it has as much authority as it claims to have. And it is undeniable that a relativistic philosophy encourages this state of affairs. This is the solid element in the idea that a relativistic philosophy weakens social authority. It does; it weakens the hold of institutions which do not serve the ideals of their members.

But, as Damon Runyon might have said, is this bad? What is

69

needed under these conditions is social reform, and not a dirge on the loss of faith. To blame a relativistic philosophy when men stop believing that their social institutions serve legitimate ideals is a most curious procedure, and hides a quite extraordinary value judgment. If it is discovered that a social order causes avoidable suffering or fails to satisfy interests that could be satisfied, this state of affairs is not the result of the inquiry which reveals it. It is the fault of the social order. There is a natural tendency in most of us to be a little angry with the dentist when his probe touches a sensitive spot in a decayed tooth. I am afraid that Professor Maritain's assertion that the denial of absolutes is "the cause" of the decline of authority in the modern world is a case of blaming the dentist.

Liberalism, in a word, did not come into the modern world to undermine the foundations of authority. It came into the modern world to bring a new kind of authority to social institutions—an authority that rests, not on the a priori arguments of a philosophy or on the ex cathedra statements of those who claim a special access to eternal truths, but on the tested capacity of these institutions to serve living human interests. These words now sound banal; but it is such a conception of authority that the appeal to absolutes would replace. And when this conception of authority was introduced it represented a revolutionary venture in social organization, a new notion of how men ought properly to be related to the societies in which they live.

The new conception of social authority which was introduced by modern liberalism was a part of the general attempt of liberalism to take a social ethic whose classic sanctions had been religious and to reformulate it on a secular basis. Such an attempt is a very radical adventure in the organization of society, and is bound to have its difficulties. It entails a conception of authority which puts men's social arrangements under a more constant test, and inevitably implies a greater tension and strain

70

in society. It means that men see the social systems under which they live as human arrangements, as options to which there are alternatives. It puts the rulers of society under constant pressure to meet new demands. It makes it more difficult to maintain fixed social positions or fixed ideas. Finally, it runs against the whole weight of the absolutistic traditions of the West, and of the unconscious habits of thought and sentiment which those traditions have left with us. There can be no doubt that we have not yet entirely accepted it intellectually, and that only relatively slight pressure is needed to make us yearn for older and more orthodox styles of thought. And it has been repeatedly con· demned for this reason. Those today who, like Professor Maritain, are critics of philosophical relativism do not generally share the authoritarian political views of those who, in the past, have criticized a humanistic and empirical approach to moral issues.* But they share the same nostalgia for absolute Authority, the same nagging and impossible desire to escape the curse of fallible individual judgment.

The revival of the doctrine that eternal values are necessary for moral decency, and agreement on first and final things indispensable for social order, constitutes one of the hallmarks of our distracted time. Thirty years ago, John Dewey wrote, "Thought at every moment puts some portion of existence into peril." It is a remark which suggests how much has changed in the present atmosphere. We do not want thought to put some portion of existence into peril: existence seems to be taking care of this itself, and without our help. We want thought to help shore things up, to fix things again, to lift us above our oppressive sense of drift without meaning and flux without limits. American

* Professor Maritain writes, for example, "A genuine democracy cannot impose on its citizens or demand from them . . . any philosophic or religious creed. . . ."

thought was once marked by a genial willingness to take a chance on a hypothesis. This will to believe has now become increasingly an unhappy anxiety to believe.

It is not hard to see why. "When the whole earth trembles beneath our feet," wrote Lucretius, "when cities are shaken and fall or threaten to fall, what wonder if the sons of man feel contempt for themselves, and acknowledge the great potency and wondrous might of gods in the world, to govern all things?" The pace of contemporary experience has been unprecedented, and its shocks cumulative and pervasive. In the last forty years there has not been a major European capital from London to Moscow which has not seen revolution or war in its streets. In an orderly society men carry around with them the unconscious expectation that things will go so far and no farther, that habit, tradition, good manners, or the simple inertia of the *status quo* will be able to draw the line. The experience of the last forty years, in which the unimaginable seems to have become real, has deeply shaken this sense where it has not completely destroyed it.

It is natural, therefore, that men should wish to find some way out or round or through, that they should feel the need for rules and discipline, and that they should turn, with a heightened preoccupation, to the search for a faith or a cause. There is nothing wrong with this, and a great deal that is right; and, in any case, it is unavoidable. Professor Maritain's theory of modern history rubs the spot where it hurts the most. It picks up the problems of social reconstruction at precisely the point at which most of us feel the pressure of the present crisis in our everyday lives—in our confusions and doubts, in our need to find a defense against our fears, in our anxiety to believe.

The demand for a faith or a cause is an insistent and massive feature of the present social scene. It presents the contemporary social philosopher at once with his initial opportunity and his ultimate test. It is not something which can be controlled simply

72

by appeals for sweet reasonableness, or by rehearsing the horrors which the ideological fever of the twentieth century has wrought. This is the great temptation, and the great weakness, of contemporary liberalism. It can only be met by giving men a cause that is exciting; it can only be controlled by giving them one that is reasonable. Professor Maritain speaks to this need—and this is his strength, and the reason for his appeal. But he has not given men a reasonable faith; he has merely exhorted them to have faith in faith. He has given them, in place of a cause, empty and indignant words.

For a liberal and relativistic philosophy is perfectly capable of giving men guidance in the choice of their goals. It can give them this guidance in a more objective and public way than any absolutism. It can do so, too, without begging any moral questions, except perhaps the question whether man is so inordinately sinful that we ought simply to determine what he wants, and then see that he does not get it. And it is as competent as any other philosophy to fortify a man's faith—when that faith is worth fortifying. It is inferior to absolutism in only one way—it cannot be used to fortify any and every faith. For this small weakness we may all give thanks.

V.

LIBERAL SOCIETY
AND ULTIMATE VALUES

W E HAVE considered the reasons for believing
that a philosophy of human history which takes a relativistic
view of human values is perfectly capable of guiding men responsibly in their affairs. If relativistic liberalism has led to disasters, these have not been due to its inherent logic. But when
men adopt an idea, they do not act on its logical implications
alone; they respond to it emotionally. Men are passionate and
impatient creatures and logic is not everything. In the history of
man's doings and sufferings on this planet it is not very much at
all. And just as there are foods that can poison man's body,
there may be ideas that are poison to his soul.

Is the denial of absolutes one of these poisonous ideas? Does
the liberal attitude toward history fly in the face of something
fundamental in human nature? Does liberalism propose a practical policy for the organization of any human society? These
are questions which are asked today, and they have been asked
repeatedly, I suspect, by men of liberal inclinations in the past.
So there is still a further issue to be considered in connection

74

with the theory that our present difficulties go back to the rejection of a belief in eternal truths.

In the end, Professor Maritain and other partisans of the Absolute do not criticize liberalism simply on the logic of its case. They also say that a question of elementary psychology and sociology is involved. There are certain permanent demands of human nature, they claim, and certain unchanging necessities in human society, which govern the effects that an idea has in history. Men want to believe that what they do is part of an eternal design; they want to feel that their accomplishments and their hopes are not all bound to be swallowed up by time; they want to be convinced that history is not, by its very nature, just a parade of lost causes. A purely secular and relativistic philosophy may have logic on its side; but, its critics point out, it has a deeper biologic against it.

A few exceptional individuals may be able to live with modern liberalism's conception of human destiny; but for most men—for "the common consciousness"—it provides a dismal picture of life. As Professor Maritain says, the dialectic of ideas in history "involves a movement much swifter and much more violent than that of abstract logic. Positions that are tenable in theory (whether rightly or wrongly) are swept aside, because they appear *unlivable* in practice—I do not say for a particular individual, but for the common consciousness." For there is a "natural Platonism" to the human mind, a natural inclination "to admit the existence of eternal truths and transcendent values." And every philosophy must satisfy this spiritual demand on pain of failure.

What is there to the notion that a liberal, relativistic philosophy takes the oxygen out of the spiritual air?

In all societies, human institutions, from the family to insurance policies, from the writing of history to the treasuring of relics

75

from the past, from science to religion, suggest that men's values transcend the limits of their own lives on this earth. Man has the distinctive capacity to contemplate his own death; and his daydreams, his poetry, his philosophy, and the recurrence of messianic ideals in his politics, all suggest that there is in him a thirst for another world to live in, for a perfection that is immune to that perpetual state of dying which, as Plato observed, conventional opinion calls "life." Man's reach, there is little doubt, perennially transcends his grasp. Whether a philosophy that narrowed men's horizons to what is attainable in the here and now would deny a permanent need in man I do not know; but it would be a mean and small-minded affair.

But what does all this prove? So far as the necessity for a belief in absolute truth goes, it proves very little. There is a simple, classic error in Professor Maritain's theory. It is the error of assuming that when men have an appetite, that appetite can be satisfied in only one way. Men obviously need to take in liquid to keep alive; but they can satisfy this need with wine or water. And similarly, if men do have the need which Professor Maritain calls "natural Platonism," this can certainly be satisfied in other ways than by the particular philosophical doctrine in which Professor Maritain happens to be interested. The desire for "the transcendent" does not require that men believe in absolutes, and it is not denied when the belief in absolutes is denied. Men can still believe that there is an independent order of things which is unaffected by human beliefs or desires. They can still pursue values that transcend "the pomp and vanities of this wicked world." They can still try to look at things, as far as it is in their power, under the aspect of eternity. It would be a very strange world indeed if there were in human nature a peculiar and exclusive propensity for one particular technical philosophy or one special religious outlook. What Professor Maritain has done has been to convert an historical circumstance—the tradition of philosophical abso-

76

lutism—into a necessarily permanent feature of the human scene. It is a peculiar and revealing paradox that those who dream of total escape from the temporal perspectives of history end by turning local and temporary conditions into eternal verities.

What, after all, does it mean to say that men are naturally inclined to believe in "eternal truths and transcendent values"? Does it mean they are inclined to believe that what is true is true, and cannot be changed? A secular philosophy does not deny this. Does it mean that men may in fact hold some ideas that are true, and will stand the test of all future experience? A secular philosophy does not deny this. Does it mean that men want to pursue, and should pursue, values that transcend the urgencies of a moment or of a generation, and will give their lives constancy and a steady sense of direction? This is precisely what the liberal outlook on history aimed to give a secular world. All it denied was that men could ever say with certainty that they were in possession of any eternal truths. It asserted that there was a larger realm of truth, independent of human beliefs, which human beings could never say they had grasped definitively—a larger world by which all human creeds and ideals must always be checked. This is an assertion that there are things that transcend the human scene; it is not a denial of it. And it is precisely this allegiance to a realm of truth which is always larger than the realm of human knowledge that led to the rejection of the belief in absolutes.

The same point applies to Professor Maritain's conviction that men's religious emotions are necessarily attached to an absolutistic creed. The institutions of religion have traditionally given men another world to live in. They have offered men symbols of a perfection that cannot be reached in this world, and have stood as reminders of the gap that must always exist between what men can actually accomplish and what they aspire to do. In any society which retains its humility and sense of humor, it may be hoped, there is a role for such institutions. But in a secular society which retains its freedoms, they cannot perform this task so long as they hold that the beliefs on which they rest, and the ideals they espouse, are not subject to the same tests as apply to all other beliefs and ideals. They do not then integrate a society, or pull men's lives together. They stand as divisive agencies, and as invitations to men to think one way on weekdays and another way on Sundays.

For there is, after all, a simple difference between an idea of perfection and a perfect idea. If there is a "natural Platonism" in man it leads him to the first; but there is no way by which he can attain the second. Religious institutions which set themselves apart from secular tests confuse the human image of perfection which they incorporate with perfection itself; and without stretching the phrase too far, they may be said to be committing "the sin of pride." Man's image of a perfection that transcends this world can expand his imagination, chasten his hopes, and discipline his emotions. But it is an invitation to fanaticism and self-indulgence when it is mistaken for anything but a human image. The "natural Platonism" in man does not require us to go that far.

But there is still a second question about the role of the belief in absolutes in human history. Must there not be in any society some basic integrating faith, some unquestioned commitment to first principles and ultimate ends? Can men live together cheerfully and peacefully in society, can they work together with spirit on common projects, unless they agree on final values?

Plato, who seems to have expressed all such notions first, said, "Where there is only private feeling, but no feeling in common, a state is disorganized." From this he drew the conclusion that general agreement on ultimate goals is essential for social cohesion. Plato used this idea to formulate an authoritarian theory of society, but the idea has persisted in our thinking about the nature of free societies as well. And this idea that a free society must share some ultimate convictions about first and final things if it is not to collapse before its enemies or dissolve into anarchy is undergoing a considerable revival. Diplomats need such convictions, it is believed, in arguing with their opponents at international conferences; citizens need them to resist the lures and deceptions that are placed before them by the enemy. A desire for an orthodoxy, and for a cosmic reassurance that one is right, has always been strong in societies whose established institutions are undergoing a fundamental change, or which feel themselves endangered by an external enemy. The argument for the social necessity of absolutes cuts deep into our present disturbances of mind.

Accordingly, the feeling is now widespread that traditional liberalism, with its willingness to leave ultimate questions alone so far as politics go, was simply unprepared for the trials of the modern world. As Professor Maritain says, "Nineteenth Century bourgeois democracy was *neutral* even with regard to freedom. Just as it had no real *common good,* it had no real *common thought*—no brains of its own, but a neutral, empty skull clad with mirrors: no wonder that before the second world war, in countries that fascist, racist, or communist propaganda was to disturb or to corrupt, it had become a society without any idea of itself and without faith in itself, without any *common faith* which could enable it to resist disintegration."*

* The same view, or something very close to it, has been adopted by a considerable number of social and political thinkers, many of them men of pronouncedly liberal tendencies. The late Karl Mannheim, for example, wrote, "The age of Liberalism was rather exceptional in thinking that change could be accomplished without bothering about religious and other forms of basic integration. . . . We now realize that a social order can only maintain itself satisfactorily on the basis of a sound statement of belief that performs in a new way the role of the old dogma. We have learned from the chaos through which we have passed that certain things must remain exempt from doubt, even if only for a while. . . . Certain unchanging aspects of the human mind seem to indicate the need for a transcendental religious foundation in society; and several factors make this need even more urgent in our present situation."

The essence of this idea was expressed by Chesterton in a metaphor:

Modern society [he wrote] is intrinsically insecure because it is based on the notion that all men will do the same thing for different reasons. . . . As within the head of any convict may be the hell of a quite solitary crime, so in the house or under the hat of any suburban clerk may be the limbo of a quite separate philosophy. . . . Now whether or not this sort of variety is valuable, this sort of unity is shaky. To expect that all men for all time will go on thinking different things, and yet doing the same things, is a doubtful speculation. It is not founding society on a communion, or even on a convention, but rather on a coincidence. Four men may meet under the same lamp post; one to paint it pea green as part of a great municipal reform; one to read his breviary in the light of it; one to embrace it with accidental ardour in a fit of alcoholic enthusiasm; and the last merely because the peagreen post is a conspicuous point of rendezvous with his young lady. But to expect this to happen night after night is unwise. . . .

But would giving men the same ultimate ends and the same sound statement of belief really guarantee that they would meet amicably at their pea green lamp post? It is an attractive idea, this notion that complex human communities can be organized like a communion of saints, and it has bemused human beings for centuries—bemused them, that is, when it hasn't killed them. For agreement on ultimate ends or on an abstract philosophy is a purely verbal affair. It does not guarantee that men will employ the same means to reach these ends, or that they will interpret the words of this philosophy in the same way. A statement of ultimate faith will produce general agreement in a society only if there is also an agreed-on institution which can enforce a single interpretation of that faith. It is one thing to agree to a general philosophic outlook; it is quite another thing—as the Hundred Years' War or the recent troubles between Stalinist and anti-Stalinist Marxists suggest—to agree on who is giving the proper interpretation of it.

80

And when force is used to make men accept a common faith, it is frequently a very unlovely brand of force.

There are two fundamental errors in the idea that every society must have an orthodox creed, that joint social activities cannot be maintained on a voluntary basis unless there is some agreement on the ultimate ends of life. The first is the error of overintellectualizing human behavior. Men do not simply seek definite goals, arranged in neat, hierarchical order, ending with "ultimate ends." They are creatures of habit and routine, they are moved by traditions, they respond to their friends and neighbors; they may even have moral principles, which they simply observe because they are uncomfortable when they don't. Men do not have to love the same ultimate good to live at peace with one another; good manners will do the job perfectly well. Even Senators, who are said to be men who know what they want, are not motivated only by their political ambitions or by the interests of their constituents; happily, most of them are also governed by the reflection that they belong to a gentleman's club with a common code. Most of all, perhaps, men respond to common symbols—to words or flags or rituals or remembered events—which draw them together in a common cause without evoking any articulate beliefs. In a word, men frequently observe rules, and work well together, without thinking about ultimate ends, or, indeed, any ends at all. If one wishes, one can call these habits, symbols, and codes which hold men together "common values." But they are not ultimate goals, and they do not depend on a common philosophy. And the attempt to impose such a philosophy has been one of the perennial, and least necessary, causes of human suffering and social disruption. "Even if there were only two men left in the world," one of Frank O'Connor's stories begins, "and both of them to be saints, they wouldn't be happy even then. One of them would be bound to try and improve the other. That is the nature of things."

The second error in the view that a common faith, or agreement on ultimate ends, is indispensable to the unity of any society is suggested by Chesterton's metaphor of the four men who meet at the corner under the lamp post, each with his own private purpose in mind. Even assuming that they do not get to like one another, or to develop a group spirit, they may still develop a common interest in that corner. They may all want it well il-luminated, for example, and may happily form a pressure group to see that this is done, so that the painter can paint well, the monk read his breviary more easily, the drinker keep from bump-ing his head, and the young lover from accosting the wrong girl. In short, even though men do not have the same ultimate goals, their interests can nevertheless intersect and overlap. Men do not have to agree on the same ultimate ends in order to co-operate willingly on a common project. They must merely feel that this project serves their own purposes as well as the purpose of others. There can, after all, be crossroads and public thoroughfares which have an indefinite number of possible destinations, but in which we all have a common interest.

Indeed, the failure to see that men can work well together without the same ultimate goals leads to a failure to take account of the most distinctive technique of a liberal society for maintain-ing voluntary co-operation—the technique of compromise. For compromise does not only take place when men are bound by a common creed. It takes place at least as often for a much simpler reason—that men have other values besides those that are in dispute. As a result, they do not choose to risk everything on a single issue. The fact that men prefer to hedge if they can, that they do not like to put all their interests in one basket, is not, perhaps, a very exciting trait; but it is one of the simple reasons why diversity and social cohesion can exist side by side.

Thus, the fundamental cohesion of a liberal society does not depend on its enunciation of any "sound statement of belief." It is not true that there has to be some system for the integration of

82

ultimate values. Social integration in a liberal society does not come from integrating ultimate values. It comes from organizing secular institutions in such a way that men's "ultimate" values—their consciences, their sense of the meaning of life, their personal dignity—do not become elements of public conflict. More positively, it depends on the ability of a society to organize itself pluralistically, with a number of vital centers of power within it which are accessible to the individual. For when power is so organized, and all of men's interests do not pile up around a single issue, conflicts of interest can be localized, and ultimate and unresolvable disagreements avoided. A society in which compromise is a regular and standard pattern for attaining co-operation and consent does not just happen. It has to be planned for, and deliberately constructed and maintained. The language of "ultimates" does not help in this process.

There are, indeed, certain very definite risks in our present passion for solving our problems by reaffirming our faith. Men generally begin to state their ends or goals in a formal and explicit way only when the established patterns for their joint activities are breaking down. If the enunciation of ends is a practical prelude to the actual reform of social institutions, it is necessary and desirable. If it remains merely a statement of faith, however, it can accelerate the course of the disease. For men are told that they have, or ought to have, a "common faith" at precisely the moment when their common habits are in decline. And this may only heighten their sense of the gap between the alleged and the real, and further encourage the growth of cynicism, hypocrisy, and that general state of affairs which the sociologists call "anomie"—life without norms. Abstract moralizing is a pleasant enough occupation; but it frequently aggravates the problems it sets out to cure.

Nor can these consequences be avoided by trying, as so many now seem inclined to try, to formulate some very elementary, limited, and innocuous statement of faith—the kind, it is said, which might be appropriate for a free society. The vaguer the terms, the more likely it is that every man will try to interpret these sacred articles of faith in his own favor. The result is not unity, but the throttling of discussion—an inverted Tower of Babel in which everybody uses the same words, and nobody means the same thing. The simple decline of our political language into rhetoric and ritual—or into a preface to selling soap or automobiles—is itself one of our major political problems.

For social cohesion certainly depends on men's ability to communicate to one another. Words stop communicating when the realities they designate begin to fade; these realities cannot be recovered by repeating the words in a louder tone. The mutual understandings and common loyalties that sustain a social order emerge out of men's daily habits and routines, out of the concrete institutions that frame their lives. Our present widespread interest in restating the ultimates on which a faith in democracy depends is an attempt to do with words what must mainly be done by practical programs that will restore these institutions. And it misleads men about something fundamental—that a liberal social order is not a communion of saints all loving the same ultimate end, but a society of men who are diverse and various and love different things, but have the elbow room that permits them to live cheerfully together. The search for a unitary creed is a symptom of our troubles, not their cure. The blessed in heaven sing; it is the men in hell who make speeches justifying themselves.

VI.

THE REDISCOVERY OF SIN

An entire generation of thinkers and writers —New Conservatives and New Liberals—has rediscovered the truth in the ancient doctrine of original sin. The adventure of modern liberalism began with the dream of human perfectibility; it has ended, they point out, in a spectacle of human wickedness raised to a new level of sophistication and efficiency. And this awful denouncement has proved that liberalism was wrong about the one thing about which it is supremely important for a social movement to be right—human nature itself. This is the basic and insoluble problem.

When there is evil in the world, we are reminded, it is not just the result of social institutions or human ignorance. It comes from something deeper and more enduring—a perversity in the human soul itself. When the human intellect errs, this is not just the result of human fallibility, but of human egoism and pride; when there is injustice or cruelty in society, this mirrors a maliciousness in the human spirit. Liberalism, with its faith in human intelligence and its zeal for improving social conditions, did not see what the illiberal Dostoevsky, with his more-than-rational wisdom, was able to see—"the underground man" who has come to the surface in the twentieth century. As a result liberals and men of good will have been unable to understand, or to stand up to, the hard realities of life in this century. "Cursed is the man who has faith in man," the maxim of Jeremiah, has emerged as a new touchstone of political realism.

On this insight a whole new approach to politics and society has been constructed. In the United States, the best-known, and the most forceful and authoritative, spokesman for this approach is Mr. Reinhold Niebuhr. In a long and successful series of books, Mr. Niebuhr has applied the idea of original sin to American history, to international diplomacy, to the revolutionary and reformist movements of our time, and to current psychological and sociological doctrines. He finds in all of these fields the same lingering illusion about human benevolence; and this illusion, he believes, is the major reason for the impotence of liberals and men of good will on the contemporary scene. Mr. Niebuhr has developed the theme of original sin into a comprehensive vision of human nature and destiny, and has constructed an incisive philosophy of history whose principal object is to replace the liberal faith in the perfectibility of man with what he regards as a more sober and tough-minded view of human possibilities.

Mr. Niebuhr writes, for the most part, as a professional theologian, which he is. He is interested in criticizing not only the liberal fantasies of circles outside religion, but the liberal fantasies that have invaded modern theological circles as well. But his interests are primarily practical and political, and his influence extends into circles that are not even amateurishly theological. In his practical judgments he has exhibited a combination of courage, imagination, and shrewd common sense which have made him a leading spokesman for liberal groups. And while his pages are adorned with Biblical references, and reverberate to the tunes of old theological controversies, the terms he uses—"radical evil," "the transcendent," "the absolute,"—have a resonance that is borrowed, not so much from Saint Augustine or Calvin, as from Kierkegaard, Marx, Freud, and contemporary sociology. Because Mr. Niebuhr wishes to restore the doctrine of original sin to a central position, in opposition to recent trends in American religious thinking, he is usually called "neo-orthodox." But the "neo" is the operative term, for Mr. Niebuhr's doctrine of original sin could only have been conceived by a contemporary mind. Its tone is the tone of the contemporary disenchanted liberal or radical, the man whose hopes have been disappointed because they have not been achieved, and disappointed even more when they have been achieved. Its purpose is, at once, to rebuke us for the utopian illusions in which we have indulged ourselves and to keep us from losing faith altogether.

The questions with which Mr. Niebuhr's philosophy of history starts are the questions that no liberal or sensitive mind has been able to avoid since World War I. Why have the great hopes of the modern era been so utterly disappointed? How was it possible for men to lose themselves so completely in perfectionist dogmas, to put so much trust in the benevolence of human beings, or so much power in the hands of a few leaders? What went wrong with the modern dream? And Mr. Niebuhr's answer is straightforward. The dream was a fantasy to begin with. It was an attempt to escape an unpleasant fact about the human scene, a fact that cannot be changed or mitigated no matter how much we multiply our mechanical gadgets or psychological panaceas or social programs. That fact is the fact of original sin. It is the basic fact of human history from which all its other main features derive. And it is rooted in the unalterable nature of human beings and the human environment.

For even in the best of all possible worlds, Mr. Niebuhr says, human life would still incorporate a standing paradox. On one

87

side, man is a finite creature; on the other side, he is infinite in his desires. He is mortal, but can look beyond his own death, limited, but able to see beyond his limitations. No matter how men try, they cannot help but be caught up in local circumstances, a parochial outlook, and a personal, all-too-personal, self. There is bound to be egoism even in their highest flights of altruism; there is bound to be something personal, self-enclosed, and partisan about their thinking even when they believe they are being most objective. And yet, despite the fact that men are captives of necessity in this way, they are also free. They cannot hold any point of view which is not relative, or have anything but a limited grasp of perfection. But they can know that there is a perfection beyond their grasp. They can see beyond their own local circumstances, recognize that some other point of view is possible, and believe that there is such a thing as impersonality and objectivity. In short, man is a creature living tensely between two worlds: one is the actual, limited world in which he lives, but from which he cannot help but feel alienated; the other is an ideal world for which he longs, but from which he is permanently excluded. To be disappointed idealists is the common and eternal fate of all men. Man's whole moral life requires him "to seek after an impossible victory and to adjust himself to an inevitable defeat."

What is the consequence? The consequence, Mr. Niebuhr believes, is that men must live out their lives with one basic and defining emotion—the feeling of anxiety. Anxiety is not a fear of something definite. It is not caused by specific things so that it can be cured by practical measures. It is the inexpungable sense in all men of their distance from the Absolute. Anxiety is "the dizziness of freedom." It shows itself in men's feelings of homelessness and alienation, in their perennial sense of dissatisfaction, in their imponderable feeling that things are wrong but that there is no way of setting them right. This feeling of anxiety is the psychological source of all great human achievements. If men could not see beyond the immediate, if they were not goaded by the feeling that something else and something better is possible, none of their triumphs could be imagined. Anxiety is the essential condition of intellectual and artistic creation, personal nobility, self-sacrifice, and everything that is finest in human history. To wish to eliminate anxiety is to wish to eliminate the emotion which is the mark of human freedom and power, and sets man off from all other species.

But anxiety is also the source of something else. It is the source of man's sinfulness. For the pain of anxiety drives men to try to escape it. They sink into sensuality in the effort to forget that there is anything beyond the immediate. They lose themselves in fanaticism in the effort to convince themselves that they have brought the Absolute to earth. They try to cut down their aspirations and fall into cynicism, or to inflate their powers and fall into pride and arrogance. In a word, they try to identify their own limited and relative powers with the Absolute. And this is original sin. Sin is the narcosis of the soul; it is a perennial temptation to which men must inevitably succumb.

Thus, there is in man, as Mr. Niebuhr sees him, a connatural perversity, a discordance in the human spirit that echoes a larger disharmony in the relation of man to the universe. And this produces a basic ambiguity and irony in all human history. For the source of all man's achievements is also the source of all his wickedness and folly. His vices and his virtues have the same origins. And so there is a taint in whatever human beings do. Their triumphs tempt them to forget their weakness; every growth in their powers leads them into pride and dogmatism. Human wickedness is not the product of bad education, or mental disease, or unjust social conditions. Specific human misdeeds may be, but not the fact of human evil. This is *original:* it is uneliminable from human nature in all times and circumstances, and is the

89

ultimate source of bad education or mental disease or unjust social conditions.

Human history, therefore, is a somber affair which enacts a basic moral drama. It is the record of men's recurrent efforts to overstep the bounds which have been set upon their lives; and what happens in history is the comment, ironic and inexorable, on this human pretension. For Mr. Niebuhr, the great events of history—the rise and fall of social institutions, the breakdown of old social classes and the emergence of new ones, the revolutions and wars, the great hopes with which social movements begin and the great disappointments with which they end—are neither episodes in a meaningless cycle of birth and decay, as ancient Hellenic wisdom had it, nor agents, as modern liberal culture has insisted, in the progressive realization of truth and goodness. They are the executors in history of the judgment of the Absolute, witnesses to the fact that men strive for a fulfillment they cannot find, and are punished for doing so. "In history," says Mr. Niebuhr, "God always chooses 'the things which are not, to put to nought the things that are.' . . . History is . . . not a realm of indeterminate growth and development. It is a realm of conflict. . . . New forces and forms of life are a reminder to the established forms and powers of the contingent character of all historic configurations and a judgment upon the pretension which denies this contingency." Man, the aggressor, is always trying to cross his natural frontiers; the nature of things is always putting him back in his place. Cold war is not just a passing phenomenon in world politics. In Mr. Niebuhr's philosophy of history, it becomes a permanent feature of the politics of the cosmos.

For while human history is carried on in the sphere of things that are mortal, it goes on against the backdrop of perfection. There is an Absolute, Mr. Niebuhr affirms, that stands outside history, an inscrutable standard that men can neither understand nor approach, but whose existence they cannot help recognizing.

90

History goes on before a mysterious presence, whose face we never see, but which tells us that there is something that is a lie in all human affirmations and ideals. When we forget that there is such an Absolute we fail to see that we are relative and mortal creatures, and we deprive human history of any meaning or unity. When we fail to see that such an Absolute stands irretrievably *above* and *outside* history, we commit the sin of pride and act as though the purposes we seek *in* history are universal and final. We cannot attain the Absolute or even know what it is; but inevitably we must live by it. It warns us that every human triumph is a temptation, and every human achievement an invitation to contrition and repentance.

Mr. Niebuhr's philosophy of history thus lies tensely between the poles of time and eternity, change and permanence, skepticism and dogma. With Professor Maritain, he agrees that there is an Absolute; with modern relativists, he agrees that such an Absolute is unattainable. He has gone part way down the road from absolutism, still clinging to absolute ideals, but convinced that they are not for the world of fallible men. And his criticism of the liberal approach to history is therefore the reverse of Professor Maritain's. Where Professor Maritain condemns liberalism for its tendency to make everything relative, Mr. Niebuhr condemns it for its tendency to forget that nothing is absolute.

For modern liberalism, and with it the entire modern era, Mr. Niebuhr believes, has committed the greatest sin in the whole calendar of sins—the attempt to deny sin. The idea of progress, the belief in the indefinite perfectibility of man, represents the most systematic effort in all of human history to get around the facts and deny that man is a limited and finite creature. It is the very principle of Sin, converted into a philosophy. And it has left the modern era without an outlook that can deal with the real world—a world in which men's motives are inevitably mixed,

91

in which the pure at heart are also likely to be the most ruthless, in which malice and self-aggrandizement are permanent facts, and in which anxiety is incurable.

The liberal belief in the perfectibility of man, says Mr. Niebuhr, is the single article of faith which has most distinguished modern culture. It is responsible for the follies, self-deceptions, and arrogant hopes on which the modern era has misspent its energies. List the characteristic weaknesses of the liberal mind—its futile pursuit of purity in politics, its conviction that history is a struggle between the enlightened and the unenlightened, its faith in objective reason and its conviction that there is such a thing as disinterested good will—and we see the practical consequences of the liberal approach to history. The belief in the natural goodness of man explains why modern liberals were so late in recognizing the true nature of Fascism. The belief that evil is social in its origins and can be eliminated by changing society explains why so many have been seduced by Communism. The belief that when man progresses in knowledge he also progresses in virtue explains why science has been erected into a false Messiah. The liberal faith that everything will be washed clean by the waters of time explains why modern liberalism has had a manic-depressive character, moving from bouts of utopian enthusiasm at one extreme to bouts of startled disillusion and despair at the other. Never has a social movement allowed itself such exorbitant hopes, or placed such faith in human nature and human reason; and never, as a result, have the hopes of any social movement been so completely and terrifyingly refuted by events. "In one century," Mr. Niebuhr observes, "modern man had claimed to have achieved the dizzy heights of the mastery both of natural processes and historical destiny. In the following century he is hopelessly enmeshed in an historical fate, threatening mutual destruction, from which he seems incapable of extricating himself. A word of Scripture fits the situation perfectly:

92

'He that sitteth in the heavens shall laugh: the Lord shall have them in derision.' "

It is a philosophy which seems to have the shape of truth. It provides a framework within which we seem to be able to explain and digest our disappointments, and it speaks with force and point to the doubts that beset us. But let us ask what in fact Mr. Niebuhr's philosophy of history teaches us. For while the doctrine of sin is a very old doctrine, the wickedness of man is an even older fact. Men who have not believed in original sin, after all, have also recognized this wickedness. And other ages, which have believed in sin, have had their disasters too—including the disasters of messianic politics. What does a belief in original sin allow us to understand about human history which we cannot understand without it? How will it guide us in our political thinking, or keep us from making the errors we have made in the past? In just what way did the modern era go wrong when it forgot to remember original sin?

Let us consider original sin, first, in its traditional form as a psychological doctrine. It is exemplified by the words of Saint Paul: "For the good that I would I do not: but the evil which I would not, that I do." As a psychological doctrine, original sin asserts that there is a propensity in man to do evil in spite of his knowledge of what is right, and, indeed, precisely because he knows it is wrong. It denies that men's vices can be put down just as mental aberrations or the result of faulty social conditions. It asserts that if men could not glut themselves on good food, they would glut themselves on bad—and not for the sake of food, but for the love of gluttony. It asserts that if men had no moral principles, they would have to invent them, merely for the sake of being faithless to them. "I had not known lust, except the law had said, Thou shalt not covet."

Now this is not a very flattering view of human nature, but

93

there is a good deal of evidence to support it—at any rate, in the behavior of members of societies that believe in original sin. It is a theory which grows out of a psychological experience which has been recurrent and insistent—the experience of the divided and impotent will, hating itself for what it is and yet unable to be what it wants to be. It is the experience not only of Saint Paul and Saint Augustine, but of Rousseau and John Stuart Mill and William James, and it has left its mark not only on our religions, but on our philosophy, our political institutions and ideals, and our practical policies in everything from education to criminology and social work. It would take more evidence than we now have to show that men in all cultures exhibit the traits which this doctrine describes. But no historian can underestimate the importance of the experience or the type of mentality to which it refers, particularly in the history of Western society. It is obvious that egoism, malice, mixed motives, and acute anxiety are facts which make a difference in human behavior, and which any realistic historian or practical politician must take into account. Something is missing from the simple notion that virtue is knowledge and vice only ignorance.

But once we recognize all this, we may well ask what it does or does not imply. And it does not imply that liberal hopes have been based on an illusion. For the doctrine of original sin, when interpreted as a purely psychological doctrine, is perfectly compatible with liberal hopes. It merely describes a human disposition, like the physical disposition to grow old. And just as the progress of medicine has gradually retarded the physical processes of senility, so the progress of knowledge might be able to mitigate the consequences of this tendency in man to do evil for its own sake. In short, Mr. Niebuhr and the many others who have rediscovered original sin must mean a good deal more by the idea than just this psychological theory. For from their point of view, original sin is not like other facts about human life. It stands by itself. It does not have specific causes and conditions, and it cannot be handled in the way that senility, or any other human trait, can be handled. We can prevent a glutton from overeating by limiting his supply of food; we can keep a potential murderer from killing by locking him up. But no matter what we do, we cannot keep men from sinning, or even slow down the rate of sin. Sin, Mr. Niebuhr tells us, is always present, and is even behind our benevolent impulses. It contradicts the very nature of man to conceive of human life without sin. And it is only when we see that sin stands apart from all other facts about human life, and that it cannot be mitigated by any rational or practical technique, that we grasp the essential insight for which the doctrine of original sin stands.

Now why does Mr. Niebuhr believe that sin has this unique status in human life?

The ultimate fact about human life, says Mr. Niebuhr, is that evil, which does not exist in nature, exists in human history. And only the doctrine of original sin, he believes, can explain this fact. For it shows us that sin arises out of a fundamental and insoluble contradiction in which human life is caught—"the paradox of human freedom." Man is limited, subject to causal necessity, bound to finite conditions. And yet he is also free, able to introduce novelty into the universe, to choose his own path for himself, and to be held responsible for his actions. On one side, man is a mortal creature, put into a world he has not made, and which limits and determines what he does at every turn. On the other side, man is able to transcend the bounds of his creaturely existence. By some strange illogic in the universe, he is free, and able to overstep his limits; and when he does, he sins. Unless we see that human existence incorporates this standing contradiction, that the basic conditions of human history transcend the canons of human logic, we cannot explain why evil is the defining and indelible characteristic of human experience.

95

It is, then, Mr. Niebuhr's belief in "the contradiction of finiteness and freedom" which underlies his conception of original sin. He believes that there is a logical paradox in believing that men can be free and at the same time subject to external causal conditions; and for this reason, whenever men do make a free choice they overstep their limits and inevitably sin. What are the logical credentials of this conception of freedom on which Mr. Niebuhr's entire system stands?

It involves a fundamental mistake. For the question of whether an action is determined by external conditions or not has nothing at all to do with whether it is free. The difference between unfree behavior and free behavior is not a difference between behavior that has external causes and behavior that does not. It is a difference between being coerced and having some choice about the conditions that govern one's behavior. Consider a simple example. In a totalitarian election, we know that the ruling party will win no matter whether there are bad economic conditions, or an unpopular war, or corruption in government. The minds of the voters are influenced not by these things but by other factors such as fear of the police. In a free election, on the other hand, we have to know something about existing economic conditions and the like, and we must have some theories about their influence on the minds of the voters, before we can foretell the outcome. But this plainly means that the mind of the free voter is *determined* by certain external conditions. And no free voter would consider himself more free if he could "transcend the conditions of his creaturely existence" and keep his mind from being influenced by such things as the economic or foreign policies of his government.

There are two main errors behind Mr. Niebuhr's conception of freedom. The first is an animistic conception of causation, an assumption that a causal law is like a command. But a causal law does not *make* things happen; it merely describes how they

96

regularly do happen. And it does not even say that things will inevitably happen in the way its describes. It says that they will happen in this way only if certain appropriate conditions are present. The man who chooses to use a parachute when he leaps from a plane does not break the law of falling bodies or exceed his "creaturely limits." His knowledge of the physical properties of parachutes merely gives him a great deal more freedom of choice about how he will come down. And if parachutes, air, and falling human bodies were not subject to certain fixed causal laws, our parachutist would not have more freedom of choice. He would have none at all. For the existence of stable laws and fixed conditions in our environment is absolutely essential if we are to make any plans or decide in a responsible way what we want to do. Mr. Niebuhr's "paradox of freedom" confuses freedom with chaos and causation with fate.

But man is creative, says Mr. Niebuhr. He introduces novelty into the universe and does unique things. Must his actions, then, not elude any generalizations? If they are predictable, how can we say they are "unique" or free?* This is the argument to which Mr. Niebuhr returns repeatedly to support his portrait of human nature and his theory of human history. But it involves the second error in his conception of freedom. For while it is of course true that human beings do all sorts of unique and novel things (including a great many which might better have been left undone), this by no means proves that we cannot generalize about human behavior or that it breaks free from the laws of cause and effect. For in the first place, uniqueness does not appear only in the sphere of human behavior. If the "uniqueness" of events made them insusceptible to generalization, this would destroy the possi-

* "The freedom of the human agents of action," writes Mr. Niebuhr, "results in diverse and novel modes of behavior and action which make scientific generalizations, based upon the observation of recurrence, much more dubious and hazardous than the generalizations which constitute the stuff of natural science."

bility of generalization in the natural sciences as well as in history and the human sciences. And in the second place, generalizations are abstractions. They relate things only in certain selected respects. They do not relate them in every respect. And so one can generalize about things perfectly well without destroying their uniqueness. When biological mutants appear, they do not break the laws of evolution; they exhibit these laws. And while Shakespeare's plays have no precedent, he clearly did not exceed his limits when he wrote them. One can recognize perfectly well, in other words, that human beings are sometimes free and creative actors without denying that their actions are also subject to environing conditions and causal generalizations. In brief, there is no such "paradox of freedom" as Mr. Niebuhr believes. It is an invented paradox. And the "fact" of original sin, which Mr. Niebuhr derives from this paradox, is not a fact at all, but the result of a basic confusion about the meaning of terms like "freedom" and "causation."

For all the alleged hard-headedness of his doctrine of sin, Mr. Niebuhr has in the end been bewitched by a sentimental idea of freedom—the idea that perfect freedom means the absence of all limitations on our behavior. It is only this "perfect" freedom that is contradicted by the idea of causal necessity; and it is only our inability to have this "perfect" freedom which leads Mr. Niebuhr to talk about the inevitable wretchedness and sinfulness of human existence. But it is not really a "perfect" freedom at all. If it were attainable, it would not feel like freedom but like a lunatic's nightmare, in which everything happened at random and nothing at all could be counted upon. Men generally begin to think about freedom when they are suffering from some limitation on their behavior which they do not like. It is temptingly easy to move from this to the complaint that there are any limitations on human behavior at all. But while we can sometimes be freer by getting rid of certain limitations, it does not follow that we would be absolutely free if we got rid of all limitations.*

But what about our basic problem—the ultimate mystery of evil? Can we really get around this mystery just by saying that a little logical clarity would eliminate the problem? For it is all very well, Mr. Niebuhr points out, to do what modern liberal culture has done, and to talk only about specific evils and their specific causes. As a way of dealing with specific evils, Mr. Niebuhr agrees, this is perfectly valid. It explains them and helps get rid of them. But it is a systematic evasion of the basic problem. It fails to explain why evil, which does not exist in nature, has come to exist in human life. Is it not plain that logic and common sense are not enough, and that we stand here before a mystery which only a belief in original sin can illuminate?

But to say there is a problem here is like saying there is a problem in the fact that crime exists only when there is law, divorce only when there is marriage, and headaches only when there are heads. Naturally evil appears only in human history: it is human beings who introduce moral standards into the universe. It is always possible to say, I suppose, that a cure for migraine is an evasion of "the ultimate problem," because it leaves the head still there, subject to all the other ills that heads are heir to. But a

---

* The kind of argument on which Mr. Niebuhr's "paradox of freedom" depends is illustrated by a Sphinx-like statement of Kierkegaard's, which Mr. Niebuhr quotes as a "succinct" and "excellent" statement of the problem: "Truth [in the human situation]," says Kierkegaard, "is exactly the identity of choosing and determining and of being chosen and determined. What I choose I do not determine, for if it were not determined I could not choose it; and yet if I did not determine it through my choice I would not really choose it. It is: if it were not I could not choose it. It is not: but becomes reality through my choice, or else my choice were an illusion." This illustrates Kierkegaard's maxim that things have become too simple and it is necessary to make them difficult again. Of course, I could not bring something into existence if none of the causes on which its existence depends were present; but this does not begin to imply that I myself may not be one of these causes.

99

man who offered such an argument (outside the pages of a philosophy of history) would be credited with little but a talent for contrived nonsense.

In short, it is difficult to see what insight into human history Mr. Niebuhr's theory gives us beyond a fact that we already know —that man is born, and suffers, and dies. The doctrine of sin is presented by Mr. Niebuhr and its other current protagonists as a ubiquitous and inevitable fact about the human scene. But it is so ubiquitous and so inevitable that it explains, with equal ease, what has actually happened in history and what has actually not happened. If Mark Antony had not lingered with Cleopatra, if Caligula had been gentle and meek, if Louis XIV had not been extravagant, but had left Versailles and entered a monastery, "sin" would explain it as easily as it explains what actually happened. It is a doctrine which is equally consistent with statements that are true and statements that are false.

For as Mr. Niebuhr reminds us, the taint of sin is present even in our benevolent actions. It is not just that all human motives are mixed. It is that no clear distinction can be made even in principle between good and bad motives. What genuine guidance can such a doctrine give us? It warns us that we are always trespassing beyond our limits, and then tells us that we cannot know what these limits are. It says that if we try to set any fixed limits to our aspirations, we are sanctifying what exists, and turning a temporary state of affairs into an absolute; but it also tells us that if we do not set any limits to our aspirations, we are denying our mortality and weakness and committing the sin of pride. We are damned if we do and damned if we don't. This is an antidote to moral complacency which substitutes moral hypochondria. And it presents us with a disturbing question which it leaves entirely unanswered: If everything we do is inevitably tainted by sin, if even the moral standards by which we distinguish between good and bad are tainted, what is the point of having any standards at all? As an alternative to our current illusions, Mr Niebuhr's theory of history is no alternative at all.

But exactly what have our illusions been?

Liberalism, it is said on all sides, has forgotten to take human egoism into account, and has been utopian in its conception of what can be made of man. This picture of liberalism has become one of the standing commonplaces of current discussion, and is shared by the New Liberal and the New Conservative alike. "Practically all schools of modern culture," says Mr. Niebuhr, ". . . are united in denying the obvious fact that all men are persistently inclined to regard themselves more highly and are more assiduously concerned with their own interests than any 'objective' view of their importance would warrant." But the belief in the undying egoism of human beings, and the persistence in any society of the struggle for power, has in fact been the distinguishing feature of the liberal approach to politics. "The principle of human nature, upon which the necessity of government is founded, the propensity of one man to possess himself of the objects of desire at the cost of another, leads on, by infallible sequence, not only to that degree of plunder which leaves the members (except the instruments and recipients) the bare means of subsistence, but to that degree of cruelty which is necessary to keep in existence the most intense terrors." These are not Mr. Niebuhr's words. They are the words of James Mill, the liberal and utilitarian, writing on the foundations of government. The idea that philosophical liberalism has been committed to a perfectionist theory of human nature is in fact a parody of liberal thought.

In general, the British liberal tradition has taken most of its ideas on the behavior of political man from Thomas Hobbes, who described man as *homo lupus*—a predatory animal. Even those figures who, like John Locke, have taken a more genial view of

101

human nature, have nevertheless regarded the irrepressible tendency of each man to favor his own cause as a major reason for substituting a politically organized society for "the state of nature." And in the twentieth century, that arch exemplar of liberalism in thought and action, Bertrand Russell, has tried to base an entire political theory on the strength, uneliminability, and remarkable variety of men's demands for power. Nor is it only British liberalism that does not fit the portrait that is now drawn of classic liberalism. The philosophers of the French Enlightenment are repeatedly described as boundless optimists and visionaries. But is it really possible to say of Rousseau who wrote the *Confessions,* or Diderot who wrote *Rameau's Nephew,* or Voltaire who wrote *Candide,* that they entertained great illusions either about their own goodness or the goodness of other men? Even the philosopher Helvetius, who was most extreme in his hopes about what could be done with human nature, and who was looked upon as a little strange by most of his liberal contemporaries, wrote: "In order to love mankind, we must expect little from them."

What, then, is the reason for the belief that modern liberalism has traditionally entertained exaggeratedly optimistic notions about human nature? There are two apparent bits of evidence. If we take Condorcet's *Outline of the Progress of the Human Mind,* the book which, more than any other, exemplifies the classic liberal interpretation of history, we find in it two central theses. One is the idea of "the perfectibility of man." The other is the belief that human happiness and virtue will be augmented with the progress of knowledge. Let us see whether Condorcet's argument in this book necessarily implies an innocent conception of human nature.

Condorcet wrote *The Progress of the Human Mind* while he was in hiding from the Jacobin Terror. It is one of the classic testaments of faith to be found in Western literature, and is essentially a religious book—a reflection, in the face of death, on what is mortal and what is immortal in human life. And what is immortal, Condorcet affirmed, is the progress of the human mind, and the consequent indefinite perfectibility of mankind. To participate in this enterprise of progress is to participate in something which gives an undying point of reference to human affairs; and to contemplate the spectacle of progress is to be redeemed from the vanities and consoled for the sufferings to which human existence is heir. Condorcet has regularly been singled out as the very model of the woolly-headed liberal transported by an impossible dream. But the idea that a belief in the indefinite perfectibility of mankind exhibits a naïvely optimistic view of human affairs comes from a simple failure to understand (or perhaps to read) what Condorcet actually said on this subject. The phrase, "the indefinite perfectibility of mankind," is ambiguous, and can be easily—not to say eagerly—misinterpreted. But on the question of what this phrase means Condorcet took great trouble to be precise and clear.

What, asks Condorcet, is the extent of the improvement in the human situation for which we may legitimately hope? What does it mean to say that man is indefinitely perfectible"? Condorcet raises this question specifically in connection with his prediction that in the future the average life expectancy of human beings will be steadily increased. "Doubtless," he writes, "man will never become immortal." But "the progress of preventive medicine, more healthful food and lodging, a way of life that will develop the body through proper exercise without damaging it by overwork, and, finally, the destruction of the two most active causes of physical degeneracy, extreme poverty and extreme wealth," can be expected to bring "a time when death shall be no more than the result of extraordinary accidents or of the ever more gradual decay of the vital forces." Now, is there any limit which can be set to this process?

Condorcet answers this question by introducing an important distinction between two meanings of the term "limit." It is a distinction which his critics wholly overlook.

The average length of life [he writes] may grow either in accordance with a law by which it continually approaches a certain definite magnitude without ever reaching it, or in accordance with a law by which the length of life, in the long course of the ages, steadily surpasses every determinate figure which has been assigned to it as a limit. In the latter case, such growth would be truly indefinite, in the strictest sense of the word, because there would exist no bounds which it cannot pass. In the former case, however, it would be indefinite *for us,* since we cannot state the limit which this growth must forever approach but cannot absolutely reach; and this is particularly the case if we only know that this increase in the length of human life is endless, and cannot even say in which of the two senses of "indefinite" this term is applicable to it. This is precisely the state of our present knowledge concerning the perfectibility of the human species. Such is the sense in which we can call this perfectibility "indefinite."

In short, there is nothing utopian about Condorcet's conception of indefinite progress. He does not assert that there are no limits to human hopes. He merely asserts that we can never say that we have reached these limits. This is a point in which he is in total agreement with Mr. Niebuhr.* Mr. Niebuhr's quarrel with the doctrine of the indefinite perfectibility of man is a quarrel he has invented for himself. The principle of the indefinite perfectibility of man is simply the denial that there are any absolutes which the human mind can safely affirm. It is not a prediction about the future; it is the statement of a policy for guiding human behavior—a policy of putting the *status quo* on the defensive, and

* Mr. Niebuhr writes, "Actually human power over nature and history is both limited and limitless. It is limited in the sense that all individual and collective forms of life are subject to mortality. No human achievements can annul man's subjection to natural finitude. But human power is also limitless in the sense that no fixed limits can be set for the expansion of human capacities."

of refusing to decide in advance that any given problem is beyond the power of human beings to solve.

Let us turn now to Condorcet's belief that progress in knowledge promotes virtue. As his account of how men in the past used their knowledge to exploit their fellows suggests, Condorcet recognized that knowledge gave men powers that could be used for better or worse. But in talking about "the progress of knowledge," he meant among other things the *diffusion* of knowledge; and he did believe that this would promote virtue. But it was not because knowledge necessarily makes the man who possesses it more virtuous. It is because knowledge makes that man better able to protect himself against other men's vices. Condorcet's belief that the diffusion of knowledge would improve human behavior rested essentially on the common-sense assumption that if men have enough information to know what is going on and how their own interests are affected, the inveterate egoism, greed, and cupidity of their rulers could be more easily controlled. The practical, political application of the idea that diffusion of knowledge leads to moral progress is not in the development of a "scientific system of morality," but in plans for public education, for the development of a free press, and for the maintenance of civil liberties. And if the moral progress which Condorcet envisaged has not taken place to the degree he expected, this does not prove that moral progress does not follow from the diffusion of knowledge. It may only indicate the development of social conditions which make the diffusion of knowledge extraordinarily difficult. Condorcet did not foresee the emergence of such conditions. But he was not wrong to believe that it should be a basic objective of a liberal society to work for their avoidance. And to talk about the wickedness of man as though it were uncontrollable merely diverts attention from this issue.

If we judge the liberal philosophy of history by its most representative spokesman, the belief in the progress of man was not made up out of whole cloth, and the men who held it were not suffering from an *idée fixe* about human goodness which prevented them from recognizing plain facts. In Condorcet's hands, the belief in the perfectibility of man was really a belief better translated into English as a belief in the *improvability* of man. And the ideals it projected point the way to our crucial problems, and give us a framework that is still valid for our social thinking.

That Condorcet's enthusiasm was aroused by this vision, and that many liberal writers in the eighteenth and nineteenth centuries (and an even greater number of illiberal ones) were stimulated by it into utopian or quasi-utopian dreams is undeniable. They lived in the fine glow of a major revolution in human affairs, and they recognized this revolution for what it was. If they were overly optimistic, it was a matter of mood and temper and circumstance. It was not a matter of fundamental philosophic principle. To take a patronizing attitude toward the men who held these dreams is to reveal a failure of historical imagination. For these men were living through a scientific and technological revolution which gave promise that for the first time in human history men would be able to get off their backs in the struggle with nature—that men could finally, to put it in unadorned terms, eat adequately and live in reasonable comfort and health. To have been dazzled by the prospects which this revolution held forth is not only understandable; more, the men who were dazzled, and who wrote the passages at which the New Pessimists now scoff, were performing the important function of announcing the new possibilities for the moral and intellectual improvement of mankind which this very real material revolution had set loose. In the light of what was contained in human experience up to that time, to do this took courage and imagination; and not to have done it would have been a greater error, a more sizable failure to provide directing ideas to modern culture, than to have played the old tune of original sin.

106

There is, in fact, a quite fundamental confusion in the idea that the liberal doctrine of "the goodness of man" reveals an impossibly naïve theory of human nature. It is a confusion between a scheme of moral values and a psychological theory. The slogan, "the goodness of man," is indeed an alternative to the doctrine of original sin. But it is not primarily an alternative description of human behavior; it is an alternative frame of moral reference— a dramatic device for freeing practical questions of politics or historical explanation from control by the ideal of salvation and the value judgments that follow from it.

For the doctrine of original sin defines "good" and "evil" with respect to the final goal of personal salvation. By calling man "evil" or "sinful," it means to say that man, through his own efforts alone, cannot be immortal, or free his mind or soul from dependence on a corrupt body, or be infallible in his intellectual judgments, or perfectly saintly in his behavior. And liberal philosophers would have agreed with all of these statements of fact. What they were doing in speaking about "the goodness of man" was simply to assert the legitimacy of talking about human traits in some other context than this context of sin and redemption. From the point of view of being saved from sin, for example, egoism might be evil; but from an economic point of view it might be good as a pivot for ambition; or from a political point of view it might be good as a defense against despotism; or, indeed, it might be neither good nor bad, but simply what has to be taken into account in governing human affairs. "Moralists declaim continually against the badness of men," wrote Helvetius, "but this shows how little they understand of this matter. Men are not bad; they are merely subject to their own interests." It is this "transvaluation of values," this introduction of a new context for the assessment of human traits, which is involved in statements about "the goodness of man."

It is Mr. Niebuhr's failure to see this point which explains his

107

caricature of liberal views of human nature. On Mr. Niebuhr's accounting, Hobbes and Locke, Hume and Rousseau, rationalists and romantics, all turn out to have entertained essentially the same overestimate of the "goodness" of man. But it is plain that if there is anything that unites these men, it is not a psychological theory, nor even a common set of value judgments; it is only a common disposition to place whatever value judgments they make in a humanistic setting, to refuse to impose standards on man which are irrelevant to what he wants and what he can do. The liberal attack on the doctrine of original sin was a phase in the transition of social thinking from preoccupation with the classic problem of "theodicy"—the justification of God's ways to man— to a preoccupation with concrete, individual problems in morals and society. It set the problem of man's transcendent perversity aside; it set the problem of man's other-worldly destiny aside; it dropped the question of salvation out of the group of questions which must be examined before a social program can be developed. In arguing for the possibility of greater happiness in human affairs, philosophical liberals were not talking about redemption through history. They were not talking about redemption at all. For "happiness" is not a synonym for "salvation," and "progress" is not a synonym for the journey of the soul to God.

But if the difference between a belief in the goodness of man and a belief in original sin is mainly a difference in the mood with which we approach human affairs and the language we employ to discuss them, it is a difference which has tremendous practical consequences for political strategy and for the quality of a culture. And the ultimate practical issue which Mr. Niebuhr's philosophy of history poses is a choice about just such issues as these.

To begin with, the introduction of the slogan, "the goodness of man," was part of the general effort we have already mentioned to diffuse political authority more widely. The new partisans of original sin tell us that pessimism about human nature will prevent the placing of too much power in the hands of a few leaders; but in the eighteenth and nineteenth centuries it was usually pessimism about human nature that was used to justify keeping power in the hands of a few. The doctrine of original sin is not necessarily an antiliberal or antidemocratic notion; but no more extraordinary reversal in the history of human ideas can be imagined than the present ingenious claim that it is necessary to a sound democratic philosophy. When liberalism asserted the goodness of man, it was saying that the mass of men could be trusted with responsibility and that the diffusion of authority was better than the monopoly of authority. The New Pessimists are merely saying, more lugubriously, that the few cannot be trusted with responsibility, and that the monopoly of authority is worse than the diffusion of authority.* The content of the two statements is the same. It is the mood that is different.

But it is a difference that is important. For there were, and are, other motives as well behind talking about "the goodness of man" instead of "the sinfulness of man." The dictum that "man is good" changed the initial questions with which social thinkers began their work. It gave the first move to the reformer, and shifted the burden of proof to those who wished to say that human pain was necessary or desirable. For human intelligence and energy have been consistently diverted from dealing with specific evils

* Mr. Arthur Schlesinger, Jr., writes: "It is a moderate pessimism about man which truly fortifies society against authoritarianism—because such pessimism must apply far more strongly to a special elite or a single party, exposed to the temptations of pride and power, than it does to the people in general. 'Sometimes it is said that man cannot be trusted with the government of himself,' Jefferson once wrote. 'Can he, then, be trusted with the government of others? Or have we found angels in the form of kings to govern him?'" But the quotation from Jefferson is revealing. Jefferson is the most characteristic of Enlightenment figures—a liberal, rationalist, and philosophical optimist par excellence.

and specific pains by generalizations to the effect that Evil is inherent in human nature and Pain is its merited punishment. The *philosophes* of the eighteenth century and the Philosophic Radicals of the nineteenth century came into a world entangled in a mass of verbal rituals, authorities descended from the past, high-sounding abstractions, and immeasurable human wretchedness. In talking about "the goodness of man" they were demanding that man's living interests be taken seriously, and that human pain be regarded as a problem initially inviting compassion and practical effort, and not higher dialectics about its necessity. This notion that existing human preferences should be consulted in determining social arrangements may now seem a trivial platitude. But as a concrete proposal for reassessing existing social arrangements, it has usually been greeted with massive indifference, and not infrequently with active hostility. If it is now a platitude, we have the idea of the goodness of man to thank for it. It was an essential instrument in the domesticating of reform in Western society.

Further, in talking about the *natural* goodness of man, liberal philosophers were wrestling with the problem of how to release the ethical feelings of Western society from supernatural sanctions. Religion had helped create a common fund of moral feeling. But it had also indicated that men could not be virtuous without the support of the supernatural; and in doing so it had entangled moral feelings in religious controversies. The slogan, "the goodness of man," was an attempt to free these feelings from the controversies which had weakened and divided them, so that they could be employed effectively on common problems. To talk about the goodness of man was a way of dramatizing the fact that there was an existing basis for practical agreement underneath the controversies between the members of different religious sects. And it was a way of saying that there was a fund of

110

general moral feeling which could be used to support concerted movements for political reform. As Whitehead has said,

> For two thousand years philosophy and religion had held up before Western Europe the ideal figure of man as man, and had claimed for it a supreme worth. Under this urge, Jesuits had gone to Patagonia, John Woolman had denounced slavery, Tom Paine had revolted against social oppression and against the doctrine of original sin. These Jesuits, these Quakers, and these Freethinkers differed among themselves. But they owed their emotions towards men as men to the generalization of feeling produced by the joint influence of philosophy and religion. Jeremy Bentham and Auguste Comte accepted these generalized emotions as ultimate moral intuitions, clear matter of fact, requiring no justification and requiring no ultimate understanding of their relations to the rest of things. They discarded metaphysics. In so doing, they effected an immense service to democratic liberalism. For they produced a practicable programme of reform, and practical modes of expression which served to unite these men whose ultimate notions differed vastly.

Finally, "the goodness of man" has expressed a preference for a different cultural atmosphere. It is not inevitable that a culture in which the belief in original sin is dominant will be harsher to children, more vindictive toward criminals, more unbending and unrealistic in its moral demands. It is conceivable that the recognition that men are all brothers in sin will make men more humble and charitable, less demanding on others, and stricter with themselves. It has had this effect on individuals; and it has been associated with such attitudes particularly in Latin cultures, where it has taken a subordinate place, on the whole, to a larger belief in God's love. But when the doctrine of the goodness of man arose, it arose to combat an idea which had also been used in support of ruthlessness, intolerance, and cruelty. When liberals talked about the goodness of man, they were attempting to make education more responsive to the needs of children, to convert the treatment of lunacy from a scourging of devils into a medical art, to make penology something more than an exercise in sadism.

111

For whatever may be said in its favor, the belief in original sin is not a belief that has spread much joy. It establishes transcendent standards for human behavior, and then calls human nature to account for failing to meet them. In contrast, the belief in the goodness of man means that we should look first into the nature of man, into his interests and capabilities, and build our moral standards accordingly. It is a way of saying that human nature, the complement of drives, instincts, and desires which human beings carry into the world, is not an obstacle to be overcome, but the raw material with which the parent, teacher, or legislator is compelled to work. And the belief in goodness recognizes the limits of human nature more profoundly than does a doctrine which asserts that human nature has certain intrinsically evil properties, and which is therefore forced to make crucial to its whole moral outlook the need for a total conversion of the human spirit.

The lineaments of Mr. Niebuhr's philosophy of history coincide peculiarly with the lineaments of contemporary experience. The liberal and democratic revolutions have encouraged us to feel a responsibility for what happens, and a duty to have a moral opinion about it. Public education and the progress of communications have made us increasingly aware of what is going on in the world, have heightened our sensitivity to human suffering, and have aggravated our impatience with the bad show that men are making of their affairs. And yet everything seems to have contrived to make this new knowledge and these heightened moral impulses appear irrelevant. The growth of a mass society, and the breakdown of the smaller groups through which individuals could make their attitudes felt, has aggravated the individual's sense that his conscience is isolated and his ideals without a social anchor. Mass unemployment has left a generation of men in every country who have had the experience of feeling superfluous. And the mechanical routines of industrialism, the anonymity of cities, and the impersonal horrors of war have all tended to submerge personal relations and individual achievement, and to give men the feeling that even their most modest personal ideals have an anachronistic and quixotic flavor.

The displaced person, as a consequence, has become a peculiarly symbolic figure in contemporary experience. The sense of estrangement, of living in a hostile world, is no longer the special possession of the adolescent, the neurotic, or the mystic. It has become an insistent and familiar mood in the lives of countless ordinary men and women. It has been caught in our most characteristic poetry and fiction—from *The Waste Land* to *1984*, from Kafka to Hemingway, and from Saroyan to the latest detective story, with its lonely and beleaguered hero. Mr. Niebuhr's philosophy of history speaks out of this experience. It expresses the frustrations, and the sense of simple irrelevance, which must beset the mind of any sensitive man in the modern world. For events like those at Buchenwald have not merely aroused moral feelings; they have stupefied them. Terms like "murder" do not cover their impersonality, terms like "mass hysteria" or "lunacy" fail to convey their planned, organized, and premeditated efficiency. Mr. Niebuhr comes to us in these circumstances, when we feel that we do not even have the words to express our feelings, and speaks to us of "the self which stands outside itself and the world [and] cannot find the meaning of life in itself or the world." He provides us with a metaphysical image of our sense of impotence and estrangement. With his emphasis on "the essential homelessness of the human spirit," Mr. Niebuhr speaks for the displaced and unemployed conscience of our times.

His achievement is to have restored a voice to that conscience. His philosophy converts the cold abstractions of contemporary

113

psychology and sociology into terms that have a moral meaning. In his interpretation of history, class struggle becomes the image, writ large, of human egoism and vanity; imperialism becomes the reflection of the imperialism in everyone's soul; domestic politics and international affairs become the stage on which the internal dissensions within each individual's spirit are revealed. Our ruined moral attitudes are reinstated by Mr. Niebuhr's philosophy of history. It tells us that what has happened is a judgment and a punishment, and so restores a moral meaning to events. It tells us that we are all sinners, and so it cheers us with the feeling that we are all involved in what has happened, and are not quite so helplessly out of things as we had thought. Mr. Niebuhr's philosophy of history does what any good sermon should do. It makes the individual take the problems of the world into his own heart; it makes him feel responsible for what happens; and it redeems him from his sense of helplessness and unimportance by making him feel that his struggle with his own soul is the essential element in social change.

But for all the poignancy and pertinence of Mr. Niebuhr's ideas, for all that they share in mood and theme with our present sense of the push and pressure of things, one cannot avoid the conclusion that, in the end, they obfuscate and mislead and confuse. To disabuse us of the belief that reason and good will have a cosmic guarantee behind them, it is not necessary to show that there is a cosmic conspiracy against these ideals. This is the same undisciplined romanticism, merely turned inside out. And it exhibits precisely that confusion of the relative and the absolute, of our own situation with the total hang of the universe, which Mr. Niebuhr's philosophy has come to cure. Indeed, it conjures up a cosmic mystery and absurdity when we have more than enough mystery and absurdity in our daily lives. It imposes an additional, and unnecessary, burden of anxiety on us beyond the anxieties we already have good reason to feel. Anxiety has

114

not, after all, been the basic emotion of men in all ages; it is not the basic emotion of all men even in the present age. And it is certainly not something to be celebrated. To make anxiety, as Mr. Niebuhr does, a standard of normality and sobriety, and to intimate that it is a path to a deeper insight into the nature of things than is offered by logic or common sense, is to add a new chapter to the long sad history of man's love affair with foolishness.

It is not very much, after all, to be told that all human ideals are partial and imperfect. This is something one can find in the secular liberalism which Mr. Niebuhr rejects. But it is less than nothing to be told this when we discover that the standards that are being used cannot be defined, and have in fact been chosen because they are more than human and more than rational. We do not need ideals whose only point is to make us strive after an "impossible victory" and suffer an "inevitable defeat." This is masochism, not wisdom. We need ideals that will allow us to distinguish in practical terms between a better cause and a worse one. We need principles that will help us to get something done, and to get it done responsibly and decently.

In the end, to believe in "the goodness of man" is not to commit oneself to any particular description of human behavior. It is not to say that men's good deeds outnumber their evil deeds, or that benevolence is a stronger disposition in men than malice. It is, quite simply, to adopt a policy—the policy of looking for cures for human ailments, and of refusing to take No for an answer. "You see, my dear boy," says Undershaft in Shaw's *Major Barbara,* "when you are organizing civilization you have to make up your mind whether trouble and anxiety are good things or not. If you decide that they are, then, I take it, you simply don't organize civilization; and there you are, with trouble and anxiety enough to make us all angels! But if you decide the

115

other way, you may as well go through with it." And for those who feel that anxiety strengthens character and brings wisdom, he adds, "Our characters are safe here. A sufficient dose of anxiety is always provided by the fact that we may be blown to smithereens at any moment."

VII.

CAN HISTORY
TELL THE TRUTH?

"I KNOW it is the fashion to say," George Orwell once wrote, "that most of recorded history is lies anyway. I am willing to believe that history is for the most part inaccurate and biased, but what is peculiar to our own age is the abandonment of the idea that history can be truthfully written." We have looked now at two philosophies of history. One has argued that the great blunder of the modern era is to have rejected eternal truths. The second has said that there is an eternal truth, but that the error of the modern world is to believe it can discover it. But there is a third philosophy which has given up the ghost, and denies that there is any such thing as objective truth at all. It completes the circle in the search that contemporary men and women are making for their historical bearings. Professor Maritain has suggested that we can find our bearings by grasping an eternity that never changes; Mr. Niebuhr has suggested that we accept our dilemma for what it is, live tensely between permanence and change, and be skeptics and dogmatists all at once; this philosophy proposes to take change as the ultimate beyond which there is nothing.

117

It is a philosophy so characteristic of our times, so expressive of our doubts, that it is part of the air we breathe. In a world in flux, it asserts that even truth fluctuates. In a world in which men are encased in hardened ideologies, and regularly talk past one another, it asserts that all human thinking is ideological—committed to the shifting perspectives of an age or a class, biased, partisan, and subjective. In a world in which the *ad hominem* argument has become respectable, it tells us that ideas are events in the life of a competitive and predatory animal, and are to be considered as weapons of struggle, and not as neutral and immaculate reports of the nature of things. The simple speed with which fashions change, the rapidity with which new ideas are taken up as gospel and then put down as superstition, the tendency of all issues to become politicalized—these have suggested to the contemporary mind that every human belief is the convention of a day, and that objectivity and truth are specious and impossible ideals. This attitude, given a rationale and a doctrine, has been turned into a full-dress philosophy of history. But it is more than just an expression of this attitude; it is an effort to build a new conception of truth and objectivity out of our very doubts and disillusionments.

In its main lines, this philosophy is part of a general movement of ideas in the modern world which goes back to Hegel, and whose technical name is "historicism." The concepts that play so large a part in our thinking—"the spirit of an age," "the wave of the future," "the path of history"—are drawn from this current of ideas. Historicism holds that history —the study of change—is the queen of the sciences, and that all human thinking must be evaluated, not against the standards of a timeless truth, but against the historical necessities of a given time and place. As the phrase "historical necessities" may suggest, historicism generally argues that there is an over-all structure or movement in history, an embracing law of historical

118

development to which all men are inevitably bound. And so it is only by keeping in step with the movement of history, by adopting the ideas that are required for the next stage in the development of man, that we can stay afloat amidst the flux of events.

Instead of proposing that we escape from history to the solace of the unchanging, historicism proposes that we immerse ourselves completely in the flux—get into the swing of things. Not only must each age find its own social ideals and moral standards; but each age must also find its own canons of truth and reason and argument. For human ideas are not descriptions of an independent reality; they are strategies for staying alive. And the belief that there is a truth which stands above historical change and circumstance is itself only the protective strategy of one particular historical era, and has no validity beyond that era.

Marxism, in certain of its versions, is the most conspicuous example of historicism in the modern world. But Marxism owes at least some of its influence to the fact that it is part of this larger current of ideas which has had such a peculiar appeal to the contemporary mind. Under the name, "the Sociology of Knowledge," historicism has received a straightforward formulation. The Sociology of Knowledge is a doctrine which has taken some of the most influential ideas in the modern world and brought them together in a single framework. It borrows from Marx, Freud, Veblen, and others who have stressed the unconscious drives and partisan interests that lie behind men's ideas. It is part of the whole trend in modern thinking which has replaced the traditional notion of mind as a pure and disembodied thing with a conception of intelligence as something practical and creative, a tool by which a vital creature adapts himself to a changing environment.*

* The phrase, "the Sociology of Knowledge," stands for two quite distinct things. It stands, in the first place, for a particular branch of ordinary sociology —the study of the social conditions under which ideas are developed and communicated. In the United States in particular, careful and detailed studies

119

The Sociology of Knowledge has been most fully and uncompromisingly developed by the late sociologist and social philosopher, Karl Mannheim. The simple physical facts of Mannheim's career rehearse the problems with which he was concerned throughout his life—the disintegration of Western civilization from within, the rise of unreason in a society that had prided itself on its rationalism, the disappearance of genuine communication in a society whose technical instruments of communication were at an unequaled level of development.

Mannheim was born in Hungary, and was twenty-one when World War I broke out. Even more than intellectuals elsewhere, Central European intellectuals took the war as a symbol of the end of an era, and the sense that an old world was completely dead, but a new one as yet unformed, never left Mannheim in all his thinking. After the war, Mannheim moved in the revolutionary Marxist atmosphere that prevailed among young intellectuals in Hungary. But with the defeat of Communism in Hungary and the rise of a right-wing regime, Mannheim moved to the Germany of the Weimar Republic. There he came under the influence of German sociologists like Max Weber and Max Scheler, and eventually succeeded Scheler as the occupant of a chair in sociology at Frankfurt am Main. It was here that Mannheim developed his Sociology of Knowledge, and wrote his most important book, *Ideology and Utopia*.

With the advent of Hitler in 1933, Mannheim left Germany and went to England, where he became a leading influence at

---

of the development of ideas, the media of communication, and the formation of public opinion have been carried on under this heading, and the results have been interesting and promising. Such investigations are scientific inquiries like any others, and have no intrinsic philosophical implications. But the phrase, "the Sociology of Knowledge," has also been used to stand for a philosophy of history and a theory of human knowledge which denies the classic belief that there are objective truths about human affairs. This is the aspect of it in which we are interested.

the London School of Economics, and where he remained until his death in 1947. Mannheim's English experience was a major event in his life. He found in England a liberal social order with a cohesion and durability his experience in Central Europe had led him to believe was impossible. And much of his thinking after that time was an attempt to blend together what he took to be the peculiar virtues of Anglo-Saxon liberal society with the ideas he had developed on the Continent with its more rigidly ideological politics and its hostile class arrangements. Mannheim's diagnosis of our ills, like the work of his great predecessor, Max Weber, is an attempt to bring together certain key ideas in Marxism with certain classic liberal ideals. No social thinker in our time has taken the crisis of liberalism more seriously, or looked more deeply for its causes. And no one has proposed as comprehensive a program as did Mannheim for salvaging a liberal society and, in his phrase, "planning for freedom."

That program begins with an attempt to rebuild the intellectual outlook of modern man, and to provide him with radically new categories for viewing his history. In Mannheim's Sociology of Knowledge we find some of our deepest suspicions and doubts faced courageously, and the anatomy of a major intellectual mood laid bare. His philosophy enunciates a dominant tendency in current thinking, and offers, at once, the best case that can be made for it and the purest clinical specimen of it. In examining Mannheim's philosophy we are examining, in their best and most consistent form, ideas that are in the minds of most of us. And we are raising the question whether the traditional philosophy of liberalism, with its belief in the rationality of man, rested on as complete an illusion as our contemporary mood of disenchantment suggests.

The central problem in Mannheim's philosophy is a problem that is decisive for contemporary liberal thought. "The func-

121

tion of the nineteenth century," G. M. Young has written, "was to disengage the disinterested intelligence, to release it from the entanglements of party and sect—one might almost add, of sex —and to set it operating over the whole range of human life and circumstance." To recapture that intelligence, and to give it an anchor in our institutions, is the overhanging problem of twentieth-century liberals. This is the problem with which Mannheim was concerned. His philosophy was an attempt to provide a program for modern society which would permit that application of organized intelligence to social affairs which had been the classic liberal dream. But Mannheim was convinced that this liberal idea could be realized only if the liberal philosophy of history was revised at one of its central points.

Why, asks Mannheim, has the liberal ideal of applying organized intellectual methods to human affairs proved such a failure? It is, he says, because liberalism denaturalized reason, detaching it from the living urgencies of the human psyche and the human social situation. It regarded reason as something static, detached, and timeless, and it set as the goal of human thinking the pursuit of an objective truth from which all the bias and partiality of an historical creature struggling with practical affairs had been removed. Dazzled by achievements in mathematics and the natural sciences, liberalism worked with a model of human reason that was based upon this kind of formal and abstract thinking. But this ideal of an impersonal truth about social affairs which is like the objective truth found in the natural sciences is clearly an illusion. In trying to apply a pristine ideal of reason, liberalism merely succeeded in rendering reason impotent. For the kind of detached thinking one finds in mathematics or physics, Mannheim was convinced, lacks the vitality, flexibility, and commitment to values which thinking must have if it is to make any practical difference in the world.

Modern society has been unable to control the hidden rigidi-

122

ties of thought and the outbreaks of ideological fanaticism which have prevented the peaceful resolution of social conflicts, Mannheim believed, precisely because the liberal ideal of reason has denied the practical origins and limitations of human thinking. For all social thinking, Mannheim emphasized, is inevitably determined by unconscious assumptions and unacknowledged commitments. The unconscious controls the thinking of individuals, as Freud has shown. But even more, whole social classes wear blinkers, and view events from only a limited point of view. Men occupy distinct social positions or social habitats; their social experience brings them into contact with only a limited range of events; and when they think about these events they employ the system of ideas which their social habitat gives them. Human thinking is a social act. It employs a language which is a social product, and moves within a conceptual framework that belongs to a group. As a result, all social thinking, according to Mannheim, represents a particular angle of vision on human affairs, and is inevitably partial.

An exciting Japanese movie of a few years ago, *Rashomon*, offers a peculiarly apt ilustration of Mannheim's central thesis. The movie is in the form of a story told by a woodsman, who is in despair at what he has seen and heard, and has lost all his faith in man. He reports that a Japanese lady and her husband have been set upon in the woods by a highwayman. The lady has been raped, the husband killed. And then he repeats in turn the accounts he has overheard at the police station, where the highwayman, the lady, and the dead husband, speaking through a medium, have had to tell the events that transpired. Each participant tells a different story, each subtly arranges the events in a pattern that will put his own position in the best light. As each of these stories is re-enacted before our eyes, our tension mounts. We are not sure whether what really happened was

123

murder and rape, whether the lady was treacherous or loyal, the husband cowardly or heroic, the highwayman an aggressor or a victim. Each time we move to the next story we hope to get closer to the truth, and each time we are put off. But suddenly we seem to see an opening. For it turns out that the woodsman, who has claimed to be merely repeating the stories he overheard at the police station, has been an eyewitness to the actual scene in the forest. So the woodsman tells his story. But, once more, we hear a story which has something subtly off-center about it. A dagger is unaccounted for. And then it turns out that the woodsman has stolen it. He has not been a neutral bystander; he too is a participant.

This notion that we are all participants in what happens in human history, and that there can therefore be no such thing as objectivity about history, is the central theme, and the central problem, in Mannheim's philosophy of history. We never see what "really" happens, and in fact it makes no sense even to ask. The affairs of men take place in a hall of mirrors, each with its own angle of distortion; and all we can report is what we see in the mirrors, for there is nothing else to see. All social thinking is inevitably the thinking of men who have a role in events, feelings about them, and a limited perspective upon them. Every belief comes labeled with the date, place, and social pedigree of the man who holds it. And the idea that there is an objective truth about human affairs, independently of who asserts it, is only one element in the special perspective of liberalism.

To express this conception of history, Mannheim employed a term which is now, partly through his influence, very much part of our common parlance. It is the term "ideology." Mannheim's account of the history of this term illuminates his own use of it. In the period of the French Revolution, a group of philosophers, carrying on the antimetaphysical tradition of the Enlightenment,

124

conceived the project of founding "a science of ideas," for which they coined the name "ideology," much as the term "psychology" designates the science that studies the mind or the term "biology" designates the science that studies living organisms. Napoleon, however, discovering that this group of philosophers opposed his imperial ambitions, used this term contemptuously and dismissed them as "ideologists."* And this derogatory use of the word stuck. Like the term "doctrinaire," the term "ideology" came to stand for thinking that was impractical and unrealistic as compared with the point of view of political men of action.

Karl Marx, as Mannheim reminds us, made this notion of "ideology" part of a general theory about human thinking. Man's thinking, Marx argued, was determined by the actual economic organization of society; men's ideas are the products of their social institutions; their social institutions are not the product of their ideas. The failure to recognize this is the essence of ideological thinking. In Marx's hands, therefore, the term "ideology" did not merely apply to the illusions of individuals, but to the illusions of entire social classes. Men develop systematic theories which put their own class interests in a favorable light, and which mask the fundamental facts of economic class struggle behind high-sounding and allegedly neutral abstractions.

But according to Mannheim, Marx did not go far enough. Despite the fact that Marx argued that *all* thinking was socially determined, he continued to think that there might be a kind of thinking which was not partial or ideological—for example, his own. And this was to draw the line arbitrarily. The notion of "ideology" cannot be used just as a polemical weapon for disparaging the ideas of one's opponents. It applies to all social ideas without exception. And when this is seen, said Mannheim, "what was once the intellectual armament of a party is trans-

* There is a fellow-feeling that crosses the front lines in these matters. Wellington referred to intellectuals as "the scribbling set."

formed into a method of research in social and intellectual history. . . . This sociologically oriented history of ideas is destined to provide modern man with a revised view of the whole historical process."

As seen from his own point of view, therefore, Mannheim's distinctive contribution was to have replaced the classic liberal conception of an objective, unbiased truth—a conception which even Marx retained—with a new theory which emphasized the incurably ideological character of all thinking about history and human affairs. There can be no disengaged intelligence seeking a universal truth. Intelligence is inevitably earth-bound, practical, and biased. The questions men ask about social affairs are always selected questions that are suggested by some particular point of view and serve some special interest. The answers men accept as satisfactory are always partial answers with an inescapable element of arbitrariness in them. And even the standards of truth that men employ are limited by the social perspectives in which they are framed. To know whether an idea is "true" we have to know the social position of the man who holds it, the circumstances under which it was developed, and the practical functions it serves. "Truth," in short, has an historical character, and what is true for one age or from one point of view is not true for another age or from another point of view.

Skeptical as it may seem, Mannheim's purpose was anything but skeptical. The problem that concerned him, in the words of Yeats, is that

> The best lack all conviction, while the worst
> Are full of passionate intensity. . . .

Mannheim's criticism of traditional liberalism was not an effort to disparage intelligence. It was an effort to revitalize the modern

126

social intelligence by cutting it loose from what Mannheim considered to be false ideals, an attempt to make men aware that all thinking must be committed to some practical, social cause. On the one side, ideological passions prevent men from solving the problems of modern society rationally; on the other side, the resources of intelligence and good will we have at hand are chronically unemployed. And both of these states of affairs, Mannheim was convinced, are the products of the liberal belief that there is a kind of truth which stands above the conflict. Liberalism hoped to introduce reason and moderation into the discussion of human problems, and to put man's social intelligence to work. But the ideal of reason it employed actually accomplished the reverse. It turned the inevitable partisanship of all human thinking into fanatical partisanship by encouraging men to identify their own ideologies with universal truth; and it encouraged men who did not wish to be partisan to pursue an unrealistic ideal of disinterestedness, and to hold themselves apart from practical affairs. Only an explicit recognition of the inevitable ideological character of all human thinking, Mannheim felt, could cure this situation.

Mannheim thus wished to introduce a radically new conception of objectivity. Objectivity, according to Mannheim, is not the sort of detached and impersonal standpoint that liberalism has made it. Ideas are not "objective" because they are free from the perspective of a given social habitat or historical situation. If we take the inevitable ideological character of thinking seriously, we see that ideas can be "objective" only in a very different sense. "Only when we are thoroughly aware of the limited scope of every point of view are we on the road to the sought-for comprehension of the whole." Men become more objective when, aware of their own prejudices, they begin to enter sympathetically into other ideologies than their own, and to see things from the other fellow's point of view. The "truth" for an age is not something that stands apart from the perspectives of that age. It is the unified perspective which brings them all together.

But if each man has a distinct social position, and can see things only from the point of view which that position gives him, how can such an inclusive perspective be created? To create it, Mannheim felt, was the specific mission of a distinct class in modern society—the intellectuals. We come here to the practical strategy of social reform with which Mannheim's Sociology of Knowledge culminates. Intellectuals are recruited from all social strata, and they are only loosely anchored in the outlook of any class. So it is the intellectual who can break down the rigid ideologies that separate men, and do the essential work that needs to be done if modern society is to recover its cohesion. Freed from the futile liberal ideal of truth, and armed with the Sociology of Knowledge, the intellectuals of modern society can systematically expose the partiality of all ideas; they can close up the gaps between men and build a common creed that will bring men together; and they can exercise an influence in human history which intellectuals have never had before. Mannheim's philosophy of history represents a manifesto for the modern intellectual, a declaration of principles which will finally save the professional thinker from his hereditary position of being above the battle and beside the point.

Mannheim's influence has been as great as that of any sociologist of this generation,* but his importance is more than something that can be measured in terms of his direct influence on other thinkers. It is the importance of a man who has taken a style of thought that is one of the most conspicuous elements in the present intellectual climate, and has stated it explicitly

---

* The distinguished liberal historian, Charles Beard, for example, was strongly influenced by him; and it must be evident how much Mr. Niebuhr's philosophy of history is saturated with Mannheim's ideas.

and clearly. Like Moliere's *bourgeois gentilhomme,* who discovered that he had been speaking prose all his life without knowing it, a great many of us have been speaking the language of the Sociology of Knowledge without knowing it. Popular versions of Freud's ideas have led us to suspect that all thinking is wishful thinking, and that all our social ideas are the projections of our inner—and, indeed, infantile—lives. Ideological warfare has engendered the feeling that neutrality is impossible and disinterestedness a sham. And even Mannheim's quaint idea that intellectuals might give us a "total" perspective that takes account of all partial perspectives is a reflection of the popular notion that truth is discovered by listening tolerantly to all points of view and putting them together. Mannheim has laid bare the grammar of a language which has become a modern idiom. And it is an idiom which challenges the traditional liberal approach to history at one of its most fundamental assumptions. Is it an idiom that makes sense? Is it really impossible to be objective about the human scene?

Basically, the idea that we cannot be objective about human affairs employs two main lines of argument. The first of these rests on a sharp distinction between the study of nature and the study of human affairs. The second rests on an assumption about the meaning of terms like "partiality" and "bias." Let us look at each of these in turn.

Mannheim drew a sharp distinction between the study of nature and the study of human affairs for two principal reasons. Consider, says Mannheim in effect, how we get our knowledge about the behavior of our fellow creatures. Human behavior is purposive, goal-seeking behavior. If we want to understand why men act as they do, we have to understand their motives and see things from their point of view. But this requires that we use our imaginations, that we project ourselves into the minds of the men whose behavior we are studying and share their feelings

129

and values. In short, empathy or imaginative sympathy, which is not necessary in the study of the physical world, is necessary in the study of human affairs. And so the whole logic that guides the writing of history and the formulation of our ideas about social affairs is different from the logic we employ in other fields.

It is an appealing argument. It speaks to a sense of outrage stirred in all of us when we are talked about as though we were inanimate objects; and it is plain that most of those who have made any contribution to our sum of knowledge and wisdom about the human scene have been men whose faculties of sympathy and fellow-feeling were highly developed. But it is an argument which neglects a crucial distinction. The method of imaginative sympathy is a method by which we get our ideas about what makes human beings tick or the world go round; but it is not a method by which we *prove* that these ideas are true. You may understand another man better by identifying yourself with him. But when you come to explain his behavior, you do not offer as evidence the fact that you have identified yourself with him. You offer evidence which other men can check. For while sympathy and fellow-feeling are useful faculties, they are not infallible. For one thing, when we think we have identified ourselves with others, we may only have imposed our own feelings on them. For another thing, if we do succeed in projecting ourselves into the minds of others, seeing things exactly as they do, we must then also share their self-deceptions. If we really believed that we can only prove the truth of a theory about human behavior by taking the attitude of the human beings we are talking about, we would ask paranoids to verify our theories about paranoia. In brief, techniques of inquiry may differ from field to field, but the *logic* of proof does not. Whatever special techniques we may use in the study of human affairs, the evidence we offer for our social ideas does not differ logically

130

from the evidence we offer for our ideas about the physical world.

Mannheim, however, had still another reason for drawing a sharp line between the study of nature and the study of man, and it is a kind of reason which is repeatedly employed to show that an objective science of society is impossible. It is possible to talk about impersonal objectivity when we study nature, Mannheim believed, because there are fixed and regular patterns in nature which one can discern without imposing one's own point of view. But the distinctive sphere of human behavior which we are trying to understand when we think about social affairs is the sphere of politics. And here, by definition, we are dealing with a sphere in a state of flux. Politics is the realm in which men are constantly dealing with new conditions, and are constantly having to make decisions in situations that are not covered by set rules. How is it possible, therefore, to speak of any fixed, objective pattern in political events? Where human behavior is governed by an established routine, as in the case of a judge applying a law to a specific case, or a factory worker performing his assigned task on the assembly line, one might conceive of making objective statements about human affairs which approach the kind of statement we find in the natural sciences. But in the crucial sphere of politics, such objective patterns cannot be discovered. If anyone finds any order in politics, it is an order which he himself has imposed, and which incorporates his own secret wishes and values.

There is a certain wry truth in the notion that any man who finds an "order" in politics is engaging in a species of wishful thinking. Certainly most political theories in the past have not been explanations of political behavior, but ideals which hope to suggest a rationality in politics which is not apparent to the naked eye. Nevertheless, Mannheim's argument rests at bottom on a mistake as crude as that of the ladies in one of Moliere's plays.

131

Full of the latest scientific theories, these ladies scold a servant for falling after he has been taught the law of gravitation. Mannheim's mistake is to have confused rules which men deliberately introduce and follow in their behavior with laws that govern their behavior whether they know of their existence or not.

Freud remarks somewhere that the study of pathological behavior was delayed for generations on the ground that, since such behavior is irrational, there are no laws governing it. The same error is present in the belief that a science of politics must be different from the normal kind of science. Even if we assume the worst, and classify political behavior as pathological behavior, it is now evident that pathological behavior follows regular and predictable patterns. We are putting the cart before the horse when we think that a science of politics must be different from other sciences because political behavior is random and haphazard. It is not because political behavior is random and haphazard that we do not have much objective knowledge about it. It is because we do not have much objective knowledge about it that it seems random and haphazard.

The reasons, then, which Mannheim and so many others give for drawing a sharp distinction between the natural sciences and the social sciences are open to considerable doubt. There are obvious differences between the behavior of human beings and the behavior of physical things; but they do not justify setting these two in separate worlds, or suggesting that the ideals of truth and reason we apply to the physical sciences do not apply to the study of human history. The natural sciences, after all, have also had social origins and social consequences. The anthropomorphism of early astronomy is notorious; the religious motives that inspired Newton are well known; Darwin drew his idea of the struggle for survival from the regnant Malthusian economics of his day. Ideological bias, compulsive inattention to facts that later seem obvious, the failure to draw implications that are there, and the repeated drawing of implications that are not there—all these are part of the physical scientist's life as well as of the historian's or sociologist's. Physical science is not the immaculate product of the disembodied mind any more than social science is; but this has not prevented men from attaining what everyone accepts as objective knowledge in the study of the physical world. It is difficult to see, therefore, why this should be absolutely impossible in our social thinking. The simple point is that all thinking has its physical, psychic, and social determinants; but this in no way implies that human beings cannot be objective.

But if it is true that all human thinking is socially determined, it will be asked, does this not make the very conception of an impersonal truth a contradiction in terms? For if all thinking is socially determined—that is, determined by accidents of time, place, or social class—then, as Mannheim says, it must incorporate perspectives that are limited and partial. And even the standards of truth and validity we employ must be part of such perspectives. How is it possible, then, to speak of a truth which transcends the point of view of an age or a culture?

These questions are the second line of argument on which the Sociology of Knowledge depends. But they rest, quite simply, on an unwitting play on the word "partiality." Every human perspective, it need hardly be said, is limited and selective, and human knowledge must always be incomplete. This is partiality —partial truth. But this is a far cry from saying that all knowledge must inevitably be distorted or biased. For to see only part of what is to be seen does not mean that whatever we do see is partial in the sense of being prejudiced. Partial knowledge does not necessarily mean false knowledge.

Consider some examples from the writing of history. Historians must inevitably be selective in what they write about, and for this

133

reason it is frequently said that they cannot avoid imposing an arbitrary pattern of meaning on events. But it is difficult to see why the mere fact of selection in history implies bias. If you are writing the history of cavalry, for example, you may say that mechanized warfare meant the end of cavalry. This is, to be sure, a narrow and highly selected interpretation of the meaning of mechanized warfare. But it is a perfectly true account; and it would not be any truer if you digressed from the subject, and explained all the other consequences to which mechanized warfare had led. Similarly, we can interpret the meaning of World War II with relation to the acceleration of scientific research, the breakdown of colonialism, the defeat of Nazism, the polarization of world power between the Soviet Union and the United States, the increase of social mobility, the final breakdown of the free market, the rise of juvenile delinquency, and the increase of cigarette smoking. Each of these is a perfectly legitimate, though partial, point of view; and none falsifies what actually happened unless, of course, it can be shown that World War II did not actually have the consequences which a given point of view says it has.

In fact, all knowledge is selective. If we insist, on the basis of this truism, that all knowledge is therefore biased, we imply that we can never learn the objective facts about anything until we are omniscient. More, we contradict the very idea of knowledge. For all knowledge involves generalizations, and therefore abstractions. By its very nature, then, it is selective, and if it were not selective it would not be knowledge. When we apply the term "biased" to our beliefs merely because they are selective, we are using the term "biased" in such a way that the distinction between being biased and being unbiased loses all meaning.

But how, it will be asked, can we justify the selections we make? History consists of an indefinite number of individual events connected in an indefinite number of ways. When we select only certain events, and weave them together into a connected story, are we not imposing a pattern which history itself does not have—a pattern which is a projection of our own interests or assumptions, and not of the facts themselves? If something always has to be assumed before we ask any questions or make any inquiries, is it not senseless to talk about an objective, unbiased approach to any subject?

These are the considerations which led Mannheim, for one, to his conviction that incomplete knowledge is necessarily biased. But they rest on a mistaken assumption about assumptions. It is a truism that every inquiry, whether in history or the natural sciences, must proceed by taking something for granted. But this does not mean that in every inquiry we take the same assumption for granted. What we leave unquestioned in one context we can very well question in another. The fact that we must make assumptions proves only one thing—that none of our knowledge is certain. But while we can never attain absolute certainty, we can progressively correct the assumptions we make. There is no single, unquestionable assumption, no "total ideology" or "act of faith," on which the entire structure of our thinking depends. In short, we do not have to risk everything on assumptions that are absolutely right or absolutely wrong. We can simply make limited assumptions, which leave something standing even if they turn out to be wrong. This, quite simply, is how we avoid dogmatic ideologies and their attendant disasters.

In the end, indeed, there is an embracing paradox about the idea that all ideas about human affairs are true only from the point of view of a particular culture or social class. This statement is itself an idea about human affairs. If, like all other such ideas, it is a doctrine which is true for some people but false for others, there is no reason why people who hold a different point of view should pay any attention to it. If, on the other hand, it is not limited in its validity, then it is an exception to the very

135

generalization it utters. It is one example of an idea whose truth transcends the historical circumstances in which it is uttered. And if there is one such idea, it seems arbitrary to suggest that there can be no others. In short, it is not easy to dispense with the traditional notion of objective truth. Even the Sociology of Knowledge implicitly invokes it.

Logically, then, Mannheim has not proved the impossibility of an objective social intelligence. But there is still a practical question to be asked. Even if we grant that objectivity is a meaningful ideal, it is far from an easily attainable one. Who today can claim to be free from prejudices? And if anyone is, will he not be a voice crying in the wilderness unless some way is found to restore rational standards to society at large? Under these circumstances, is not some technique like the Sociology of Knowledge, which will bring the unconscious prejudices of whole classes to light, indispensable to the reconstruction of modern society?

It is unquestionably difficult to resist the appeal of this idea. We have become accustomed to psychoanalysis, which brings to light the unknown distortions that impair the power of individuals to deal objectively and rationally with their problems. It is a short step from this to the idea that we could recover our collective rationality by some form of mass socioanalysis which would bring the unconscious prejudices of whole classes to light. If everyone recognized his own prejudices, it seems apparent, we would all be able to see things more easily from the other fellow's point of view. And out of this process by which all perspectives are considered sympathetically but critically for the partial things they are, it might appear that a larger and more "objective" truth would emerge.

Appealing as this idea may seem, however, it rests on a very curious idea of how truth is found. In fact, when men have

136

different perspectives, they come to agreement about the objective facts by appealing to considerations which stand apart from all their perspectives. Consider an analogy from the field of everyday visual perspectives. Suppose there is an object suspended in the sky. A man in Germany says it is shaped like a ball; a man in Rhodesia says it is an oval; a man in Alaska says it is triangular. To bring these different perspectives together, we do not merely enter sympathetically into each one of them. We invoke something quite independent of all of them—namely, what we know about the behavior of light. With the help of this knowledge, together with the information that each observer gives us, we construct a hypothesis about the objective shape of the entity in question. We then go back and see whether an object with such a shape, seen from the vantage points in question, would look as each of the observers says it looks. If the perspectives do not fit, we check for individual aberrations—for blind spots, or untruthfulness, or defective instruments, and the like. And if we find no individual aberrations, we go back and reconsider the idea we have framed of the object. Under certain circumstances, we may even reconsider our ideas about the behavior of light. But we keep on with this process until we arrive at a conception of the shape of the object in question which will explain, in accordance with more embracing laws, why it appears to men as it does.

The ultimate shape we attribute to our object, therefore, is independent of the point of view of any particular observer, and not wholly dependent on all three points of view taken together. It is constructed, not simply by consulting the perspectives of individual observers, but by employing certain general beliefs that are independent of the particular perspectives in conflict. And it is only because we have such objective ideas that we are ever able to correct the bias or distortion of individual points of view. Knowing something about the behavior of light, for example, we know that a straight stick normally looks bent in the water. If a man tells us that such a stick, suspended in the water, nevertheless looks straight to him, we do not accuse ourselves of having only a partial perspective on things, and tolerantly proceed to build a new perspective which takes his observation into account. We take the man to an oculist.

What is involved, then, in the idea that we can all become more objective if we only recognize how subjective we really are, is a mistaken conception of objectivity and how it is attained. To gain objectivity, we do not need a separate Sociology of Knowledge standing outside all the other sciences. We do not even need to be reminded, as Mr. Niebuhr suggests, about the original sin that taints all human achievements. For there is no master science, and no celestial medicine for the mind or the soul, which guards us against ideological bias. When we attain objectivity, it is in the course of organized inquiry itself, and is a result of the internal controls and self-corrective methods of the inquiry. We become objective about the facts by focusing on the facts, not by focusing on the individuals who are observing them.

The failure to see this is the reason why Mannheim's philosophy of history misses the essential significance of science as a social phenomenon in the modern world. Strangely enough for a sociological doctrine, the Sociology of Knowledge construes objectivity exclusively in psychological terms. It means by objectivity a psychological *attitude*—the attitude of a man who gives the same weight to other points of view that he gives to his own. But objectivity is achieved in human thinking, not primarily as the result of the attitudes of individuals, but as the result of deliberately established social arrangements. There are two principal reasons why scientific ideas are objective, and neither has anything to do with the personal merits or social status of individual scientists. The first is that these ideas are the products of a co-operative process in which the individual has to submit

138

his results to the test of public observations which others can perform. The second is that these ideas are the results of a process in which no ideas or assumptions are regarded as sacrosanct, and all inherited ideas are subject to the continuing correction of experience.

Individual scientists, accordingly, are likely to be just as jealous of their reputations, attached to their own ideas, and incapable of taking the ideas of others seriously, as the rest of the human race. But the ideas that come to be accepted by the scientific community *are* objective; and they are objective in the precise sense that they meet impersonal standards which are independent of the peculiar perspective of any individual. "Rational Man" does not designate an original fact about human nature with which we begin; and the belief in "Rational Man" is not destroyed when we show that men as individuals are benighted, dream-ridden, and provincial creatures. "Rational Man" is the name for a social achievement.

The mistake of defining "objectivity" in terms of a psychological attitude, or in terms of the content of a particular doctrine, rather than in terms of certain public rules and procedures, is not just a blunder of interest to the logicians. It is a blunder with profound practical implications for education, law, and social policy. It is responsible for our failure to see that the outbursts of irrationality that have taken place in this century are not symptoms of biological or mental decline but of dislocations in our social institutions. Political irrationality does not require new medicines or old mystiques; it requires practical political reforms. And the notion that objectivity is exclusively a psychological trait is responsible also for many of our current misadventures in domesticating science in our lives. It explains, on one side, why so many reject the idea of applying science to human affairs on the ground that this implies a Brave New World like Mr. Huxley's. It explains, on the other, why so many men with

139

humanitarian impulses have tended to think about social planning in terms of a society organized and controlled by a select group in possession of the One True Doctrine.

Mannheim's doctrine is not quite one of these, but it is perilously close. Because he thought that "objectivity" designates only a psychological attitude, and not the conformity of an idea to certain public rules, Mannheim thought that the recapturing of reason in modern society was the business of a specific social class—a class which had the right attitude. The nineteenth-century liberal ideal of applying organized intelligence to human affairs was in the main an institutional ideal—an ideal of devising social arrangements which would encourage the dissemination of information, which would place individuals in a position to judge this information, and which would balance the division of social power in such a way that equitable and nonviolent procedures would govern the resolution of social conflicts. Mannheim took this ideal of applying organized intelligence to human affairs, and converted it into the ideal of applying organized intellectuals to human affairs.

There can be no doubt about the depth of Mannheim's aversion to authoritarianism. But in the end, his philosophy of history, for all its liberal sympathies, and for all the wealth of sociological insight it contains, is a version of the oldest kind of philosophy of history. It is the kind which assigns to a Chosen People the task of doing the great work of history, and finds in some one group of men the lone point of view that can save us all from our troubles. It substitutes for Plato's conception of an absolute and unchanging truth a conception of a "truth" which is constantly changing and growing, and which is discovered, not by resolutely turning away from the myths that prevail in the practical world, but by studying them assiduously and sympathetically. It lacks the utopian overtones, the expectation of a perfection to be achieved, which have usually gone with

140

Platonism. But at bottom, it is a return to the ancient Platonic dream that the cities of man will not cease from ill until philosophers are kings.

Paradoxically, the Sociology of Knowledge is the descendant of the liberal philosophy and history-writing of the Enlightenment. It was the philosophers and historians of the eighteenth century who began the modern custom of tracing ideas back to their origins in ordinary experience. They did so to expose and unmask prevailing ideas, and to show that they rested on accidents or superstitions or mere conventions. But at the basis of this criticism was the assumption that there was an objective truth about the human scene that transcended any age or culture. In exposing the bias and partiality of the inherited ideas of their time, eighteenth-century philosophers and historians were measuring these ideas against what they believed were universal canons of science and reason. What the contemporary Sociology of Knowledge has done has been to carry the critical methods of liberal philosophy and history one step farther, and to subject these allegedly universal canons of science and reason to precisely the same criticism as liberalism leveled against ideas in religion, politics, and society. The Sociology of Knowledge represents a peculiarly ingenious use of one of the classic methods of liberal philosophy and history to unseat the basic assumptions of liberalism.

In Mannheim's case, the motive was to set all our thinking about history and human affairs on a revolutionary new basis. But there have been other motives as well behind the increasing vogue of this approach to our social thinking. On its conservative side, a good deal of the Sociology of Knowledge has not been skepticism at all, but only the use of skeptical arguments to reinforce old beliefs that have been endangered by the rise of science. The Sociology of Knowledge represents another attempt

141

in the modern world to show that the methods and standards of science do not apply to the realm of human behavior. Modern science is the proudest achievement of the modern West, and it has been thought to be the way by which men could divest themselves of bias and attain an impersonal objectivity. A good many of the current partisans of the Sociology of Knowledge are telling us that science itself is merely the shared illusion of an age, a kind of convention or normal madness which works in a practical way, but is as arbitrary and partial in its presumptions as any other department of human activity. Professor Sorokin has informed us that we live in a "Sensate" era, and that our science, with its emphasis on observation by the senses, is only the expression of a limited point of view, and lacks the wisdom that can be found by other techniques. In a more moderate way, Professor Northrop has spoken of a "meeting of East and West," and has suggested that we would have, not simply more joy in life, but a deeper idea of *knowledge* if we gave as much attention to the Oriental emphasis on the immediate, aesthetic quality of experience as we do to our own Western emphasis on generalization and theory. Western science has been precisely that feature of Western culture which has been seized upon most avidly by other cultures; but a major theme among recent sociologists of knowledge has been that science too is relative, and that it is, indeed, the very symbol of our limitations, provincialism, and moral inferiority.

But all of these soft impeachments of science rest on the view that science, like any other body of belief, depends on certain "ultimate" or unquestioned assumptions—that it is, in a word, another ideology. And this involves a fundamental misconception. For science is not a single, unified creed, and it does not rest on any wholesale presuppositions. It makes no advance commitments which it is unprepared to discard under any circumstances. The so-called "metaphysical foundations of science," about which we hear so much, are at best a misnomer for the historical origins of scientific ideas, and have nothing to do with the content or truth of these ideas. For science, quite simply, is not a creed in competition with other creeds; it is not the view of a sect. It is a way of bringing all creeds to the test of certain common techniques and methods. And when we reject it for being provincial, we reject the one language which has been able effectively to cross boundaries and to draw men together. In the simplest terms, the only effective world community that now exists is the community of science. In this respect, if in no other, the vision of eighteenth-century liberal philosophers has been achieved. For the progress of science, as they saw, is not the progress of some one creed at the expense of others. It is the progress of a set of rules and procedures which allow men to co-ordinate their thinking and to co-operate in the search for truth.

The achievement of such an institutional technique for achieving objective beliefs is, indeed, the signal intellectual achievement of modern liberal society. It is the one point at which that society differs most fundamentally from other societies. There are techniques in all societies for fixing men's beliefs, and for bringing them into some sort of agreement on the facts. All of these methods involve accepting something without question—custom, a revelation, the superior judgment of selected individuals; most of them also contain an element of coercion; none of them are self-corrective in a steady and deliberate way. The institutions of modern science, in contrast, represent a radically new technique for co-ordinating men's ideas without coercion, and for bringing unquestioned assumptions or "ideologies" under criticism. The emergence of such a revolutionary institution in the modern world represents a turning point in the way in which human society achieves its beliefs. This is what the liberal philosophy of history celebrated, and why the classic liberals believed

143

that the progress of the human mind had become a legitimate and attainable ideal.

The decline of a public, the disappearance of a reservoir of good will and common understanding, the rise of rigid ideologies on one side and of apathy on the other, the collapse of the ideal of public participation into the practice of public relations— all these challenge the hopes which the rise of science provoked. But they are not the result of these hopes, and they do not prove that these hopes are illusions. They are the results of fundamental changes in the institutions that frame our lives. The increase of social mobility has made men more aware of the differences between their own points of view and the points of view of others; the breakdown of respected patterns of competition has encouraged men to think that there are no common standards by which these different points of view can be judged; the daily assault which the media of mass communication make on men's pocketbooks, anxieties, and beliefs, has led men to develop protective mechanisms against being taken in, and to suspect that everyone has an angle and that there is no such thing as truth anyway. The results may be seen in the popularity of muckraking and debunking, in the hostility and suspicion that has come into our political discourse, in the language of "psychic gestures," "myths," and "vital lies" which our intellectuals have increasingly substituted in their discussion of ideas for the old language of logical consistency and correspondence to the facts.

But we cannot introduce reason and objectivity into our public life if we give up the ideals of reason and argument. Freud, whose authority is most frequently invoked to support the view that rationality and objectivity are illusions, once uttered a prophecy. If we reject it as a prophecy, it still expresses the only ideal by which a serious man can live:

144

We may insist as much as we like that the human intellect is weak in comparison with human instincts, and be right in doing so. But nevertheless there is something peculiar about this weakness. The voice of the intellect is a soft one, but it does not rest until it has gained a hearing. Ultimately, after endlessly repeated rebuffs, it succeeds. This is one of the few points in which one may be optimistic about the future of mankind. . . . The primacy of the intellect certainly lies in the far, far, but still probably not infinite, distance.

VIII.

THE PROGRESS
OF THE HUMAN MIND

A MAJOR theme has been lurking in the background of most of our discussion up to this point. It is the theme of intellectual progress—what it means, how it takes place, what its moral and social consequences are. The belief that intellectual progress, and particularly progress in science, is the key factor in the progress of civilization has been central to the traditional liberal view of history. But each of the philosophers we have studied so far has argued that the intellectual progress of the modern world, as represented by progress in science, has had relatively little to do with the moral or social progress of man. Professor Maritain argues that in all the essential questions of morals and politics what we seek are absolutes that stand above change and progress. Mr. Niebuhr urges that the incurable sinfulness of man sets an impassable barrier to what objective and disinterested intelligence can do in human history. That human reason does not develop the power to determine its own independent course is the fundamental theme of historicist philosophies like Mannheim's.

146

In expressing these views, these philosophers speak for the increasingly widespread suspicion—indeed, it is much stronger than a suspicion—that the intellectual and scientific progress which has been the proudest achievement of modern man is a snare and a delusion, and that the modern world has given a central place in civilization to a department of human life which is, at best, only a very minor department among those that contribute to human progress. The enslavement of human reason to unconscious wishes, to passion, and to "the veiled, vague chaos of the human soul," is the theme of most of our present thinking about the prospects of modern man. Condorcet's and Mill's enthusiasm for modern science, their faith in reason and their hopes for the future, are dismissed as the fantasies of men with a thin view of human nature and a flat conception of the possibilities, and the dilemmas, of human life.

Let us bring these issues to a focus and consider what it means to believe that human reason progresses, and that such progress can be an independent and decisive variable in human history.

"The state of the speculative faculties, the character of the propositions assented to by the intellect," wrote John Stuart Mill, "essentially determines the moral and political state of the community, as . . . it determines the physical." These words express a cardinal tenet of the liberal view of history. But they are not easy words to defend. Men's behavior, it is plain, is determined mainly not by articulate beliefs, but by wishes, impulses, customs, habits, routines, and social institutions. "The state of the speculative faculties, the character of the propositions assented to by the intellect," has repeatedly reflected the quite unintellectual moral and political state of the community, and has helped freeze that state rather than determine it. The reverse of Mill's proposition is as easy to believe as Mill's proposition itself. And yet if we cannot make any sense at all out of this proposition, the conse-

147

quences are grave. For if human reason cannot exercise an independent influence in history, or if the progress of the human mind is unconnected with moral or political progress, then human freedom in any meaningful sense disappears from the stage of history.

What, then, does it mean to talk about "the progress of the human mind" as liberal thinkers have done in the past? What are the origins of organized thinking in ordinary human activities? What changes does it introduce into these everyday activities? What contribution to human progress do these changes represent? What, in particular, is the place of modern science in that calendar of deliberately selected and cultivated goods which we call civilization?

If we take the modern university as an example, "the speculative faculties" of man engage in three principal types of enterprise. There is, first, the sort of research and teaching that concerns itself with objects that arrest the mind or delight the eye or ear, with experiences that exercise the emotions, and with symbols that express human ideals and aspirations. Secondly, there is a type of activity which has to do with keeping the memory of the past just, alert, and alive. Finally, there is a sort of enterprise which attempts to organize and explain events by general principles. The first of these may be called "criticism," the second "history," and the third "science." But while these are now highly organized, professional activities, they come into the world with a natural pedigree and a practical vocation. They are the ordinary concerns of a creature whose energies are not natively in balance with the world he inhabits, who is not brute enough to proceed on instinct alone and not divine enough to see or do all things at once.

Consider criticism. It is not originally an esoteric or specialized activity, a hobby for collectors, a pursuit for lovers of beauty, or even a way of life for creative spirits in the arts. It begins in the

148

ordinary activities of discrimination and selection which are forced upon the human creature by the fact that he has manifold wants and only limited resources for satisfying them. And it becomes orderly and systematic in the efforts to refine and organize perception and taste which life in a precarious world makes necessary. There is, to be sure, an irreducible element of personal preference in all criticism. What is good wine for one man merely spoils the taste of coffee for another. This has perennially disturbed professional critics and philosophers, who have tried repeatedly to promulgate universal canons of taste. But if it is understandable that salesmen should find the irreparable contrariness of human tastes discouraging, it is not easy to understand why others should. For idiosyncrasy of taste is one of the few gifts nature has given to man, the political animal, to make his way easier in life. If we all had the same tastes, we would all be scrabbling over the same food, walking in the same parks, and fighting over the same women. Diversity of preferences is not only pleasant; it is a social necessity.

The difficulty, however, is that the objects that satisfy taste are sometimes fuzzy and sometimes evanescent, that tastes frequently frustrate one another, and that tastes are communicated and are socially contagious. Personal preference, therefore, is not all there is to criticism. If everything delightful could be paused over, if the consequences of one choice were the same as the consequences of any other, if we never really had to pay for anything and had all the time in the world besides, there might still be preferences, but there would be no such thing as criticism. The gods in Homer are immortal, and while they may be wounded they are never permanently scarred. It is just as it should be, therefore, that although they have marked preferences, they are notorious for their bad taste. The only exception is Hephaestus, who is lame.

Human beings, in short, cannot merely like what they like, for

149

they usually find what they like surrounded by circumstances which distract their attention, or marred by blemishes which disturb their enjoyment. The individual finds that his tastes are fleeting when he has not clearly fixed the objects that satisfy them, the centers around which they are organized, or the edges that separate them from other things. He finds that he must not only purify and stabilize them, but put them into some sort of order so that they will not mutually frustrate one another. And he finds also that he must find the proper words for them, not only because words are indispensable to thinking about them, but because he wants to communicate his tastes and enhance his enjoyment in them by sharing them with others. Criticism, in short, though it has an indelible trace of what is subjective and a-rational, is a public and rational affair. The native bent of the individual spirit, its brute preferences and aversions, are not the pre-established desiderata of criticism, but the problems with which it begins. Criticism, indeed, is precisely the process by which what is private and solitary is chastened and socialized by being made to move out in a public world.

The motives that sustain the writing of history are similarly ordinary and continuing. History may be, as it was with Herodotus, an attempt to keep the glorious and amazing events of the past from being forgotten. It may be, as with Thucydides, a half-despairing effort to keep men from repeating old mistakes. But, just as criticism is rooted in the precariousness and diversity of tastes, so history is rooted in the precariousness and diversity of memory, and is an attempt to keep memory alert and to give it an order. There is rudimentary history, perhaps, in the meanderings of the dreaming mind, conjuring up its past. But history begins more clearly when the individual organizes his past in a definite pattern, and gives it a beginning, a middle, and an end, so that he can identify and locate himself, or keep from repeating himself wastefully. And history emerges most clearly as a regular public

150

activity in the stories by which a group communicates its collective experience, celebrates the signal events in its past, and encourages and sanctions the repetition of its established ways.

If criticism begins in the effort to organize preferences, and history in the effort to organize memory, science begins in the effort to organize work, in the activities by which men try to move efficiently to desired ends. In its earliest form, science is a list of tricks of the trade. The interest in the uniform conditions and general laws under which events take place is initially the interest of men who want to plan and organize their behavior on the basis of what is dependable in their environment, and the earliest repository of these generalizations is in the lore of the arts and crafts, in the farmer's knowledge about the seasons, in the sailor's about the movement of the stars, in the inherited tricks of workers in wood, stone, and metals who know something about the stable properties of the elements with which they deal. To those who remember Descartes, or who are dazzled or disturbed by the cold, chiseled façade of modern mathematical physics, science may seem more intellectual and remote than either criticism or history. But, in fact, its origins are, if anything, even more democratic. For at its origins it is associated with the work of the lower classes rather than with the leisure of the upper classes; and it is an ancillary and servile activity, committed to the antecedent values that custom and tradition lay before it, and restricted to the summarizing of past experience. It is the slave of human practice, and not its master. The control of nature or of human behavior which it makes possible is haphazard and sporadic, and, on modern models of science, it is, indeed, hardly science at all, but something much closer to what we now call technology. That technology is now so widely taken to be the whole of science suggests, in fact, how much the origins of science in ordinary experience continue to dominate the image we have of it.

151

Criticism, history, and science are thus everybody's business. They emerge together in the context of daily routines and emergencies, and they continue together in all sorts of practical activities like the bringing up of children, sport, or politics. Such practical activities involve a *mélange* of values, precedents, and rule-of-thumb principles about the durable traits of children, footballs, or human ambition. And for most purposes there is no pressing reason why criticism, history, and science should not retain this amateur status, or why practical thinking should not remain an undifferentiated mixture of emotion, memory, and precept. The simple, flexible language of everyday life, with its ambiguities and vaguenesses, is a better medium for the conversation of lovers than the language of mathematics. The working familiarity of the doctor with the ordinary range of symptoms and medicines is frequently preferable to the more articulate, but abstract, analysis of the chemist. And just as a book of etiquette is not a substitute for tact and good feeling in human relations, so we can ordinarily expect practical men to do a better job repairing an engine or writing a novel than the theoretical physicist or laboratory psychologist.

Nevertheless, so long as criticism, history, and science are only everybody's ordinary business, they remain restricted by the practical necessities that first generate them. And so long as they remain bound in this way, they are not quite satisfactory even for practical purposes. They serve practice but do not control it. They are provoked by its demands, but they are also hurried, harassed, and hemmed in by them. Criticism swings between yesterday's custom and today's fashion; history remains a pragmatic device for celebrating pre-established values; and science neither breaks old routines nor forestalls new emergencies. The consequences can be seen in the immediate quality of men's experience. To take an example, history, in its primitive condition, usually depicts the present as a simple re-enactment of the past; or, when custom and habit are crumbling, it rewrites the past with every minor tremor of passion or fashion. The consequence is that the line between the present and the past fades. But since this is also the line by which we normally separate what is irrevocable from what can be changed, the consequences for behavior are profound. To the modern mind, the dances, the rituals, the sudden bursts of emotion, that mark simpler societies often seem like reflections of a greater freedom, instances of unburdened, or unbuttoned, spontaneity and animal vitality. But they can only be understood against the background of the enveloping monotony of primitive life, and the oppressiveness of existence in a society which has not yet distinguished what it remembers from what it can do.

What is necessary, in short, is that the endless circle of practice be broken. And it is when this circle is broken that the turning point in the career of reason appears, and human intelligence becomes an independent factor in history, able, within limits, to control its own development and to change the dimensions in which human history goes on. The instrument by which this change takes place is the development of *theory*. It is the failure to understand the difference between theory and practice that constitutes the fundamental oversight in Mannheim's view of the social determination of knowledge, and in most of the present inclination to disparage the prospects or the moral significance of intellectual progress. For human thinking may begin with some practical need, or some overriding moral impulse. But to the extent that it is successful, thinking yields a set of inclusive ideas; and the logic of these ideas carries the mind to issues that lie beyond the immediate and practical questions that originally set it in motion. The mind becomes speculative; it considers new alternatives, and far-reaching possibilities. It theorizes.

In its origins human inquiry is no doubt a practical affair, provoked by the breakdown of working routines, or the unexpected advent of something new. The methods which lead to theory are

153

the end products of a long evolution that begins with the fumbles, trials, and errors of practical men. And the truth of a theory is in the end a matter of experiment and observation in the ordinary world of the five senses. But if theory and practice are not separate and independent, the line between them is nevertheless a large one. Theory has remarkable consequences for practice precisely because it is not just a duplication of practice on a higher level. Compare the sailor's knowledge of navigation with the theories by which the astronomer can move from one phenomenon to another separated from it by vast reaches of space and time. Or, to trace the movement of theory a step higher, compare the description of the separate elements we learn in elementary chemistry with the periodic table which orders the elements in terms of the more embracing ideas of atomic structure, and turns the differences in their behavior into illustrations of the same set of laws. Practical judgment is rough and ready, theoretical judgment precise. Practical thinking is provoked by problems it has not created, theoretical thinking deliberately seeks ideas that will make further questions possible. Practical knowledge leaves the world segmented and divided, with the farmer, sailor, and mechanic each living in his own little universe of uniformities. A theory joins separate worlds and brings us all under the same sky.

And the sky is larger. We are in the habit now of thinking of theory in terms of its practical applications—in terms, that is, of the conveniences, and even more of the terrors, which technology has visited on the human race. But these are the by-products of theory. On its own account, the difference that theory makes is a difference in the quality of our experience of the world. Copernicus, Bruno said, "emancipated our knowledge from the prison from which, as it were, it looked at the stars only through small windows." It is natural, therefore, that we should resist the impact of theory, and that there should be an ancient warfare between theory and practice. Small windows go with small rooms and dark corners. It is easier to keep warm in small rooms and to live in dark corners. In coming into the world theory upsets the old familiar terms and the intimate, comfortable dimensions of practical life. It arouses all the latent animosities of the Old Adam, who is an inveterate *petit bourgeois* attached to his little securities and familiar terrors. But theory has this unsettling impact precisely because it releases men's imaginations from bondage to what is close at hand, and gives them the power to extend the range of their experience by their own deliberate choice. Theory is the great instrument by which the human mind comes of age, and in some measure becomes self-directing and self-controlled.

It is intelligible, therefore, that so many who have felt the impact or revelation of theory in their lives have thought it a divine thing, separate in its origins and independent in its truth from the gross world of ordinary men. It is the freedom that comes with theory, the release from the prejudices and demands of the mundane order, that Plato ultimately celebrates 'in his distinction between opinion and knowledge, in his metaphor of the cave, and in his myths about philosophy, love, and immortality. And it is the sense of the remarkable power which theory gives, of the compulsions it exercises on thought against all the pressures of interest and instinct, which led that other Platonist, Descartes, to condemn history, deny his memory, and doubt his senses. Plato and Descartes erred, because they took the remarkable independence from practical urgencies which theory gives as a sign of its logical separation from the everyday world. But it was an understandable and exciting error; and if it had not resulted in so much bad philosophy, it might almost have been a useful one. For the advent of theory is a turning point in the drama of human progress. It is what converts the history of the

155

human mind from a series of routines interrupted by emergencies into a deliberately adopted and orderly career.

The great triumph of the theoretical mind, and its best example, is modern science. It is usual to damn modern science with faint praise as only a powerful form of engineering, a subordinate and practical craft whose only justification is its usefulness for manipulating things. Science is portrayed as the opposite of art, of imagination, and of the humanistic disciplines in general. And it is condemned for having taken us in, for having imposed on the modern mind a thinned-out map or skeleton of the world, with none of the world's fullness, and with no intimation of its possibilities. All of these parodies of modern science start with a failure to see the difference between theoretical inquiry and practical inquiry.

In fact, theoretical science is a deliberate, creative enterprise, in which the human mind actively selects and constructs a home for itself. For a scientific theory is not discovered simply by vibrating sympathetically to the tunes of the universe. It is a deliberately constructed device for organizing inferences and for leading to new observations. Even elementary scientific procedures, such as the measurement of time, illustrate the creative character of scientific thinking. To time an event means to measure it against some process which has a periodic character—like the movement of the hands of a clock around the face. And any one of an indefinite number of such processes might be chosen to be our standard of time—the falling of sand from one container into another, or the famous walks which Kant took around Königsberg, walks so regular that the townspeople set their clocks by them, or, to take a not implausible contemporary example, the heartbeat of some political Big Brother. Depending on the standard we took, different laws or correlations between events would turn up, and some would be very interesting indeed. For example,

156

every time Big Brother got sick, all citizens working the standard 250,000 heartbeat day would find themselves growing increasingly tired. This would create a community of suffering with Big Brother, would demonstrate that his power reached into the most intimate details of daily life, and would ensure that all citizens would rejoice at his recovery. But these generalizations, while politically useful, would not have the sweep or the intellectual elegance that comes from employing other standards, such as the rotation of the earth on its axis. These permit us to move across great stretches of experience in a stable and economical way. It is to increase the power of the human mind to do just this that theories are formulated.

A scientific theory thus makes a positive contribution to human experience. When men approach their world within the framework of a theory, their experience has a dimension which simple observation alone cannot give it. The primary function of theory is to lead to new experiences, to be an instrument by which men can deliberately and intentionally expand their horizons. Scientific theory is not the opposite of imagination. It is a product of imagination, and an instrument for emancipating it from enslavement to the familiar, the routine, and the here-and-now.

And it is an instrument, as well, for stabilizing and disciplining the human imagination. The mathematical side of modern science is probably responsible for the popular impression that science is cold, mechanical, and remote. But the mathematical side of modern science is in fact a remarkable example of how the human imagination can be at once liberated and disciplined. Mathematical methods are ways of overcoming at least four weaknesses to which our ordinary everyday experience is liable—its grossness, its instability, its idleness and disorder, and its idiosyncrasy. Far from being less refined than the qualitative judgments we usually make, quantitative techniques permit us to make more minute and precise distinctions; they allow us to render the same

157

verdict on things at different times and independently of how we feel; they enable us to put our perceptions in a definite order so that we can reason from them with more assurance and to more far-reaching consequences; and, perhaps most important, they provide a way of transcending the idiosyncrasy of different perspectives and of bringing the experience of different men together. Mathematical methods thus represent not merely professional techniques, but social inventions, man's own instruments against his obtuseness, waywardness, and egoism. Their emergence constitutes a sociological phenomenon of first-rate importance—the emergence of a new technique for co-ordinating human experience and for bringing men into uncoerced agreement.

Theoretical science, in short, is an example par excellence of a liberal art—a deliberate, selective reordering of experience, which releases men from the narrowness and urgency of their routine affairs, carries them beyond the limitations and accidents of their lives, and makes it possible for their commerce with the world to have scope, order, and systematic consequences. It has been used as an instrument of industry and of war, but its primary function is more humane and, as it were, aesthetic—to cause human experience to be fruitful and to multiply. And its relation to practice is the relation of any fine and liberating art—it carries men beyond the foreground of their experience, and enlarges the dimensions of human choice by acquainting men with the alternative possibilities of things. Quite apart from its technological applications, it represents, to use an old philosophical expression, a "final good"—something which has its own inner dynamism, goes its own way, and can give stability and direction to the rest of our lives.

In what way, however, does the emergence of theory affect the "speculative faculties" other than science, and change "the character of the propositions assented to by the intellect"? What are the implications of theoretical science for history and criticism?

Unlike science, history is not mainly concerned with formulating theories. Its business is different—to report the singular events that make up the past. But the emergence of theory nevertheless holds fundamental implications for the writing of history. For it radically alters the picture that man keeps of his ancestry, and transforms his relationship to the past.

To be sure, the power of theory to affect history is as yet largely potential because our theories of human nature and society are still on the whole unformed or on a relatively low level of development. Nevertheless, something of what such theories might mean can be gathered from the impact which theories of the natural universe have already had on the writing of history. The emergence in the modern world of large-scale astronomical, physical, and geological theories has probably been the most significant single event in the history of history itself. For the bare knowledge that such theories were possible profoundly altered historical perspectives. In the light of what is constant in nature, the past took on the same dimensions as the present, with the same physical environment and the same human material. The myths and legends departed, the gods receded, the heroes were cut down to size. In the light of what is universal, the stories of all human groups were put on the same level, subject to the same tests and explicable by the same principles. Eighteenth-century history, the prototype of modern history-writing, no doubt underestimated the differences between men; but it was not a mere moral prejudice of the Enlightenment to join the word "humanity" with the words "reason" and "nature." In seeing the history of all groups as explicable by the same set of embracing laws, the historian gave a meaning to the conception of human brotherhood which expressed not only a social ideal but a meth-

159

odological commitment. And this methodological commitment had a moral impact. Those who ask what moral influence the theories of modern science have had would do well to begin by noting the humanitarianism, the toleration, the feeling for human equality, which inform the histories that were first written under the stimulus of Newtonian physics.

The potentialities of theory for history derive from the fact that a theory represents a framework which allows us to follow out the implications of a fact systematically. It tells us what is possible. So, on the one side, it checks imagination, sifts out the fanciful, makes memory less shifting and willful, more stable and reliable. Knowledge of the invariant enables the historian to assess the authenticity and meaning of the documents, reports, and ruins with which he begins his work, and to make inferences from them which lead to the unearthing of new materials. And when he constructs a connected story out of these materials, theory limits the hypotheses he can reasonably formulate, and imposes upon him the necessity of making his story square with a larger, independent body of ideas. But, on the other side, in leading to knowledge of what is possible, theory also liberates memory, releasing it from its provincialism and innate partisanship, making it more sensitive to the alternative paths that are possible in human life, and more generous in what it retains. The historian G. M. Young has said that the great tragedy of English-Irish relations was due to the fact that what England could never remember Ireland could never forget. The historical imagination which could have prevented this catastrophe is certainly a rare gift. Theory makes it possible for it to be deliberately cultivated.

Theory, in a word, carries the promise that history can become a critical enterprise. Primitive history, as we can partly confirm by remembering our own early lessons in history, swings between the poles of brute contingency and absolute inevitability—between the extreme of telling us what simply and inexplicably has been and the extreme of presenting the human record as the working out of some master plan in which everything has a necessary meaning. In one case history is a mystery, in the other case a miracle; in both cases there is no room for the critical intellect to make out what might have been in the past, or to discern the limits and possibilities of the present. When theory is applied to history, however, events are interpreted as the consequences of general laws on the one side, and of contingent circumstances on the other. So history ceases to be an exercise in memory or in piety, and becomes a critical enterprise which disengages the essential from the accidental in the record of human affairs. Aristotle to the contrary notwithstanding, history need not be less philosophical than poetry.

Such history can fundamentally alter man's innermost feelings about his past. For theory allows men to rise above the limited range of what has happened and to move in the larger range of things that might have been or might still be. In its light we can see more clearly the accidents that have gone into human history, the opportunities missed, the good causes spoiled. We become more aware of the awful waste that dominates the record of man's career on this planet, and more sensitive to the wonder of his few glimmering, tormented achievements. Theory, in brief, releases us from domination by the past; but it also saves us from making our picture of the past a mere image of our own fitful interests or creeds. For while history is the record of what passes, with the aid of theory it can rise to a level on which it will be something more than a shifting reflection of shifting things. The study of history can steady us, making us more alert to man's continuing aspirations, more generous in our understanding of the forms they take, more patient and humorous in our loyalty to them. And it can chasten us, reminding us that men and their affairs are an episode on a larger stage, that men have not set the broad conditions under which their history takes place, and that they convert

161

these conditions into opportunities only by understanding them and acquiescing in them. The progress of the human mind toward theories about human nature and social structure would allow the study of history to bring stability to men's memories and a greater amplitude to their ability to select in the present.

But, in the final analysis, the relation of intellectual progress to the more general progress of man must be measured by its consequences for criticism. For criticism is a name for human choice. And it is because the progress of the human mind in the construction of theories fundamentally alters the character of our choices that intellectual progress represents the essential element in the story of human progress.

Theories, of course, are not logically sufficient grounds for critical judgments: the soundest and most inclusive theory can only tell us what is or what is not possible; a critical judgment expresses a preference or an imperative. When men embellish their aesthetic tastes or political preferences with statements that "science" gives them absolute support, they are merely employing a new dodge in the old game of putting off on some higher authority the responsibility for the choices we make. But if theories do not absolutely guarantee any of our choices, they can at least make them more responsible and circumspect. And they can alter our choices in the most powerful way by enlarging the context, the set of alternatives, from which we choose.

Ideally, the use of theory in criticism chastens criticism by an awareness of the objective limits to human preference and aspiration; and it freshens criticism by a larger vision of what it is possible for man to do and be. When illuminated by theory, criticism rises above the level of convention and fashion, and gives the life of a civilization spark and *élan* by presenting it with objects of aspiration that do not emerge within the narrow and

162

pressing urgencies of everyday behavior. Just as in the case of history, the deliberate, direct use of theory in criticism is still largely something to be achieved. Wherever it has been achieved, however, it represents the liberation of the human imagination from domination by the close-at-hand, and its partial triumph over its own willfulness and waywardness.

There can be no question that the progress of "the speculative faculties" in the modern world has presented us with a range of choices for which there is no precedent. This is not a gift which has been universally welcomed. The increased freedom of choice which this intellectual progress has given to modern man has undoubtedly added to his sense of strain, to his consciousness of his failures, and to his feelings of guilt. But this is because he may more justly hold himself accountable for his actions than could his predecessors, and it is a measure of his opportunity and of the powers that are available to him. If there is a dynamism and restlessness in modern culture, it is in part because that culture has a wider sense of its limits, and a more imaginative view of what it is possible for human life still to become.

This is the sense, I think, in which it can be said that "the state of the speculative faculties, the character of the propositions assented to by the intellect, essentially determines the moral and political state of the community, as . . . it determines the physical." For it is the progress of the theoretical intellect that lifts human behavior and human institutions out of the staleness and flatness of the routine to the level on which men may deliberately enlarge the scope of their experience and deliberately select the goods they pursue. The progress of theoretical science in the modern world is not just the progress of a useful—or dangerous —tool or technique. It represents the growth of the human imagination, and of the potentials of discipline and order which men have at their disposal for the cultivation of their feelings and the pursuit of their aspirations.

163

IX.

MR. TOYNBEE'S TRANS-FIGURATION OF HISTORY

ARNOLD TOYNBEE'S *A Study of History* brings together all the criticisms of the contemporary outlook on history which we have examined, and puts them in the framework of a majestic theory of the direction and meaning of history as a whole. In an age whose meaning no one knows, the very existence of *A Study of History* seems like a promise that there may be some light in the darkness after all. It is the testament of a man who has surveyed the course of every human civilization on record; and this man's considered conclusion is that there is a repeated pattern, a set of laws, that govern the rise and fall of human societies. In an age of drift and disaster, furthermore, this man believes that the pattern of history is a moral pattern, and that history tells a story in which there is a place for everything and everything is put in its place. History, he reports, is the scene of the trial and transfiguration of man, a way station in man's journey toward saintliness. He claims that he has reached this conclusion objectively and without prior commitments. What is more, he has ten volumes of evidence to offer for it.

164

No work in history in this century rests on so much erudition, covers so much territory, or keeps its intellectual drive or emotional freshness so steadily as this book of Mr. Toynbee's. For a history that combines so much richness of detail with an embracing theme that is never lost, one must go back to Edward Gibbon. For comparable sweep and passion, and for a moral outlook as consistent and unrelenting, one must go back to Saint Augustine's *City of God*. In style and manner, in its use of myth and metaphor, in its willingness to generalize, *A Study of History* represents a departure from prevailing modes in the writing of history as radical for this century as was Marx in the nineteenth or Voltaire in the eighteenth century. It is one of the singular achievements on the present intellectual landscape.

And its purpose is as radical as its style and manner. It is to set the history and prospects of the present age against the background of the history of every human civilization known to man, and in the process to turn the existing categories of historical thinking inside out. First conceived and plotted in 1929, and completed over the course of twenty-five years, *A Study of History* retains to the end this architectonic vision with which it began. Throughout it bears the accent of a man who is plainly convinced that he is writing a book which is not just a landmark in the history of history-writing, but an event in the making of history itself. Mr. Toynbee writes with disarming candor and modesty. But he refers to himself consistently in the third person as "the writer," making himself not simply an observer, but an actor, in the historical drama he is describing. He puts all his personal observations, even those about the contemporary events, in the past tense, suggesting that they are not merely comments on history, but part of the history that is being commented upon. He is even careful to date himself in A.D. 1946 or A.D. 1952, as though he fears that his readers in the future may misplace the present moment in the millennia that whirl through his book. And if his

165

book proves what it sets out to prove, he has not overestimated the importance of what he has done. For he will have revealed a remarkable moral pattern in the march of human affairs; and he will have shown that we have one last chance to save our civilization—provided we set our faces resolutely in the opposite direction from the one in which the modern liberal West has been traveling.

Mr. Toynbee's study of history is an attempt to see history as a living and unified process, and to treat the record of human affairs in a context which will show their essential vitality and interrelatedness. Modern society and modern history-writing, he points out, have been dominated by two institutions—the industrial system and nationalism. In a misplaced attempt to imitate the industrial division of labor, history has been written on a kind of scholarly assembly line. It has been cut up and dried out by narrow specialists concerned with minute segments of the historical process. The life has been taken out of it by men who have tried to apply the methods of physical science to the study of human affairs, and have committed "the Apathetic Fallacy" of treating living beings as though they were inanimate. Even more insidious, however, has been the influence of nationalism. Without ever stopping to think about it, modern historians have written history as though it were the story of separate and independent nation-states. And so a temporary, and already outmoded, system of international organization or disorganization has been mistaken for the permanent framework within which history goes on.

But how does one find a permanent framework that transcends the illusions of one's time and place? The events of history, Mr. Toynbee argues, have to be placed in some "intelligible field of historical study" which will allow us to see them in their living unity and in their full connections. We cannot really understand the economic history of a society unless we see it in terms of all

166

the other aspects of that society's life—its politics, its culture, its religion, its inner morale. And we cannot understand the history of any nation so long as we restrict ourselves to events that fall within its formal geographical boundaries. For the history of any institution, or of any nation, is part of a larger whole. And until we find out what that larger whole is, we are dealing with artificial abstractions, and not with reality. Mr. Toynbee's first problem, therefore, is to find the context in which history makes sense, the "intelligible field of historical study," into which the events of history actually fall.

Such intelligible fields of historical study, Mr. Toynbee claims, are civilizations. Consider, for example, the history of Great Britain. When we want to explain the history of Great Britain, Mr. Toynbee points out, we cannot stay within the geographical limits of the British Isles. The major chapters in British history— the coming of Christianity, feudalism, the organization of a national state, the Protestant Reformation, the industrial revolution —are all episodes in the history of other communities besides the British community. They are events that transcend the boundaries of the British Isles, problems that are common to a larger society. And when we have found out what the spatial boundaries of this larger society are, and how far back it goes in time, we will have found "the intelligible field of study" into which British history falls.

How do we proceed? If we look at the present British economy, Mr. Toynbee indicates, we find ourselves with a field of study which is world-wide. If we look at British political institutions, our frame of reference is only a little smaller. It is only when we come to British culture that we find ourselves dealing with a more restricted area. Here we find that Britain shares its history with only that relatively small part of the world that is populated by Roman Catholic and Protestant peoples. However, if we now trace the history of Great Britain backward in time, an interesting

167

phenomenon turns up. The economic and political frontiers within which British history falls recede much more rapidly as we go back through the centuries than do its cultural frontiers, and ultimately we come to a time when these three sets of boundaries all roughly coincide. We find a society as self-contained and independent economically and politically as it is culturally. And this society turns out to have boundaries which are approximately those established by the Carolingian Empire in A.D. 775. It is this society which is the original cradle of the civilization we now know as Western Christendom. The history of Great Britain is an integral part of the history of that civilization.

But why, it may be asked, do we not go farther back than the Carolingian Empire? Why do we take this society as the "cradle" of a *new* civilization? The answer is that if we look into the history of the Carolingian Empire we see that it originated in two things —the emergence of a universal church, and the wanderings of barbarian peoples, during the later days of the Roman Empire. And both of these are alien and underworld forces from the point of view of the ancient world. They were not taken seriously by the dominant classes of ancient society, and no historian interested in Graeco-Roman society has to pay any attention to them until he begins to chart the decline of ancient civilization. When Gibbon portrays the *decline* and *fall* of the Roman Empire, he tells the story of the *triumph* of Barbarism and Religion. In short, when we trace the origins of the Carolingian Empire back to the Graeco-Roman world, we approach that world from an angle of vision that is foreign to it.

In other words, there is a clean break, according to Mr. Toynbee, between Western civilization and the civilization of the ancient world. Western society is continuous with Hellenic society, but it is the continuity between parent and child, and not the continuity of a single civilization. Western civilization is a new member of the family of civilizations, and not just an exten-

168

sion of an older civilization. It has its own separate and distinct existence, and follows the law of its own being. And the history of this civilization, its over-all movement and direction and growth, is the framework within which all the pieces of Western history fit, and beyond which we do not have to go.

In the six thousand years during which human civilization has existed on the earth, Mr. Toynbee finds that there have been twenty-one such distinct and separate adventures in civilization. Of these, eight are still going on. They are "Western Society," "Orthodox Christian Society" in Russia, "Orthodox Christian Society" elsewhere, "Iranic Society," "Arabic Society," "Hindu Society," "Far Eastern Society" in Korea and Japan, and "Far Eastern Society" elsewhere.* The study of human affairs in terms of the history of these civilizations and their ancestors, he believes, is the proper business of the historian. It is the only way of rescuing the study of history from its present lifelessness and triviality, and of allowing us to see that the events that make up history are parts of larger processes which have their own internal integrity and unity.

The very existence of civilizations, however, poses a general

* The civilizations that are now alive, according to Mr. Toynbee, are civilizations of the third generation. In the second generation of civilizations is the Hellenic Society, which is the parent of the Western and the two Orthodox Christian Societies; the Syriac Society, which is the ancestor of the two Islamic Societies; the Indic, which is the progenitor of Hindu Society; and the Sinic Society, which fathered the two Far Eastern Societies. Behind these societies, we find a first generation of human civilizations. The Minoan Society of Crete and the Aegean areas fathered the Hellenic and Syriac civilizations; and the Sumeric Society fathered Indic Society, and also had two offshoots in Hittite Society and Babylonic Society. In the Western Hemisphere, there are the remains of three civilizations: the Andean Society of the Incas, and the Mexic and Yucatec Societies of Central America. Behind these two Central American civilizations stands an earlier one, the Mayan. Finally, standing in splendid isolation, with no apparent ancestor or descendant, is the Egyptiac Society, which has the distinction of having lived longer than any other society whose history we know.

169

problem. Civilizations, like other things, come into being and pass away. They seem to be the work of men, and yet, looking at the record, men do not seem able to keep them going indefinitely. They seem to be subject, as it were, to a higher law. What explains the birth of civilizations? What are the patterns, if any, into which their growth and decline fall? Is there any purpose to civilization? It is to answer these questions that Mr. Toynbee undertakes the comparative study of twenty-one civilizations which makes up the bulk of his book.

His story begins by singling out the characteristic that distinguishes civilizations from primitive societies. Primitive societies are dormant and inert. They do not change. Their history is all behind them or all ahead of them. Civilizations, in contrast, have an *élan*. They are on the move; they are making history. And so the first problem for the philosopher of history is to explain how this movement started. For when we consider the fact that man as a species has been on the earth at least three hundred thousand years, it is plain that the era of civilizations, which covers only the last six thousand years, is very recent, and is a very small part of the record. Something quite drastic must have been necessary to tear man loose from his customary inertia and sleepiness.

We can find the secret of this remarkable event, Mr. Toynbee avers, by taking a clue from mythology. For mythology expresses in living metaphor the actual experience of men. And in the mythologies of the most diverse cultures there appears and reappears a constant theme. It is the theme of some aboriginal cataclysm, of some static perfection that is broken in upon and upset by an external agency. This is the theme that recurs in all the myths about superhuman encounters—the clash between Yahweh and the Serpent, the challenge laid down by Satan to the Lord at the beginning of the Book of Job, the struggle between Artemis and Aphrodite on which Euripides builds his

Hippolytus. It is the theme of the Annunciation, and of the ubiquitous stories about the encounter of a virgin with the father of her child—Europa and the Bull, Psyche and Cupid, Gretchen and Faust. In every case, the essential story is the same, and it is presented as something rare and portentous.

At the beginning, we are always confronted with some peculiar perfection, some state of special ease and serenity—the Garden of Eden, or Job perfect in virtue and prosperity, or Faust perfect in knowledge, or Gretchen perfect in beauty and purity. And this balance is always upset by some sudden blow, by a temptation or a wager or an intrusion that comes from outside the human scene. But these intrusions are never merely arbitrary or destructive. For while the old perfection is lost, something else is gained. The human actors who are caught in the collision between superhuman powers go through a terrible and trying ordeal. But it is literally a *trying* ordeal, a trial, and when they accept this ordeal and respond to it with their whole souls, they come through it with new energies and powers. They come through tempered, and find themselves on a different and higher level of life. Expelled from the Garden of Eden, Adam and Eve set up the first domestic economy, and become the parents of the first farmer and the first shepherd; Job finds a deeper serenity; Gretchen is transfigured.

It is from these myths, Mr. Toynbee believes, that we can find the clue to the genesis and growth of human civilization. Human civilization is born out of a successful response to a challenge; and it keeps on growing so long as there continue to be challenges which are actively accepted and met.

The histories of individuals and communities and societies fall into successive chapters, in each of which a number of representatives of whichever the species may be are confronted by some identical challenge which imposes an ordeal. Under each of these common ordeals, the parties react in different ways. The majority succumb outright; some

171

just manage to survive, but at the cost of such wear and tear that they are good for nothing afterwards; others discover a response to the challenge which is so satisfactory that it not only carries them through the ordeal of the moment but puts them in a favourable posture for undergoing the next; others, again, follow these path-finders as sheep follow their leader into a gap which he has forced through a hedge.

The encompassing pattern that governs the birth and life of civilizations is the pattern of Challenge-and-Response. Man is moved to break the cake of custom, to stir out of the *vis inertiae* of primitive life, when he is confronted by some difficulty or obstacle which he must meet and overcome at the peril of his life, and which rouses him to make an unprecedented effort.

In short, the ordinary notion that civilization is the product of favorable conditions—a fertile soil, a mild climate, accessibility to water routes, natural defenses against invasion—is wrong. As Mr. Toynbee takes pains to show, it is possible, of course, for a challenge to be too difficult. But in general, the growth of a civilization takes place best when conditions are sufficiently difficult to stir up a high degree of energy and *élan* by way of response. When a challenge is easy, men meet it and lie down to sleep again. When it is too difficult, it either destroys them or leaves them in a state of arrested development, like the Polynesians in the Pacific, on the fine edge of an adjustment with their environment, but with no energy left over for anything else. But when a challenge is just right, it stirs up energies that give men enough momentum to keep them from drifting back to their primitive sleep. Like a sprinter who has got off to a good start, they can only keep their balance by continuing to run. "The real optimum challenge is . . . one which not only stimulates the challenged party to achieve a single successful response but also stimulates him to acquire a momentum that carries him a step farther: from achievement to a fresh struggle, from the solution of one problem to the presenta-

172

tion of another, from momentary rest to reiterated movement. . . ."

And as long as men do continue to meet challenges with ever
greater responses their civilization grows. It grows, furthermore,
in a definite direction. At the beginning, men respond to external
challenges which arouse their inner vitality. But as they continue
to meet challenges, their inner vitality grows. And so their field
of action gradually changes from the external to the internal, from
a struggle to master their environments to a struggle to master
their own souls. A civilization in the process of growth comes
progressively to set its own challenges for itself; it becomes progressively more self-determined, more individuated, more the
source of a unique style and a self-imposed drive and direction.
It has an inner integrity and unity, in which everything flows
from a single, organized center. Everything in the life of such a
civilization is co-ordinated, everything serves and reflects an
inner harmony.

This process Mr. Toynbee calls "etherealization"—the gradual
subordination of the external to the internal, of the tangible to
the intangible, of matter to life. And this direction which the
growth of a healthy civilization takes suggests what all its *élan*
and drive is for; it indicates what the whole point and purpose of
the adventure of civilization is. "The criterion of growth is progress towards self-determination; and progress towards self-determination is a prosaic formula for describing the miracle by which
Life enters into its Kingdom." Each civilization, when it is
healthy, has its own distinctive style and path; but all civilizations
have the same goal. They are attempts to transmute gross human
nature into a finer substance; they are efforts to transform "Sub-
Man" into "Super-Man," to convert the cities of this world into
the City of God. Civilization is "an audacious attempt to ascend
from the level of Primitive Humanity, living the life of a social

173

animal, to the height of some superhuman kind of being in a Communion of Saints. . . ."

But once a civilization has been born and has picked up momentum, what causes it to stop? Why do civilizations break down and die? Why do civilizations lose the power of self-determination, and fail to reach "the goal of human endeavours"?

The answer, Mr. Toynbee believes, lies in the very mechanism by which the process of Challenge-and-Response operates. In any society and in any age the mass of the human race is inert and uncreative. It follows the stale round of custom, lives by the pressure of social convention, and is basically imitative. "There is an overwhelming majority of ordinary people in the membership of even the most advanced and progressive civilization; and the humanity of all these people is virtually primitive humanity." Only a very small portion of any society is ever original or creative. And it is this "creative minority" which always makes the successful response to a challenge. The creative individual is a mutation, a deviation from the standard, the single instance of a new species of man. And he takes the rest of the society along with him by the contagion of his personality.

But as a consequence of this division of humanity into two types, there is in every human society an undertow that pulls against creativity. For when the majority follows the creative minority, it can only do so by imitation. The creative personality charms men into following him. But while those who follow him may be lifted out of themselves for the moment, they do not thereby shake off their common clay. And so, when they try to re-enact the Passion of the creative individual, they create a ritual; when they try to make the vision he embodies concrete, they turn it into a code. They can only live by conforming to a standard, and so they make a standard, a new convention, out of

174

what is unique. And this is why every victory won by a creative individual in history always has the shadow of defeat behind it.

This is the ultimate source of the breakdown and disintegration of civilizations. There is a grinding rhythm in the process of civilization against which every civilization has struggled, but which none has as yet overcome. It is the rhythm by which every creative act, when it succeeds in altering a society, also becomes something merely imitated. Dragged back by the tidal inertia of the majority, the creative minority in the end merely repeats itself, merely goes through the motions of what were once its creative activities. It hypnotizes itself by the imitative acts it has induced in others, or it comes to abuse the power which it has employed to enforce this imitation. So the institutions which embody the creative acts of the past become inert, and intractable to new challenges. This is the nemesis in creativity which catches up with creative minorities. They tend to rest on their oars, or to idolize the institutions that embody their past triumphs, or to become intoxicated by their past victories and to run amok.

So, having lost its creative vitality, the creative minority also loses its power to charm. It no longer plays the tunes to which the rest of society happily dances. And the disintegration of a society begins. Where once the society was a harmonious whole, held together by a common vision of God as seen through his saints, now class struggle and fratricidal warfare appear. The creative minority degenerates into a merely "dominant minority." There arises an "internal proletariat" within the society, which is profoundly alienated, and which has no stake beyond its own physical survival in the continued existence of the society. And all around the borders of the society barbarian hordes—an "external proletariat"—begin to press in on it. The society has entered on its "Time of Troubles." It has fallen victim to the fundamental dialectic in history, "the cosmic tug-of-war between Life and Matter." But it has broken down through its own failings, through its

175

failure to keep its creative *élan*. Civilizations never die as the result of external blows, but always as the result of self-inflicted wounds. They die, as Greek tragic heroes die, out of blood guilt, pride, and blindness.

Once a civilization has broken down, says Mr. Toynbee, it follows an inexorable and melancholy path. Just as a healthy civilization picks up momentum when it meets a challenge successfully, and goes on steadily to new and greater triumphs, so a declining civilization, once it has failed to meet a challenge successfully, goes on through the centuries repeating itself unhappily, trying to meet the challenge which it has failed to meet, and falling short more disastrously each time. A growing civilization is one that is progressively differentiated and unique; a declining civilization is one that is progressively standardized and uniform. And so the rhythm of disintegration in all declining civilizations is the same. The same phenomena occur, the same story is told.

There is, first, a Time of Troubles, signalized by an outbreak of fratricidal warfare, like that between the Greek city-states or like the religious wars in Europe during the seventeenth century. There is then a temporary truce, like the reign of Alexander the Great, or like the period in the eighteenth century when war was a mild "sport of kings." But then there is another and more violent outbreak of war, followed again by another and longer truce, brought about by the establishment of a universal state, like the Roman Empire. During this period—the "Indian Summer" of a civilization—men may be lured into a false sense of tranquillity, and imagine that everything is stable. But the existence of a universal state is itself a sign that the civilization has reached a point at which its disease is incurable. Even during the existence of this universal state, there is regularly a premonitory shudder, which reminds the dying patient, or should remind him, that his chronic ailment is still with him. In the history of the Roman

176

Empire, for example, there is the threatening interregnum between the death of Marcus in A.D. 180 and the accession of Diocletian in A.D. 284. And in the end, although the universal state recovers from this brief fever, it subsides and dies.

Thus, the rhythm of disintegration which Mr. Toynbee finds in every civilization that has died is three and a half beats: Rout (the Time of Troubles) and Rally (a temporary interlude of peace), Relapse (more violent warfare) and Rally again (the founding of a universal state), Relapse (trouble within the universal state) and Rally (its temporary elimination), and finally death. This process normally takes between eight hundred and eleven hundred years. And once a civilization has reached the stage of the universal state it is almost certainly too late for it to recover.

But death, for Mr. Toynbee, is not the end of the story. There is also rebirth. For a civilization, as it goes through its death throes, regularly develops three distinctive classes—a dominant minority, an external proletariat, and an internal proletariat. And each of them leaves something behind.

The great, though futile, achievement of the dominant minority is the creation of the universal state. And with that creation go other distinctive achievements such as the attempt to rule society by impersonal and uniform laws, and the development of rationalistic philosophy and science. The dominant minority, having lost its etherealizing vision and its ability to charm men into following it, begins to think in mechanical terms. It invents purely political strategies; it creates a civil service; it seeks on a purely intellectual level after the laws that govern all of nature; it tries all sorts of legal and administrative techniques for keeping men at peace. But all of these lack the one thing that is necessary—the spark of life and warmth. They do not meet the essential problem, which is to restore a society unified and inspired by a

177

transforming vision. The most that dominant minorities succeed in doing is to leave a legacy of law, science, and philosophy behind. And it is this legacy which later dominant minorities, in other civilizations, seize upon when they repeat their own losing battle against social disintegration.

Essentially the same story is true for the external proletariat. The external proletariat produces the barbarian religions and the poetry and mythology of the so-called heroic ages. The Homeric pantheon of gods, the *Nibelungen Ring, Beowulf* are all the work of external proletariats. And there is a vitality in these achievements, Mr. Toynbee agrees, which is absent from the work of dominant minorities. But there is also something evanescent about them. For the myths are parochial, and the gods that are worshipped are tribal gods, who are jealous, who rule by force, and who do not have a message for all peoples.

So it is to the internal proletariat, Mr. Toynbee finds, that we must turn for the peculiar institution which allows a new society to be born out of the death of an old one. Profoundly alienated from the civilization of which it is a part, the feeling of an internal proletariat sometimes turns to resentment, and takes itself out in gospels of blood and iron like Marxism. But within this alienated proletariat, there may also be some creative individuals who die to this world to be reborn in another. Seeing the walls of their cities crumble, they look beyond these cities to another city whose walls stand forever, a city which is not of the flesh but of the spirit, and which cannot die because it is outside time. And having withdrawn from a dying world, these individuals then return to it carrying with them a new vision, and preaching a new gospel of love to all men. It is these citizens of another world who "save the City of Destruction from its doom by converting it to the Peace of God."

What these men have done is to create a higher religion. And it is the transforming vision of a higher religion which turns

178

death into life, and sets a new civilization in motion. The higher religions speak in different idioms, but they all bring the same message of transfiguration to the race, reminding humanity that it is only when all men have turned away from this world in their inmost souls that the ordeal of human history will have come to an end and its purpose will have been attained. The whole point of the process of civilization is to produce, through the working of Challenge-and-Response, that tempering of the human spirit which leads to its transfiguration, to its escape from inertness and materiality, and its initiation into the communion of saints. Mr. Toynbee's ultimate message is the message of the seventeenth-century Bishop Bossuet, which he quotes: "All the great empires that we have seen on the earth have come together in diverse ways to contribute to the good of Religion and the glory of God, as God himself has declared through his prophets."

This, in very brief scope, is the philosophy of history which Mr. Toynbee puts before us. It is an encompassing view of human destiny, to which he brings a prodigious and unchallenged learning in support. And it is not just a way of looking at the past. By inference, and by explicit application, it is a diagnosis of our own times and the proposal of a cure. We have a chance to survive; but it is our very last chance, and if we forfeit it we will not have another. For all past history shows that when a civilization has passed a certain point in its decline, there is no turning back. And we have come to that point but have not yet quite passed it. The rhythm of disintegration has taken us through our first Time of Troubles, our first temporary rally, and our second outbreak of class struggle and fratricidal warfare. The next step, unless we change the course we have followed, is the universal state. No civilization that has ever entered the universal state has been able to turn back and save itself. It is the point of no return. We are on the brink of disaster and have only just time to save ourselves.

But to do so we must turn our backs completely on the path we have been following. For the modern liberal West has been committing social suicide. Everything of which it has been proudest—its humanism, its belief in the unlimited use of science, its technology, its innovations in law and social planning—all these, in other civilizations, have been the telltale marks which have revealed their mortal disease. Secular liberalism and democracy have been attempts to disregard a fundamental law of history, revolts against "the native genius" of the West. They have been trying to organize the economic, political, and intellectual life of Western society—and even its moral outlook—independently of the religious vision which alone keeps a civilization alive. And what they have succeeded in doing is revealed by the nationalistic frenzies, the Fascist barbarism, the berserk Communist idealism, which are the unmistakable signs of our civilization's breakdown. The laws of history show that this process of cultural self-immolation has now gone as far as it can go.

For modern man has had an entirely wrong view of his own history, and as a result modern society has been a study in social disintegration. The judgments and the basic assumptions which the contemporary world has inherited from liberalism are reversed by Mr. Toynbee at every key point. His philosophy of history tells us that the meaning of history is not the gradual extension of man's understanding of nature and himself through the growth of intelligence; nor is it the gradual advance of freedom and happiness in this world through law and concerted social action. The meaning of history is the conversion of men's values away from such worldly objectives, and the transfiguring of men into saints. The conditions that are favorable to material progress and to intellectual progress are precisely the conditions that endanger the true end of history and lead to a civilization's decline. Mr. Toynbee's view of history suggests that a "pluralistic society" is a euphemism for a broken-down society; that the leadership of

180

great individuals is preferable to the rule of impersonal law; that there are no such things as accident or chance in history; that the moderate reformer, who tries to change a part of a society without engaging the entire society at its heart, is the Don Quixote of social action. Most of all, it tells us that a modern era—an era which, in Matthew Arnold's suggestive terms, has a habit of criticizing what it receives from the past—is wrong *au fond*. For the basic law of history is that men cannot, on pain of death, sin against inherited lights.

If these ideas are right, then there is no case for modern man. The regeneration of contemporary society depends on rejecting all the ideals and assumptions which liberal men in the modern era have taken to be matters of almost elementary common sense. Have all our common-sense judgments been wrong? Are we on the wrong path entirely? Can we save ourselves only by admitting that the modern era has been a mistake? Let us take a common-sense look and see.

Mr. Toynbee's philosophy of history rests on three main ideas —the idea of Challenge-and-Response, the idea of an intelligible field of historical study, and the idea that a civilization must be an integrated whole. Let us begin with Challenge-and-Response.

The phrase is a suggestive one. It applies to experiences which we regard as turning points in our personal lives, and to major events in history like the response of the Greek city-states to the challenge of Persia or the response of the Dutch to the danger of the seas. It gives such events a dramatic significance, a moral focus, and a certain exciting sporting quality. For Mr. Toynbee, however, it does more. It pronounces a universal truth about history: "Whom the Lord loveth He chasteneth, and scourgeth every son whom He receiveth." The law of Challenge-and-Response stands in stark contrast to the prevailing assumption of modern times—the assumption that comfortable conditions

181

are favorable to the growth of civilization. Mr. Toynbee is preaching a harder gospel. Civilizations grow and thrive, says Mr. Toynbee, only under difficult conditions. And the effectiveness of a challenge increases in proportion to its difficulty.

Why, then, one asks, are the very highest civilizations not found in the most difficult regions? Why, for example, have the Eskimos not created a dynamic civilization? In general, Mr. Toynbee replies, a challenge is more effective the more severe it is. But after a certain point a law of diminishing returns sets in. A challenge can be so severe that it kills the challenged party; and even when it does not kill him, it can exhaust all his energies, and leave him with nothing left over for further growth. And so the law of the golden mean applies to Challenge-and-Response as it does to other things. The optimum ordeal is always a mean between two extremes: it is never easy, but it is not too hard.

But this leaves us with a decisive question. How do we determine this crucial point at which a challenge becomes too severe? To this Mr. Toynbee only replies that we can never know. One swallow does not make a summer, he points out, and the failure of one man or one group to meet a challenge does not prove that another man or another group might not meet it. What information, then, does the law of Challenge-and-Response give us? It does not tell us what "too hard" or "too easy" or even just plain "difficult" means. All we discover when Mr. Toynbee's explanation is finished is that some civilizations succeed in overcoming environing conditions and other civilizations do not.

In fact, Mr. Toynbee's own argument cuts the ground away from the idea that it is the difficulty of surrounding conditions that accounts for the rise of civilization. For he goes on to show that there are always compensations for difficulties.

For example, the superlative physical challenges from the sea which have been presented to Venice and Holland have not only administered to them a physical stimulus which their neighbors have lacked, but have incidentally served to shield them from a human ordeal to which their neighbors have been exposed. . . . And so it has been in Swiss history with the Alps. . . . The thirteen nuclei of modern Greece . . . reveal the same phenomenon of compensation in the sphere of the human environment for a challenge in the sphere of Physical Nature. In all these cases, the physical challenge of remoteness and stoniness and waterlessness and mountainousness were unquestionably stimulating in themselves, but they also had a protective value in the human sphere which was of first-rate historical importance.

In other words, a civilization's success also depends on easy conditions! This does not leave much to the idea of Challenge-and-Response. Obviously, in this less than perfect world, it is always possible to show that a successful civilization has had to overcome some difficulties. This hardly proves that these difficulties are the cause of its success.

The youthful Samuel Johnson once described, with more candor and fewer trimmings, the same facts about the human scene which have led Mr. Toynbee to his idea of Challenge-and-Response. "The reader will find here," Johnson wrote in his preface to Lobo's *Voyage to Abyssinia,*

no regions cursed with irremediable barrenness, or blest with spontaneous fecundity; no perpetual gloom, or unceasing sunshine; nor are the nations here described, either devoid of all sense of humanity, or consummate in all private or social virtues. Here are no Hottentots without religious polity or articulate language; no Chinese perfectly polite, and completely skilled in all sciences; he will discover, what will always be discovered by a diligent and impartial enquirer, that wherever human nature is to be found, there is a mixture of vice and virtue, a contest of passion and reason; and that the Creator doth not appear partial in his distributions, but has balanced, in most countries, their particular inconvenience by particular favours.

This is less striking than Mr. Toynbee's idea of Challenge-and-Response, but it seems more sensible. And in fact all that Mr. Toynbee has done has been to show that civilizations grow from complex and mixed conditions, and that what has its advantages from one point of view may cause trouble from another. He has converted this common-sense observation into the paradox that difficulty and trouble promote human progress.

In the growth of any complicated civilization, of course, there are bound to be difficulties which it has had to overcome. And as the traditions and collective memories of human societies suggest, victory over difficulties can frequently cement a society together, and give it confidence and drive. But this is a far cry from saying that suffering is the reason for human achievement. Pain may be an unavoidable by-product of most achievement; but it is not its cause. For the mass of humanity, the simple fact is that suffering brutalizes and corrupts. It does not transfigure men, it grinds them down. Most of us, as Mr. Toynbee remarks, are "Sub-Men" and not saints. But ordeals will not make us saints.

"Creation spells agony," says Mr. Toynbee, "because learning through suffering is the only means of spiritual transfiguration." Even in Mr. Toynbee's own mind, this does not apply to most of us. It is not intended to be a statement of a statistical average, but a description of the conditions for making saints. The "law" of Challenge-and-Response is in reality the proposal of a new moral standard—or, rather, a proposal that we return to an older moral standard that prevailed in a nonsecular society. It suggests that we should look upon the suffering of the many as necessary and justified because it leads to the saintliness of the few. It is a grisly idea. When human suffering was less avoidable than it now is, there may have been some justification for this standard; but no modern society, and no modern religion, can take it seriously. If the salvation of contemporary society depends on adopting this moral standard, it will look to most of us not like salvation at all, but like the decline of elementary moral feelings.

But let us turn to the second of Mr. Toynbee's key ideas. All the historical evidence which Mr. Toynbee adduces in support

184

of his theory of history is interpreted in terms of his basic category of "an intelligible field of historical study." It is an idea that begins with a perfectly plausible assumption. For historical events do obviously fall together into systems. And what we normally mean when we say that the study of history helps us to understand what is going on is that history places what is going on "in context"— that is, it places events in the systems to which they belong. If we understand something about the history of European imperialism, for example, and if we see that, as a result of World War II, European economies have lost one of their main props, we understand the present economic problems of Europe much better. If we know something about the history of colonialism in the Orient, and the long process of cultural change by which Oriental peoples took over Western ideals like technology and national self-determination, we are not likely to think that the revolution in China was all the work of a few professional conspirators. In this sense, the task of the historian is precisely the task, as Mr. Toynbee suggests, of setting events in a field of study which will make them intelligible.

But the fact that the events of history fall together into systems of events does not prove that they fall together into some one embracing system. How does Mr. Toynbee himself determine his "absolute" fields of historical study? In looking for the "cradle" of Western civilization, he examines the origins of the religious and ethnic characteristics of Europe in A.D. 775, and determines that these characteristics originated in features of the ancient world which are alien to the main interests of an historian of that ancient world. He has shown, in short, that there is a difference between the ancient world and the early medieval world; but he has not shown that this difference necessarily makes them entirely separate societies. A man may be black-haired in his youth and gray in his dotage; and the fact that he will someday be gray-haired is alien to the main interests of the biographer who tells

185

the story of his youth. But it does not prove that we have two numerically distinct men.

The question of what is an "intelligible field of study" depends entirely on the problem with which we are dealing. There is no single "essence" that defines the true character of a civilization, and no single context within which we can fit everything that happens in its history. If we are looking into the origins of the Carolingian Empire, we may find these origins in "alien" movements within Hellenic society. But if we are looking for the origins of Western agricultural techniques, for example, or of geometry, or of the idea of democratic citizenship, we will find these in Hellenic society as well; and they will not be "alien" to that society, even accepting Mr. Toynbee's way of using this term.* We will have one continuous field of study and not two.

* In a passage attempting to show that the growth of practical techniques is not an appropriate criterion of progress, Mr. Toynbee writes: "The technique of iron-working, which had been originally introduced into the Aegean at the moment of the great social relapse when the Minoan Civilization went into dissolution, remained stationary—neither improving nor declining—at the time of the next great social relapse, when the Hellenic Civilization went the way of its Minoan predecessor. Our Western World inherited the technique of iron-working from the Roman World unimpaired; and it likewise inherited the technique of writing, embodied in the Latin Alphabet, as well as the Greek science of mathematics. Socially, there had been a cataclysm. The Hellenic Civilization had gone to pieces and a social inter-regnum had ensued, out of which the new Western Civilization emerged. But there was no corresponding break of continuity in the realm of technique—at least not in the histories of the three important techniques just mentioned." In the realm of technique, then, Mr. Toynbee himself shows that Western society and Hellenic society are one civilization, and not two. He shows, indeed, that Western techniques go back even farther than Hellenic society, and that techniques in general have a continuity and durability that undercut changes in religion, governments, and social institutions. The point is not only important because it suggests that a major element in the history of man eludes Mr. Toynbee's categories. It is a point of crucial significance for the question of human progress. The discovery of fire, the use of metals, the invention of the wheel, the development of writing, the introduction of money as a means of exchange —it is difficult to say whether all or any of these are the products of transfiguring visions. But they have an ability to ride through the fashions, to move across cultural boundaries, and to live through social disasters. And they have a cumulative tendency to improve, and to engender other techniques which

Mr. Toynbee's mistake is to have taken a "field of study" which may be useful for the study of one problem, and to have converted it into a mandatory context for the study of all historical problems. He has turned an intellectual distinction which has been made for a specific purpose into an absolute historical law.

And in the process he has put history—and us—in a strait jacket. For the whole point of Mr. Toynbee's "intelligible fields of study" is to show that the essence of a civilization is fixed at its creation, and that one departs from this essence only on pain of death. It is the cardinal point, and the cardinal fallacy, of that whole tradition of thought we have called "historicism." For as we have seen, the question of the "origins" of a civilization depends on what strand in that civilization we are examining. And even after we have found out what these origins are, they do not tell us what the "essential" nature of that civilization is. The origins of the species called "Man" go back, after all, to creatures that did not stand erect. No doubt this is a useful bit of information to have. It explains, among other things, the oversize head that sits on top of our weak spines, and gives us our pains in the back. But none of this proves that it is the essence of man to walk with his knuckles touching the ground.

Mr. Toynbee's conception of an "intelligible field of study" denies, in effect, that anything significantly new can arise in the history of civilization and change its proper course. It is a kind of argument that is becoming increasingly familiar to all of us. We are constantly being recalled to *the* tradition of the novel, to the *essence* of real music, to the *true* origins of American, or Western, or all human civilization. It is regularly implied that

---

also become part of the permanent legacy of the race. If there is any truth at all in Plato's belief that a major object of civilization is to make secure the possession of things that men prize, then the history of practical techniques, and the emergence of science (an art for the systematic improvement of techniques), cannot be put down as merely peripheral developments in the career of mankind.

187

our troubles began when we forgot the historic destiny laid down for us by the past. Such arguments thrive at just those times when nothing inherited from the past seems able to persist unchanged. And their present popularity testifies to the unsettling pace of modern change, and to its mindless insensitivity to received values. But to learn from the past, to be sensitive to its values, to recognize that what has survived over the long pull in human affairs may have more to be said for it than appears in the short view of the present—all these are one thing. To suggest that men cannot liberate themselves even partially from their pasts, to make piety a commandment of History—these are quite another. Rationalism in philosophy—a tradition that goes back to the Greeks—is for Mr. Toynbee the great "treason of the clerks" in Western history; humanism—which has an equally long tradition—is a movement which has sapped the lifeblood of Western society; even Renaissance architecture is an aesthetic failure because it is a "revolt against . . . Western Civilization's native genius." Mr. Toynbee's reference to the "essence" of Western civilization are ways of converting his private tastes into public necessities. And the past to which he recalls us is *his* past, a highly selected one, whose pedigree is no longer or nobler than the past of those things in modern society which he rejects.

But it is when we come to Mr. Toynbee's idea that human societies (unless they are dying) are integrated wholes that we touch the ultimate idea on which Mr. Toynbee's entire philosophy of history rests. For Mr. Toynbee, a healthy civilization is all of a piece. Its economic activities are not separate from its moral standards, its moral standards are warmed by a religious vision. No one part can be treated independently of the rest without throwing everything off balance. Nothing happens at random or serves no purpose; everything harmonizes with everything else and serves the unity of the whole.

188

Here is the ultimate choice with which Mr. Toynbee's philosophy of history confronts us. It is a choice between the partial, piecemeal reform of social institutions and waiting for a miraculous spiritual vision; between empirical social analysis and dependence on the superior insights of intuition and feeling; between a pluralistic society, containing many visions of man and God, and a monolithic society in which everything is part of the same chorus singing the same song. It is more: it is a choice between a view of human destiny in which chance and accident play a part, but in which human beings are free to give history the direction they choose, and a view of human destiny from which chance and accident disappear, but in which the freedom of human beings means only their perfect obedience to a course that has been laid down for them in advance. It puts before us ultimate questions about the nature of our troubles, the powers we have at our disposal for dealing with them, and the ideals at which we should aim.

It is an idea which has certain obvious attractions. Even in a highly specialized and secularized society, our lives do not fall into neatly segregated compartments labeled economic, political, or intellectual. Even minor changes in one field are likely to spill over and affect apparently remote institutions. It is obviously important, therefore, to try to see how the institutions of a society are interrelated, to take account of the unintended or indirect consequences of even limited social policies, and to see how individual problems are parts of a larger whole.* But there is,

* Even here, however, it is difficult to know how we could follow Mr. Toynbee's prescription, and study the whole before we study the parts. Mr. Toynbee writes, "In order to understand the parts, we must first focus our attention upon the whole because this whole is the field of study which is intelligible in itself." But how can we say anything at all about the whole until *after* we have looked at its parts? While it is true, for example, that the business cycle is a phenomenon of the economy as a whole, and is certainly not aimed at by any individuals, the only way in which economists can study the business cycle is by observing the behavior of individual firms in their relations to one an-

189

nevertheless, an extraordinary assumption about the facts in the notion that civilized societies, healthy or unhealthy, have been created on such a remarkable pattern that nothing is wasted, and that all parts of the society harmonize in the service of a single common purpose. To put it quite simply, this confuses human civilization with a beehive, and it is neither true in fact nor attractive as an ideal. The kind of evidence which is usually employed to show that human societies are "indivisible wholes" all of whose parts are inseparable comes mainly from the anthropological study of *primitive* societies (and it is anything but conclusive even there), whose inertia and sleepiness, as Mr. Toynbee himself sees it, sets them on a lower level of human progress than complex civilizations. A little disunity seems to be the price we have to pay for the vitality, change, and *élan* which we prize in civilization.

Indeed, we need only reflect for a moment on what we are doing when we speak of a society "as a whole" to see that we cannot possibly mean in any literal sense that everything in it is connected to everything else. Roughly, there are two ways of speaking about "wholes," and Mr. Toynbee has confused them. One is simply to enumerate everything that lies about, and when we have done to call this "the whole." The second is to show how various elements are connected together to form an integrated unit; but this requires a theory of how they are connected, and all theories are selective and are bound to leave something out. "Integration," in short, is a relative term, and a

---

other. Similarly, the ordinary historian does not proceed from an over-all theory about the Victorian Age to the facts of industrial expansion, Dickens, the Chartists, the Reform Bills, and the educational changes at Oxford and Cambridge. His picture of "the whole" is built up from his study of the parts; and if there is any substance to it, it is supported by appealing to these parts. Mr. Toynbee's notion of how history should be written involves a procedure which neither he nor anyone else could possibly carry out. In general, in all domains of human thinking, progress is only made by abstracting and isolating parts of a complex whole and focusing attention upon them.

190

loaded one. It stands for the co-ordination of *some* activities within a delimited context and with respect to some specific purpose; and its value depends on what that purpose is. Tinker and Evers were a remarkably integrated duo at second base for the Chicago Cubs. It is reported that they were not on speaking terms. It is not at all certain that they might have been a better second-base combination if they had been.

Mr. Toynbee's *A Study of History* tells the story of twenty-one separate civilizations, and yet it is an attempt to show that the story of every one of these civilizations has the same shape —the shape of high drama. When the curtain comes up, the stage is set, the characters defined, the basic problem laid out— and it is the same basic problem in every case. And through the whole story the stage stays the same, the characters of the actors set their destinies, and nothing happens which is purely acci-dental or random. In Mr. Toynbee's study of the career of civiliza-tions, there are the same dramatic unities, the same logical reversals of fortune, the same occasions for self-recognition, and the same opportunity for a spiritual salvation through suffering which we find in tragedy. And the only difference is that the story takes place, not in a day or a year, but over the millennia.

But the basis of this dramatic view of history is that each of these civilizations is an independent whole, and that no scene, no line, no character, no property, is without a function. There must be no accidents, no purely arbitrary events, no breaks of fortune and misfortune. Most important, the characters must accept their initial situation as Mr. Toynbee defines it. They can-not change the terms in which they must live out their destinies. But human civilizations do not meet these specifications, and what Mr. Toynbee's view of history gives us by way of aesthetic satisfactions it takes from us in simple realism. For human civi-lizations are not isolated and self-contained fields of study which cannot be broken in on from the outside; nor are they such perfectly integrated organisms that no element within them can ever act as an independent variable, and put the civilization on a new course. Mr. Toynbee has been looking for laws that lay down an inexorable direction in which an historical process moves, a direction which controls what happens to any of the parts of the process. It is the ancient dream of philosophers of history. But it is a dream.

For despite Mr. Toynbee's noble effort to show the contrary, our common-sense judgment is right: there are such things in history as contingencies, accidents, good breaks and bad breaks. To suggest that history follows a direction which has been laid down for it in advance turns the writing of history into astrology. For while everything that happens in history has its causes and fits into some system, not everything fits into the same system or follows the same pattern. Different causal sequences cross and crisscross and tangle one another up. Bad weather puts off a battle and gives an enemy time to recoup; societies are overwhelmed by greater force and die through no fault of their own; fools are born kings, and anonymous Miltons die mute and inglorious. And these if's and chances that surround human history are not only signs that the world is not our oyster. They are signs of the plurality of history, of its many possibilities. Given human knowledge and human will, the contingencies of history are our opportunity to give history a direction we in the present choose. Human history is open, for better or worse—which is what it means to say that we are free.

Mr. Toynbee's *A Study of History* shows us what the twentieth century has done to the nineteenth. It is the testament of a man out of the Victorian Age, hostile to our technology and stung by our violence, a spirit preaching the gentler virtues, convinced that vice should be punished and goodness rewarded, and unable to believe that there is not a deeper meaning—a higher promise

192

—behind the collapse of the hopes with which he grew up. And he has constructed a philosophy of history to support these hopes.

No summary can convey the frightening learning, the sheer narrative ability, and the beautiful sense of timing with which Mr. Toynbee unfolds this system. He never gives away a secret until it will have its maximum effect. He quotes from Greek and Latin and Chinese and Hindustani. The language of Aeschylus and the turns of phrase of the latest poet are equally at his disposal. The lives of the saints, the philosophy of Henri Bergson, the reflections of contemporary economists on the business cycle, are all grist for his mill. So are homely reminiscences from his youth, flash observations of a countryside seen from a train window, chance meetings in a wayside inn. And in addition to all this, Mr. Toynbee apparently knows the Bible by heart. His philosophy keeps before us at every turn the one thing which it is so easy to lose in our view of the past—the image of the human spirit struggling with itself and its environment. *A Study of History* restores the tradition of universal history, and restores history to the humanistic studies.

Mr. Toynbee has turned all these gifts to the single purpose of filling out a vision of human destiny which is unmatched in its audacity, and which, in the twentieth century, is nothing short of revolutionary. It does nothing less than turn Voltaire and Gibbon on their heads, and take us back to Bishop Bossuet and to Saint Augustine. It picks up every indictment we have examined of the era of modernity and liberalism, and adds something special of its own. With Professor Maritain, Mr. Toynbee argues that liberal society is insecure so long as it rests its moral convictions on purely secular postulates; but he goes beyond Professor Maritain, asserting that no higher religion has a monopoly on truth, and arguing that the present age must find its own redeeming absolutes for itself. With Mr. Niebuhr, he

193

affirms the ubiquity of original sin; but he goes beyond Mr. Niebuhr and sets as the goal of all history the ultimate elimination of original sin. With Mannheim, he asserts the relativity of all historical thinking; but he thinks that we can get beyond this relativity not through the work of intellectuals, but through the visions of saints and mystics; and he believes that it is by feeling and not by intellect that man plumbs to the fundamental truths about his situation.

But he does not offer a social policy. He offers a flight from social policy. For though he denies that there are any loose ends, or accidents, or morally senseless disasters in history, he does so only to make our power to control our destinies rest on the greatest accident of all—the coming of a new breed of men who will bring a miraculous vision with them. He does not tell us how to prepare for this event except to be humble and to endure patiently. He does not even tell us, in this day when visions are cheap and plentiful, how to recognize a true vision when it comes. And in telling us that the rational intellect is incompetent in the realm of the spirit, he deprives us of the only instrument we have for distinguishing between the voice of God and the temptations of the devil. Mr. Toynbee's philosophy of history is a reaction against the pluralism, the functional autonomy, and the decline of intimate personal relations that have come to characterize modern society. It expresses a nostalgic desire for a society in which friendship and love will do what we must now do by law and social engineering. It speaks for those who have been chilled by a mass culture, by mechanical routines, and by a world in which the individual seems powerless, and who hanker for that more primitive and warmer kind of social authority which is the authority of great individuals and not of abstract rules. Inadvertently, it suggests what some of our troubles are. But it is not a tool for social analysis; it is an instrument for denigrating social analysis.

Mr. Toynbee's attempt to prove that there is a grand moral design in history, and that chance and accident have no influence in human affairs, is an effort, in an era of awful human waste, to console us with the thought that nothing is ever wasted, and that everything in this world contributes to some higher good. It is an attempt, like similar attempts in the past, to cushion the shock of the main facts of human history in all ages—the steady frustration of the minimal demands of the great majority of human beings, the role of violence and *force majeure,* the rain of fortune and misfortune on the good and evil alike. It is not easy for sensitive minds to face these facts in any generation. But to argue that justice is already established in the laws that govern the history of this world is a strange and sorry way to preach the message of the Kingdom of God. We do not preserve our ideals by confusing them with the facts.

"We have convinced ourselves (if there is any virtue in this Study)," says Mr. Toynbee, "that the destruction which has overtaken a number of civilizations in the past has never been the work of any external agency, either human or inanimate, but has always been in the nature of an act of suicide." It would be nice to believe that everything works out with such moral finesse. But a contemporary thinker who would say something relevant about the current state of human affairs cannot be a revolted Victorian, trying desperately to believe that vice is always punished and virtue rewarded. Lincoln's assassins did not miss, and Hitler's would-be assassins did. What might have been is a saddening question. But it is an inescapable theme of history, a question which men must face if they are to understand the past or act like free agents in the present. Neither ten volumes nor a hundred will show that every civilization in history gets its just deserts. This might be, if one wishes, "the goal of human endeavors." But it has not been prearranged for us. We shall have to see to it for ourselves.

195

X.

THE REVOLUTION
OF MODERNITY

T HE philosophies of history we have been discussing speak, it cannot be doubted, out of a disquietude that
is widely shared. Ten years after a victorious war, and in the
midst of unusual prosperity, an extraordinary number of men
and women, here and abroad, are asking whether our civilization has not been on the wrong path for a long time. They are
searching for a faith or a cause, they suspect that we have placed
too much trust in the benevolence of the human will and the
objectivity of the human mind, they listen sympathetically to the
statement that a liberal and secular social order has been sinning
against inherited lights. It is time to take stock, and to ask why
these sentiments are so widely shared, and why there has been
such a notable loss of confidence, not only in our ability to
achieve the ideals that have distinguished the modern period, but
in the very validity of these ideals themselves. What I shall
say in this final chapter is necessarily only a sketch. But it points
in the direction in which I think we might look if we are to deal
with our problems.

196

Why is it said that the sickness of modern society goes back to the fact that it was born sick, and that all the signposts we have been using to measure our progress have in fact been measures of the progress of this disease? Why is it felt that something very fundamental has gone wrong? The answer is that something very fundamental *has* gone wrong. But what has gone wrong is not the result of a faulty philosophy of history. A social philosophy and a philosophy of history provide men with guidelines, a set of leading principles, that enable them to formulate their problems. There have been weaknesses and equivocations in modern liberal theory which have led men to emphasize certain factors, to select certain strategies, and to disregard other issues; and in this sense, the philosophy of liberalism, along with a great many other philosophies, and along with the absence of any philosophy, is "responsible" for our present doubts and anxieties. But at bottom these doubts and anxieties are not the result of a faulty philosophy any more than a tornado is the result of our ignorance about its causes. The collapse of some liberal hopes, the obvious threat to others, is the consequence of fundamental social dislocations that have overtaken us.

War, the business cycle, and the disorganized international scene have had an obvious influence. But there have been other tidal movements in our institutions which are hardly less important, and which stand behind the present feeling that the liberal ideas and ideals with which we grew up are on the way out. These institutional developments have given us the feeling that history is something that goes on behind our backs, that there is a power someplace we can't get at, and that the individual cannot affect the conditions of his life. They have created a kind of social experience which makes the philosophies of history we have been studying seem credible.

First of all, there is the role that technology plays in our lives. In no other age have men lived with so dizzying a sense of change,

197

or seen their basic material and social environment being made over, and made over again, so steadily. Technology, plainly, is the fundamental dynamic element in modern society. It affects everything from the size, shape, look, and smell of our cities and suburbs to the mobility of populations, the character of social classes, the stability of the family, the standards of workmanship that prevail, and the direction and level of moral and aesthetic sensibilities. The decision as to when, where, and how to introduce a technological change is a *social* decision, affecting an extraordinary variety of values. And yet these decisions are made in something very close to a social vacuum. Technological innovations are regularly introduced for the sake of technological convenience, and without established mechanisms for appraising or controlling or even cushioning their consequences.

A current example is the impact of television. It has affected education and home life, changed the patterns of congressional behavior and political discussion, and fundamentally altered, for better or worse, the operating conditions and purposes of traditional political institutions like legislative investigations and political conventions. But the decisions on how to use television, and how not to use it, have been made almost entirely by men whose area of responsibility is very narrow, and who have to think about only a very few, selected values. The engineers, we say with pride, are the true revolutionaries. We forget to add that if they came dressed as social planners many of us would regard them as tyrants. The engineers and industrialists who make decisions concerning technological changes have enormous power to affect the quality and conditions of our lives even though they do not know they have this power and have no interest in exercising it. This does not change the fact that their decisions are often decisions about basic social policy, and that the traditional liberal mechanisms of public consultation and consent, on which the authority for such basic decisions has been supposed to rest,

198

have next to no influence here. From the point of view of most of us these decisions just seem to happen; and it is one reason why so many ordinary men and women have come to feel that they are being manipulated by invisible persons whom they do not know and cannot control.

The problem cannot be met by reminding engineers of their social responsibilities, or by calling conferences to discuss the human use of human inventions. The problem is institutional. Contemporary industrial society is an elaborately interconnected affair; large-scale organization plays an inevitable role in that society. This means that decisions made in certain central places have consequences that flow out farther and wider than the decisions made by most absolute despots in the past.

> Gone are the days when madness was confined
> By seas or hills from spreading through Mankind:
> When, though a Nero fooled upon a string,
> Wisdom still reigned unruffled in Peking. . . .

And yet, despite the extraordinary range of these decisions, those who make them are frequently anonymous even to themselves. The Madison Avenue account executive does not think of himself as an educator; the industrialist who believes that men who are out of work should be willing to travel two thousand miles to find a job does not think of himself as advocating an unsettled home life. They do not know they are making the kind of broad social decision they are making; they neither intend, nor can they foresee, most of the consequences of what they are doing; they are likely to feel as much caught in the drift of events as the rest of us. As individuals they may have, of course, a sense of power and a feeling that they are making the wheels go round. But they are not likely to know, and no one asks them to care, how many wheels they are turning, or the direction in which they are carrying us along.

199

There are other institutional changes as well which have tended to throw liberal hopes in the shadow. Technological developments have eaten out the social texture of modern society. To begin with, the simple physical mobility of an industrial population makes social ties impermanent and thin. When a man's place of residence depends mainly on his job, and when jobs are changed frequently, community pressures are weakened, and community affections diluted. But even more important, the kind of social relation into which men tend to enter in an industrial society has changed fundamentally. Once individuals joined only one or two groups which took care of a wide variety of things; they now join many groups, each of which has only a single purpose. A man joins a trade association or a union to take care of his working life, a bridge club or a bowling team to take care of his recreation, and a Better Citizenship Society to take care of his unharnessed moral impulses. In each of these groups he deals with different people; and in each of them only a part of himself is involved, and the general social significance of what he is doing tends to be hidden from view. This has depleted the reservoir of community feelings and common interests on which liberal societies have counted for the resolution of disagreements.

An example of what this means is offered by the local church. Even fifty years ago, the local church in many places was still the focus of a community. Men met at the church to get the news, to enjoy themselves, to deal with common disasters, to receive or to dispense charity, to be confirmed and married and to bury their dead. When they came together to pray, it was as a community which had been meeting regularly to deal with common problems. Now, however, the local church is one more specialized association with a special business. Men get their news elsewhere, they get their entertainment elsewhere, and when they realize they have a common problem they usually form a special association—a Youth Board, for example, or a Civic

200

Association—to deal with that problem. As a result, church membership has become more formal and occasional, and prayer more abstract. The problems of our churches do not come mainly from the inducements of a rival "materialistic" philosophy. They come from the basic institutional changes that have taken place in industrial society.

Another example is the family. In preindustrial societies, the family is usually in only one of its aspects an arrangement for mating and bringing up children. It is an economic arrangement, and, even more, it is the basic form of social insurance. A marriage represents the union not of two people, but of two clans. It gives a man additional protection against his enemies, extends his influence in the community, cushions him against sudden disasters like disease or bad crops, and guarantees that he will be cared for in his old age. And it is, consequently, a relatively permanent arrangement. But in an industrial society the variety of functions which were once served by the single institution of the family have been parceled out to separate agencies. Men find their social security by investing in stocks and bonds, by joining unions, or by turning to the State. The family has been reduced in function; and with this reduction in function has gone a reduction in its size, power, and permanence.

Before we become nostalgic about all this, it is well to remember that these changes in the associations that govern men's lives have meant considerably more personal freedom for most men, and have released them from what were often stifling pressures. And a type of specialized social group has been created which is undoubtedly more efficient in achieving specific purposes. But these changes do mean that the sort of powerful, independent social group which once stood between the individual and the abstraction known as "society at large" has been progressively devitalized. The most powerful groups to which individuals now belong are mass organizations like trade unions or political

201

parties, where power is highly bureaucratized. The individual can no longer have the sense—except vicariously—that he is taking an active part in the making of public decisions that affect him. His access to centers of social power becomes increasingly difficult; he comes to experience social authority as something remote and abstract; he feels isolated and depersonalized. Allowing for exaggeration, the experience, and the world view, of the ordinary member of contemporary industrial society is the reverse of the experience of the member of preindustrial society. The major cataclysms that affected preindustrial man came from a physical world which he tended to think of in personal terms; the major cataclysms that affect industrial man come from a human world which he tends to think of in impersonal terms. Once the physical world was thought to be largely uncontrollable, something to be propitiated or cajoled or paid off. We take that attitude now toward our social fortunes. The destruction of the vigorous, multipurpose private associations that once stood as centers of power between the State and the individual has created that feeling of helplessness before the ebb and flow of massive social events which is expressed in contemporary philosophies of history.

Such changes in our institutions are the sort of thing which threatens to engulf the liberal image of a society made up of men who set their own standards, run their own lives, and co-operate as equals in dealing with common problems. The overhanging problem for contemporary liberals—a problem which challenges their courage and intelligence and, most of all, their imaginations —is this drift of decision-making authority into key positions that are anonymous, the development of an institutional structure that denies the individual genuine options, and the increasing inadequacy of our inherited mechanisms of public discussion and consent to control this situation. It is a problem to which none of the old models apply. We are not governed by what used to be called an "oligarchy." At the moment, and for the foreseeable future, most of us in the United States at any rate (with the large exception of the salaried middle class) cannot claim we are being economically exploited. And certainly there is no single design behind the policy decisions that are made. Those who occupy key positions—in industry, communications, organized labor, the military, or politics—are not a unified group, they have limited objectives, and they mutually check and restrain one another. But if it is not oligarchy, it is not what has been envisaged by modern liberal democracy either.

The problem, then, is that of restoring responsibility to the decision-making process. Responsibility is the analogue in politics and society of objectivity in intellectual affairs. And like objectivity, it is the product of definite social arrangements. A decision is responsible when the man or group that makes it has to answer for it to those who are directly or indirectly affected by it. To introduce this kind of responsibility, those who are affected by social decisions have to be in a position to ask the relevant questions; they have to know whom to ask; they have to have enough power to force their questions to be taken seriously; and, in the end, they have to have some power of free choice. They have to be in a position to take their business elsewhere if they do not like the answer they get. To create such a structure of responsibility in a mass society is the overarching problem, I think, to which a contemporary liberal program must be addressed. For what we have now approaches the organization of irresponsibility.

There is no single strategy for dealing with all the problems for which this phrase stands. On the simplest level, they call for changes in existing legislative processes so as to make party responsibility for political decisions clearer and more definite. On a deeper level, they require experimentation, wherever possible, with methods of administrative decentralization and devolution. In a secular society, symbols, rituals, and abstract statements of ideals can go only so far. The etiquette and the public spirit that are necessary to make institutions of free discussion and consent work must come out of the habitual personal experience of men and women with these institutions. And they can only have this experience if they have the chance to participate meaningfully in the work of social groups that have some independent power and are doing something important.

But most of all, the creation of a structure of responsibility requires the extension of the activities of both the State and voluntary mass associations into fields where they are not now active. The pattern of competition is the basic pattern which liberal societies have traditionally employed to make the decision-making process responsible. The problem now is to find ways of extending the area in which individuals have real choices by restoring genuine *social* competition. The major social decisions that are now made—decisions affecting a broad spectrum of values—are made by specialized agencies whose business it is to be concerned with only one or two of those values. Quite different decisions might be made by agencies whose context of activity and reason for existence are different. It would be interesting to explore the possibilities, for example, of bringing other agencies than those that are now active—and not only government agencies, but private agencies ranging from our great philanthropic foundations to our labor unions—into fields such as public communications and community planning. This might broaden the choices available to the individual at the same time as it brought more responsibility on all sides. Alternatives would be brought into the open that are now overlooked; and when social decisions were made they might be recognized as the kind of thing they are—genuine options involving a wide range of values. The essential point is to introduce a competition of powers into the decision-making process that does not now exist.

And what is required to do this is a new attitude toward the proper role of the State and of our large voluntary associations, a willingness to use them to introduce new standards and broader choices.

The great problem, in short, is to reconstruct the liberal tradition to make it applicable to an age of technical specialization, bureaucratized power, and mass movements. To do so will require a revision and amplification of the liberal tradition at two of its weakest points. There has been a tendency, on one side of liberalism, to neglect the importance for the freedom and power of individuals of secondary associations in between the individual and the State, and to overlook the possibility of any kind of collective action for the achievement of broad social purposes that is not State action. The other side of the omnicompetent State is the isolated individual. Liberal opposition to the State, and liberal dependence upon the State, are frequently two sides of the same coin. There has also been a tendency, on another side of liberalism, to take a primarily legalistic and political view of power, and to forget that property, managerial authority, and inequalities in social class or status, give men dominion over other men which needs to be controlled, not only by formal legal safeguards, but by the deliberate redistribution of social power. Free speech, for example, is not the business of the courts alone, but is also affected by the structure of the communications industry. Although liberalism in the twentieth century has gone far toward correcting both these weaknesses, it has not yet quite got over them. It has developed neither a systematic program for eliminating the growing vacuum between the individual and centralized authority, nor does it have a full-fledged theory of social power at its disposal.

But however difficult these problems with which liberalism is confronted may be, it is clear that they are institutional, not psychological—political, not moral. They cannot be dealt with

205

by reaffirming our faith in absolute moral principles, or by reducing our faith in human potentialities, or by admitting that rationality is a will-o'-the-wisp, or by waiting for spiritual transfiguraton. The revival of liberal hopes depends upon their being attached to specific programs and definite objectives; it does not depend on initially disparaging the technical powers and the secular intelligence which must be our main instruments in dealing with our problems. "So much does the soul require an object at which to aim," wrote Montaigne, "that when it does not have one, it will turn its violence upon itself, and create false and fantastic problems, in which it does not even believe, rather than not have something to work upon."

It would be absurd to deny (though it is done every day in four-color advertisements) that the hopes which the liberal outlook on history expressed have not been disappointed. But before we decide that it was these hopes that misled us, it would be well to look at the nature and quality of the disappointments we have suffered. For there is something quite distinctive about them. It suggests how very new and special these disappointments are, and what the context is in which they have arisen. And it suggests, too, that our disappointments, while real, need not be final.

There is an obvious fact about recent history which it is easy to forget. We have had wars which have involved whole populations as have no wars in the past, depressions which have left a third of the working population unemployed, and political tyrannies whose power to penetrate into the daily lives of individuals puts all past tyrannies in the shade; we live now with weapons that threaten the sheer physical survival of the race, weapons we have invented but are not quite sure we know how not to use. And yet on certain simple standards of progress, progress in the last hundred and fifty years has been unprecedented. Basic conditions of human life have changed for the better, and almost beyond recognition. The average length of

206

life has been steadily extended; illiteracy has been progressively eliminated; leisure time has grown; work, while much of it is routine, mechanical, and dispiriting, is at least less back-breaking; a certain degree of uniformity and equity has been introduced into our legal systems; special privilege, while great, is now recognized as special privilege. These may be limited indices of human progress, but only the most improbable callousness could altogether neglect them. In these respects, men's lives have changed more radically in the last hundred and fifty years than in all history before that time.

This progress throws our present disappointments into perspective. For the simple fact is that men's happiness depends upon their expectations—and the expectations of modern men have grown tremendously. This is the setting in which our present sense that we are going to the dogs must be understood. If there is now a widespread sense of guilt and failure, it is in part because humanitarian feelings have increased, and because the moral sympathies of many ordinary men and women now have an immeasurably greater scope than the sympathies of any but the most exceptional leaders of mankind in the past. If there is a sense that we in this century have a peculiar talent for sin, it is because the collective disasters we have suffered are almost all of them clearly man-made—a token of human power which represents a quite new state of affairs in human experience. If the existence of poverty oppresses us, it is because we do not think it is inevitable. If intellectual inquisitions shock our sensibilities, and seem like inexplicable eruptions of irrationality, it is because our moral expectations have been profoundly altered by the prestige which institutions of free inquiry now enjoy. And if we are worried about the chances of the human race for survival, this is painful, but it is a little like the gout. Most men in the past, most men in Asia and Africa today, have had to worry about their own short-run personal survival.

Indeed, the very bitterness with which we contemplate the difference between our expectations and our actual performance has arisen within this context. There is bound to be some difference between the professions and the actual practice of any society; in most societies this difference has been very large. But this gap between theory and practice has been what most men in the past have expected. It is precisely what their absolutistic moral codes explained and justified. The steady development of an experimental attitude toward morals and society in the modern era has meant, in contrast, that men expect human ideals and human practices to be closer together. It means that they demand that myths and symbols stand for some reality. And it has subjected both our ideals and our institutions to a more constant test, and has made it harder to maintain a gap between theory and practice without insupportable tensions.

In short, there is a sense in which the philosophies of history we have studied are right. Our present complaints have arisen within the context of a secular society, a pervasive science and technology, and a liberal outlook on human history. But those who blame this outlook for our problems are taking the very context in which we define these problems and converting it into their cause. It is like saying that the invention of arithmetic is the cause of Junior's troubles at school.

For the revolution of modernity has not been only a material revolution or an intellectual revolution. It has been a moral revolution of extraordinary scope, a radical alteration in what the human imagination is prepared to envisage and demand. And it has changed the basic dimensions in which we measure happiness and unhappiness, success and failure. It has given us the sense that we make our own history; it has led us to impose new and more exacting demands on ourselves and our leaders; it has set loose the restless vision of a world in which men might be

208

liberated from age-old burdens, and come to set their own standards and govern their own lives.

To be "modern" is not a monopoly of modern man. There have been modern men in most eras, and there have been other modern eras. At least once before, during the Greek Enlightenment, the Western mind envisaged a world in which the critical spirit would be preferred over the pious spirit, and in which doubt, not dogma, would be regarded as the leaven of a high civilization. Such modernity has been only one strain in the present era, and not always a dominant one. But it has lasted longer, gone deeper, and spread farther than has the modern spirit in any other time. No other age has gone so far in the belief that the spirit of modernity might be widely shared, and that all men might participate in the goods and responsibilities of a modern civilization. The modern spirit in Athens was a brief and glimmering thing, arising in a society based on slavery. The modern spirit in fifteenth-century Italy was an aristocratic phenomenon, limited to an elite. But our own revolution of modernity has led to the unprecedented vision of a society in which the opportunity for personal achievement and social power would be generally diffused among men, and not limited to a selected group.

And as its crowning symbol, it developed a radically new outlook on human destiny, which saw the meaning of history in terms of the progress of the human mind, and held that human history could be made to follow the direction that men chose to give it. Prometheus was the first modern. The revolution of modernity proposed to put men squarely on Prometheus' side. It is a unique venture in human affairs, and we can only relieve the strains and tensions it has created by taking it seriously. Our disappointments are real. But they are real because our powers are great and our expectations legitimately high.

ACKNOWLEDGMENTS

A writer's debts, other than his financial ones, are usually intangible, and I cannot name all those whose ideas or whose encouragement have helped in the writing of this book. My friends, Ernest Nagel, Herbert Deane, James Gutmann, Lyman Bryson, and Eric Larrabee, read the book in manuscript. Mr. Evan Thomas brought a hard head and a soft heart to the task of editorial supervision. Miss Josephine Bertelson and Mrs. Armon Glenn ingeniously deciphered my manuscript.

I am very grateful to the John Simon Guggenheim Memorial Foundation for the grant of a fellowship in 1953-54 which gave me the leisure for extended thinking and writing. I am also grateful to those responsible for the administration of the Fulbright program, both in the United States and France, for having given me the opportunity to spend a year in France as a visiting scholar. A grant from the Columbia University Council for Research in the Social Sciences aided me in defraying secretarial and bibliographical expenses.

My greatest debt is to my wife and children, who have borne the brunt of having a book written in their midst. My daughter has been a model of cheerfulness and tolerant sympathy, and my son spurred me on by asking me regularly, ball and glove in hand, whether I was getting finished. For this, and for much else, this book is dedicated to him. My wife has lived with this book as I have, and her taste, her sense of what is important, and, not least, her powers of endurance, are on every page.

Acknowledgment is due to the following publishers for permission to quote from books or articles: The Macmillan Company; Oxford University Press; Liveright Publishing Corporation; Dodd, Mead and Company; Sheed and Ward; Harcourt, Brace and Company; Putnam; Ernest Benn; Harper & Brothers; Alfred A. Knopf; Geoffrey Bles; University of Chicago Press; Princeton University Press; Charles Scribner's Sons; Columbia University Press; Houghton Mifflin Company; Yale University Press; Routledge and Kegan Paul; Cambridge University Press; *The Philosophical Review; The American Sociological Review.* Chapter VIII of this book first appeared, in slightly different form, in *The Antioch Review,* and I am grateful to the editors of this periodical for permission to use this material here.

C. F.

New City, New York
September 23, 1955

NOTES

Chapter I

p. 7: *"A philosophy of history . . . is a theory of how things get done in history, and of what men can make of their history."*

Philosophies of history have performed three main functions. In the first place, they have been essays in logic—attempts to determine what constitutes good evidence for our beliefs about human affairs. They have been concerned with questions like the following: whether an objective explanation of human events is possible, and what such an explanation would be like; how we can choose between competing interpretations of historical events; the role that value judgments play in the writing of history; the intellectual standards by which professional historians and ordinary men ought to rule themselves in coming to their judgments about human affairs. On this level, a philosophy of history is not an essay in writing history. It is *about* the writing of history. But even on this seemingly remote level, it has first-rate significance for practical decisions and social action. For the logic we employ in making our historical judgments is the same as the logic we employ in coming to decisions in everyday life; and our conception of what is or is not a rational historical idea affects the ideas we are prepared to entertain in actual social practice. No branch of logical inquiry comes closer than the logic of history to that area of human activity which is most important and least understood—the logic of practical judgment.

In the second place, philosophies of history have usually contained generalizations or theories which purport to explain what makes history go, how historical events are related to one another. Sometimes these theories have shown why all history has had to happen just as it has happened, and how it is moving inexorably in a definite direction and toward a single goal. Some-

213

times these theories have been more modest and more helpful. They have not treated history as a closed system or a closed book. Instead, they have picked out certain elements in the historical process—scientific institutions, for example, or property systems, or "great men"—and have tried to trace their relations with other elements in history, without suggesting that there are never any accidents in history or that there are no other factors to be taken into account in giving historical explanations. But in either case these generalizations about history have been ways, not simply of understanding the past, but of managing the present. They have laid down the great guidelines for the formulation of social programs. Finally, philosophies of history have been attempts to canvass in a thoroughgoing way the values and ideals that seem peculiarly durable and decisive in the long procession of human affairs. This is the level on which they speak of "the meaning of history," sometimes finding a cosmic guarantee that ensures the ultimate victory of this meaning, and sometimes offering a practical strategy by which men can give history this meaning if they choose.

Chapter II

p. 11:   "*. . . what America was doing or was capable of doing.*"
More than a century ago Tocqueville picked out this antihistorical element in the American mind, and noted how deeply rooted it was in the peculiar experience of a democratic society: "To evade the bondage of system and habit, of family maxims, class opinions, and, in some degree, of national prejudices; to accept tradition only as a means of information, and existing facts only as a lesson used in doing otherwise and doing better; to seek the reason of things for one's self, and in one's self alone; to tend to results without being bound to means, and to aim at the substance through the form—such are the principal characteristics of . . . the philosophical method of the Americans. . . . America is therefore one of the countries in the world where philosophy is least studied, and where the precepts of Descartes are best applied. . . . In the midst of the continual movement which agitates a democratic community the tie which unites one generation to another is relaxed or broken; every man readily loses the trace of the ideas of his forefathers or takes no care about them." (*Democracy in*

214

America, edited by Phillips Bradley, New York: Alfred A. Knopf, 1945, Vol. II, pp. 3-4.)

p. 19: *". . . arguments . . . among professional historians concerning the standards and values that should govern the writing of history."* For a brief account and estimate of these arguments, see the article by C. Vann Woodward, "American History," in *The Saturday Review*, April 4, 1953.

Chapter III

p. 26: *Quotation from Yeats.*
These lines are taken from "The Second Coming." (*The Collected Poems of W. B. Yeats*, New York: The Macmillan Company, 1945, p. 215.)

p. 27: *Liberal historians and liberal literary critics.*
See, for example, Arthur Schlesinger's *The Vital Center*, Lionel Trilling's *The Liberal Imagination*, and Leslie Fiedler's *An End to Innocence*.

p. 28: *"One of Ibsen's characters remarks . . ."*
The remark is made in *The League of Youth*.

p. 28: *The Eighteenth Proposition of Oxford Liberalism and the prospectus of the Rochdale pioneers.*
Quoted by G. M. Young in his *Victorian England: Portrait of an Age*, Oxford University Press, London: Humphrey Milford, 1936, p. 7.

p. 33: *". . . the gradual disintegration and devitalization of . . . independent groups under the impact of uncontrolled urbanization and industrial developments."*
Professor George H. Sabine has given a good summary account of the consequences of the disappearance of vigorous private associations. "The identification of society with mass, and of democracy with the action of individuals in the mass, is . . . a well-authenticated part of the mechanics of dictatorship. . . . It has been the formula for dictatorship of all sorts to destroy and regiment associations that had been created by the freedom to organize and that had the power to pursue a common interest by collective action. . . . A group of human beings associated according to a principle of unadulterated individualism is not a society but a rabble, and a society approaches such a condition only by being demoralized. . . . It can be ruled by a combination of force

and mass hysteria and indeed can be ruled in no other way. For its members, crowded into a structureless organization that is merely gregarious, are in effect isolated and powerless, and social isolation is incompatible not only with effective individual action but in the end with clear thinking or responsible judgment. Government tends to become a practice of applied psychiatry designed to produce rather than to cure neurosis. . . . It is of course not the case that results of this sort, when they occur, are caused by a perverse belief in a bad psychology or a doctrinaire theory of democracy. The producing conditions are objective and are unavoidable hazards that democracy under modern conditions has to meet. Organization both of industry and government on a vast scale with consequent centralization of power, urbanization and high mobility which identify residence merely with the tie of the job, the reduction of the family practically to its biological limit, and the fact that religious congregations have long ceased to be communities all tend to thin out the social medium and to increase the number of persons who in effect are socially isolated." ("The Two Democratic Traditions," *The Philosophical Review* [October, 1952], Vol. LXI, No. 4, pp. 467-68.)

p. 35: *Quotation from Mill.*
Autobiography, New York: Columbia University Press, 1924, p. 192. See also pages 157-59 in the same book. For further examples of the same point of view, see the attack on "innate ideas" with which Locke's *Essay Concerning Human Understanding* begins, John Dewey's *Human Nature and Conduct* and *Freedom and Culture,* and Bertrand Russell's *Unpopular Essays,* especially Chapter I.

p. 35: *Quotation from Mill.*
A System of Logic, Book VI, Chapter X, section 7.

p. 38: *Quotation from Hawthorne.*
From the preface to *The Marble Faun.*

p. 39: *Quotation from Hobhouse.*
World in Conflict, London: T. F. Unwin, 1915, p. 6.

p. 41: *Quotation from Henry James.*
Letter to A. C. Benson. Quoted by Lionel Trilling, *The Liberal Imagination,* Garden City: Doubleday Anchor Books, p. 67.

216

Chapter IV

p. 47: *Quotation from Chesterton.*
Orthodoxy, New York: Dodd, Mead and Company, 1908, p. 55.

p. 52: *Quotation from Maritain.*
Scholasticism and Politics, translated and edited by M. J. Adler, London: Geoffrey Bles, 1940, p. 8.

p. 52: *"Human nature 'as self-enclosed and self-sufficient.' "*
Scholasticism and Politics, p. 3.

p. 53: *" 'Man alone . . . works out his salvation.' "*
Scholasticism and Politics, pp. 6-7.

p. 71*n.*: *Quotation from Maritain.*
Man and the State, Chicago: University of Chicago Press, 1951, p. 110.

Chapter V

p. 75: *Maritain:* "*Positions . . . unlivable in practice. . . .*"
Scholasticism and Politics, p. 2.

p. 75: *Maritain:* "*The natural Platonism of the human mind.*"
True Humanism, translated by M. R. Adamson, London: Geoffrey Bles, 1946, p. 33.

p. 79: Maritain: "*Nineteenth century bourgeois democracy . . . without any common faith.*"
Man and the State, Chicago: University of Chicago Press, 1951, p. 110.

p. 79*n.*: *Quotation from Mannheim.*
Freedom, Power, and Democratic Planning, New York: Oxford University Press, 1950, pp. 286-87, 288-89.

p. 80: *Quotation from Chesterton.*
From "The Mad Hatter and the Sane Householder," *Vanity Fair,* January, 1921, p. 54. Quoted by Walter Lippmann, *Public Opinion,* Pelican Books, p. 16.
The distinguished medieval scholar, and the thinker who, with Professor Maritain, is the most eloquent spokesman for scholastic philosophy in the modern world, Etienne Gilson, has expressed Chesterton's idea in its more classic form: "What men call peace is never anything but a space between two wars: a precarious equilibrium that lasts as long as mutual fear prevents dissension from declaring itself. This parody of true peace, this armed fear,

which there is no need to denounce to our contemporaries, may very well support a kind of order, but never can it bring Mankind tranquillity. Not until the social order becomes the spontaneous expression of an interior peace in men's hearts shall we have tranquillity; were all men's minds in accord with themselves, all wills interiorly unified by love of the supreme good, then they would know the absence of internal dissension, unity, order from within, a peace, finally, made of the tranquillity born of this order: *pax est tranquillitatis ordinis*. But, if each were in accord with itself, all wills would be in mutual accord, each would find peace in willing what the others will. Then also we should have a true society, based on union in love of one and the same end." (*The Spirit of Medieval Philosophy*, London: Sheed and Ward, 1936, p. 399.)

p. 81: *Quotation from Frank O'Connor.*
From "Song Without Words" in *Crab Apple Jelly*, New York: Alfred A. Knopf, 1944, p. 42.

p. 83: "*. . . some system for the integration of ultimate values.*"
The notion that integration of "ultimate values" is indispensable in any society, and that this can only be done through a religious creed, is a recurrent theme in contemporary sociology. For example, it has been said: "The reason why religion is necessary is apparently to be found in the fact that human society achieves its unity primarily through the possession by its members of certain ultimate values and ends in common. . . . Even in a secularized society some system must exist for the integration of ultimate values. . . ." (Kingsley Davis and Wilbert E. Moore, "Some Principles of Stratification," *American Sociological Review*, April, 1945, pp. 244, 246.) For one example of the recent concern with "*anomie*" resulting from the lack of a common faith, see the work of Sebastian De Grazia; for a Marxist version of the same belief in the need for shared ultimate ends, see the later books of Harold Laski.

Chapter VI

p. 87: "*. . . Kierkegaard, Marx, Freud, and contemporary sociology.*"
Along with his colleague, Paul Tillich, Mr. Niebuhr is, in fact, the most representative spokesman on the American scene of Existentialism. The term "Existentialism" is frequently used to designate only Sartre's atheistic version of this philosophy, and

Mr. Niebuhr himself generally uses the term in this way. But Existentialism has its theistic versions as well, and no one writing in English has expressed the themes and the idiom of theistic Existentialism more powerfully than Mr. Niebuhr. The main ideas of his philosophy are the ideas of Existentialism; and he explicitly acknowledges his debt to the major thinkers in the Existentialist tradition. For example, he calls Kierkegaard, usually regarded as the father of Existentialism, "the greatest of Christian psychologists"; and he states that Heidegger, the leading German Existentialist, has given "the ablest non-theological analysis of human nature in modern times." (*The Nature and Destiny of Man,* New York: Charles Scribner's Sons, 1951, Vol. I, pp. 44, 161-62.)

p. 88: *Niebuhr: "to seek after an impossible victory and to adjust himself to an inevitable defeat."*
Reflections on the End of an Era, New York: Charles Scribner's Sons, 1934, p. 14.

p. 90: *" 'In history,' says Mr. Niebuhr, 'God always chooses . . .' "*
Faith and History, New York: Charles Scribner's Sons, 1951, p. 224.

p. 91: *" 'In one century,' Mr. Niebuhr observes, 'modern man had claimed to have achieved . . .' "*
Faith and History, p. 8.

p. 97n.: *" 'The freedom of the human agents of action,' writes Mr. Niebuhr . . ."*
Faith and History, p. 56.

p. 97: *". . . human behavior . . . breaks free from the laws of cause and effect."*
Mr. Niebuhr writes, for example: "A culture which is so strongly influenced by both scientific concepts and technocratic illusions is constantly tempted to annul or to obscure the unique individual. Schemes for the management of human nature usually involve denials of 'the dignity of man' by their neglect of the chief source of man's dignity, namely, his essential freedom and capacity for self-determination. . . . The realm of freedom which allows the individual to make his decision within, above and beyond the pressure of causal sequences is beyond the realm of scientific analysis. Furthermore the acknowledgement of its reality introduces an unpredictable and incalculable element into

the causal sequence. It is therefore embarrassing to any scientific scheme." (*The Irony of American History,* New York: Charles Scribner's Sons, 1952, p. 8.)

The argument that a belief in human freedom and creativity is incompatible with a belief in using scientific methods to study human behavior has been revived with increasing force of late. It lies behind the frequent assertion that naturalistic liberalism has really denied the reality of human freedom, and has been an unwitting philosophical prelude to authoritarianism. The late Russell Davenport, for example, wrote: "The fact that the free world must face—which by and large it has not faced—is that *if* the materialistic-naturalistic thesis is correct, *then the case for Communism is stronger than the case for the free way of life.* If man is the product of a combination of law and accident, his freedom can only be an illusion. . . ." (*The Dignity of Man,* New York: Harper and Brothers, 1955, pp. 151-52. The italics are Mr. Davenport's.)

p. 99*n.*: *Quotation from Kierkegaard.*

Quoted in *The Nature and Destiny of Man,* Vol. I, p. 163.

p. 101: *". . . the New Liberal and the New Conservative alike."*

Arthur Schlesinger, Jr., an active and effective political liberal, has written: "Why was progressivism not prepared for Hitler? The eighteenth century had exaggerated man's capacity to live by logic alone; the nineteenth century sanctified what remained of his non-logical impulses; and the result was the pervading belief in human perfectibility which has disarmed progressivism in too many of its encounters with actuality. . . . Today, finally and tardily, the skeptical insights are in process of restoration to the liberal mind. The psychology of Freud has renewed the intellectual's belief in the dark slumbering forces of the will. The theology of Barth and Niebuhr has given new power to the old and chastening truths of Christianity. More than anything else, the rise of Hitler and Stalin have revealed in terms no one can deny the awful reality of the human impulse toward aggrandizement and distinction—impulses for which the liberal intellectual had left no room in his philosophy. The conceptions of the intellectual are at last beginning to catch up with the instincts of the democratic politician. . . ." (*The Vital Center,* Boston: Houghton Mifflin Company, 1949, pp. 39-40, 165.)

p. 101: *Niebuhr: "Practically all schools of modern culture . . ."*
   The Irony of American History, p. 17.

p. 101: *Quotation from James Mill.*
   From Mill's *Essay on Government.*

p. 102: *Quotation from Helvetius.*
   Quoted by John Morley, *Diderot and the Encyclopedists,* London: The Macmillan Company, 1886, Vol. II, p. 153. This maxim profoundly impressed Jeremy Bentham.

p. 104: *Quotation from Condorcet.*
   Outline of the Progress of the Human Mind, Section X ("Tenth Epoch").

p.104n.: *"Mr. Niebuhr writes, 'Actually, human power . . . is both limited and limitless.'"*
   Faith and History, p. 71.

p. 105: *"a policy . . . of refusing to decide in advance that any given problem is beyond the power of human beings to solve."*
   No doubt, the idea of progress took an unpleasant turn in the nineteenth century. Progress came to be looked upon as something guaranteed—as an inevitable consequence of Evolution, or History, or the inexorable workings of a free market. And it was used to show, on a priori grounds, that certain problems, such as unemployment (which the early Victorians called "overpopulation") were, in fact, incurable, and should not be meddled with. But whatever we may think of this doctrine, it can hardly be called cheerful or optimistic. In fact, it goes back by direct line of descent to Malthus' attempt to refute Condorcet's belief in the perfectibility of mankind; and it represents, not a rejection of the idea of original sin, but the persistence of that idea in a secular form.

p. 106: *". . . the old tune of original sin."*
   David Riesman has remarked, "Fundamentally, I think the 'unrealistic' Godwin was correct who, in contrast to his great opponent Malthus, thought that we would someday be able to grow food for the world in a flowerpot. Technologically, we virtually have the flowerpots." (*The Lonely Crowd,* New Haven: Yale University Press, 1950, p. 35.)

p. 107: *". . . a new context for the assessment of human traits . . . involved in statements about 'the goodness of man.'"*
   In this connection, it is interesting to note that the same libera-

221

tion from the context of original sin could also be obtained by emphasizing the "evil" in man. The point of departure for Hobbes' theory of human nature, for example, is that there are no final goals or ends. Human life is a restless seeking for power after power, circumscribed by two dominating motives —the fear of sudden death and the love of glory. Hobbes emphasized that man is incurably "evil" in this way in order to show that something must be done to control his behavior here and now, and that it is irrelevant and misleading to invoke the ideal of salvation when one sets about thinking how to do so. Hobbes was not interested, as the classic doctrine of original sin was, in finding ways to redeem man from his evil inclinations; he took these inclinations, rather, as the permanent facts which necessitate political organization.

The example of Hobbes suggests that statements to the effect that "man is good" and other statements to the effect that "man is evil" may sometimes have the same *moral* content—namely, that human traits are initially neutral ethically, that their goodness or evil depends on their *consequences* in *secular* affairs, and that these consequences depend on the sort of social conditions in which human nature functions. The so-called "ambiguity" of human motivations, of which Mr. Niebuhr makes so much, thus becomes the potentiality for good *or* evil of any human trait, whether egoism or altruism, physical passion or religious feeling. And it is this secular and neutral context for evaluating human traits, fundamentally, which Mr. Niebuhr is attacking when he condemns the belief in the "goodness" of man, and includes the pessimistic Hobbes in his catalogue of thinkers who have visited naïve illusions about human nature on modern man.

Since the moral content of the phrase, "Man is naturally good," can be the same as that of the phrase, "Man is naturally evil," the question still remains as to the purpose of choosing one phrase rather than the other. A clue can be found, I think, by examining the practical circumstances under which the respective slogans are chosen, and the specific objectives of the philosophers concerned. In Hobbes' case, for example, the emphasis on the "evil" in man is a function of his essential social conservatism, his desire, in a time of civil war, to cut down the extreme hopes of men, and to expose the consequences and the duplicity of their fanaticisms. It was an attempt to save something from the wreckage, to keep things going on a minimum basis. And it was related as well to his belief in absolutism. In Locke's case, in contrast, a much gentler view of human nature is taken; and the circumstances are a successful and bloodless revolution, and a concern to cut down the claims of despotism.

p. 108: *"On Mr. Niebuhr's accounting . . . all turn out to have . . . essentially the same overestimate of the 'goodness of man.' "*
One representative example may illustrate how Mr. Niebuhr confuses two quite different things—the statement of a moral ideal and a factual description of human behavior. Mr. Niebuhr undertakes a full-dress review of modern theories of human nature in a chapter called "The Easy Conscience of Modern Man," in *The Nature and Destiny of Man*. In the course of this chapter, Mr. Niebuhr comes to the crucial case of David Hume. He quotes Hume as follows: "It is sufficient for our present purposes if it be allowed, what surely without the greatest absurdity cannot be disputed, that there is some benevolence, however small, infused into our bosom, some spark of friendship for humankind, some particle of the dove kneaded into our frame along with elements of the wolf and the serpent. Let these generous sentiments be supposed ever so weak . . . they must still direct the determinations of *our mind* and, where everything else is equal, produce a cool preference of what is useful and serviceable to mankind above what is pernicious. . . . Avarice, ambition, vanity and all passions vulgarly though improperly comprised under the denomination of self-love are here excluded from our theory concerning the origin of morals, not because they are too weak but because they have not a proper direction for that purpose." To this Mr. Niebuhr adds the observation, "Furthermore, Hume is quite complacent about the possibility of checking egotism through education. He thinks that though 'we are naturally partial to ourselves and to our friends we are capable of learning the advantages of a more equitable conduct.' " This is offered by Mr. Niebuhr as an example of "the belief that human virtue is guaranteed by the rational preference for the benevolent as against the egoistic impulses."
But, of course, Hume says no such thing. As the words Mr.

223

Niebuhr quotes make plain, Hume is not making any predictions about the eventual triumph of reason over passion, or benevolence over selfish motives. He takes great pains to emphasize that he is not engaged in weighing the influence on human behavior of generous sentiments as against ungenerous ones. He is merely talking about the origin and nature of morals, and he rules out "avarice, ambition, vanity," and the like, not because they are weak, but because they are not the defining characteristics of *moral* feelings as such. They may becloud moral judgments and they certainly affect human actions. But when a feeling is properly called a "moral feeling," it must also contain "a cool preference of what is useful and serviceable to mankind above what is pernicious." This is to define what it means to be moral. It is not to say that men ever will be perfectly moral, or that "human virtue is guaranteed by the rational preference for the benevolent as against the egoistic impulses."

p. 108: *". . . 'Progress' is not a synonym for the journey of the soul to God."*

There has been, to be sure, an apocalyptic element in many modern theories of history and politics. Interestingly enough, however, this element did not originate from the flat denial of original sin. On the whole, it came, rather, from transporting the categories and problems of sin and redemption into a secular context. The representative figure is Rousseau. Rousseau's view of human nature is the view of Pascal and Calvin and Saint Augustine. It is a philosophy which puts the classic religious emotions at the center of the stage—loneliness, the divided will, the sense of sin, the need for communion with other men, the desire for salvation from one's own willful self by submitting to a higher will that rules all men. In an important sense, Rousseau denied original sin. As Ernst Cassirer has said, he believed that "guilt belongs to this world, not to the world beyond," and that "we must therefore seek redemption solely in this world." But he was concerned with redemption from sin. And the result was that he made the problem of secular politics an essentially religious problem. He did not think of politics as the field in which men's conflicting interests are in one way or another regulated; he thought of politics as the field in which men are ultimately to be cured of private inter-

224

ests, and all conflicts of interest eliminated. Thus, he gave the State supreme function of making man moral, of saving him from sin. This is the idea of the State which has fed modern nationalism, and which lies behind the contemporary totalitarian dream that the State will one day wither away, provided we first give it the unchecked power to solve the problem of conflicting interests once and for all. It has influenced every modern political philosophy, though it has not been dominant in all of them; and it is one reason why the religious emotions of modern men and women have been channeled into political action, to the detriment of both religion and politics. But Rousseau is an equivocal figure, and not a distinctively liberal one. And if there is a messianic element in the tradition of Locke and Voltaire, the British utilitarians and the American pragmatists, it is not apparent to the naked eye. (For a fuller discussion of Rousseau's relation to the idea of original sin, see Ernst Cassirer, *The Philosophy of the Enlightenment,* Princeton: Princeton University Press, 1951, pp. 154-57. For a discussion of messianic elements in modern political thinking, see especially J. L. Talmon, *The Origins of Totalitarian Democracy,* London: Secker and Warburg, 1952.)

p.109n.: *"Mr. Schlesinger writes: 'It is a moderate pessimism . . .'"*
The Vital Center, pp. 169-70.

p. 111: *Quotation from Whitehead.*
Adventures of Ideas, Cambridge: University Press, 1947, p. 47.

p. 113: *Niebuhr: "the self which stands outside itself . . ."*
The Nature and Destiny of Man, Vol. I, p. 14.

Chapter VII

p. 117: *Quotation from George Orwell.*
"Looking Back on the Spanish War," from *Such, Such Were the Joys,* New York: Harcourt, Brace and Company, 1953, p. 141.

p. 122: *Quotation from G. M. Young.*
Victorian England, p. 186.

p. 126: *Mannheim: "what was once the intellectual armament of a party is transformed into a method of research . . ."*
Ideology and Utopia, New York: Harcourt, Brace and Company, 1951, p. 69.

225

p. 126: *Quotation from Yeats.*
These lines are taken from "The Second Coming."

p. 127: *Mannheim: "Only when we are . . . aware of the limited scope of every point of view . . ."*
Ideology and Utopia, p. 93.

p. 135: *"If something always has to be assumed . . ."*
Mannheim writes: "He who makes no decisions has no questions to raise and is not even able to formulate a tentative hypothesis which enables him to set a problem and to search history for its answer. . . . If empirical knowledge were not preceded by an ontology it would be entirely inconceivable. . . ." (*Ideology and Utopia,* p. 79.)

The idea that science or "empirical knowledge" rests on an antecedent "ontology" or "philosophy" is very widespread. Since words like "ontology" or "philosophy" are used by all sorts of people in all sorts of ways, this is an idea which is very hard to refute. But if it has any relevance to the question at issue, it means that the methods of empirical inquiry which are actually employed rest on certain prior assumptions which are not themselves subject to empirical test. And if this is the case, then there is a simple test of this view—namely, to list just one of these supposed assumptions. Consider one of the usual examples that is offered. It is sometimes said that the sciences rest on the "postulate" of the uniformity of nature. And once this is granted, all sorts of metaphysical rabbits begin to come out of the hat. The "fact" of the uniformity of nature is said to illustrate some cosmic design; or it is held to be a "presupposition" that requires some higher metaphysical justification; or it is exhibited happily as an act of "faith" which puts scientific inquiry on the same basis as any other creed. But it is difficult to see in just what way the sciences rest on this alleged postulate. They do not derive any conclusions from it in any recognizable sequence of premise and consequence. They do not even invoke it to disprove the existence of irregularities such as biological sports. They merely chart what limited uniformities they can find. The most that can be said about the principle of the uniformity of nature in relation to scientific inquiry is that it expresses the intention to seek uniformities, and not to take no for an answer. This plainly does not imply, however, that nature is under any contractual agreement to say yes. Those who say that "the uniformity of nature" is an assumption of science mistake its objectives for its presupposition.

Again, it is frequently alleged that the social sciences have accepted a world view taken over from the physical sciences, which regards the material, quantitative aspects of things as primarily real, and relegates to second-class citizenship in the universe all the familiar qualities and values of daily experience. This, indeed, is one of Mannheim's major claims. But the indictment is false on both its counts: the social sciences have not been exclusively influenced by this world view, and the physical sciences have no such view to begin with. As the example of Freud may suggest, the human sciences are by no means committed exclusively to quantitative techniques. And, in any case, such a world view is neither logically involved in the actual procedures of science, nor a legitimate deduction from the scientific enterprise. For it is difficult to see how science could logically classify the qualities of ordinary experience as a wholesale illusion since it must test the truth of its ideas by observations carried on in a world in which just such qualities abound.

p. 137: *". . . analogy from the field of visual perspectives."*
This is an analogy which Mannheim himself uses. The passage in which it occurs is illustrative of the confusions in his discussion of truth and objectivity. He writes: "When observers have different perspectives, 'objectivity' is attainable only in a more roundabout fashion [than when they have the same perspectives]. . . . The controversy concerning visually perceived objects (which, in the nature of the case, can be viewed only in perspective) is not settled by setting up a non-perspectivist view (which is impossible). It is settled rather by understanding, in the light of one's own positionally determined vision, why the object appeared differently to one in a different position. Likewise, in our field also [*i.e.,* the field of social ideas], objectivity is brought about by the translation of one perspective into the terms of another. It is natural that here we must ask which of the various points of view is the best. And for this too there is a criterion. As in the case of visual perspective, where certain

227

positions have the advantage of revealing the decisive features of the object, so here pre-eminence is given to that perspective which gives evidence of the greatest comprehensiveness and the greatest fruitfulness in dealing with empirical materials." (*Ideology and Utopia*, pp. 270-71.) But what does it mean to say that that perspective is best which reveals "the decisive features of the object"? The decisive features of the object is precisely the question over which disagreement has arisen. And why do we become more "objective" when we "translate one perspective into the terms of another"? This sounds more like a good definition of provincialism. Indeed, why should putting two perspectives together always give us more truth than we can get from one alone? A perspective that consists of two false views, instead of merely one, has not been improved. And when we take a perspective that is true, and combine it with one that is false, we are going backward, not forward.

p. 142: "*. . . science . . . the very symbol of our limitations . . .*"

From the very beginning, this emphasis on the parochially Western character of science has been a principal theme in the philosophies of history that have emerged out of the Sociology of Knowledge. It is expressed clearly and passionately by Max Scheler, one of the first leaders in this movement, and the man who actually coined the term *Wissenssoziologie*: "The crazy positivist idea that the evolution of all human knowledge has to be judged in terms of a small segment of the curve of modern Western cultural evolution must at long last be discarded. One must arrive at the insight, by means of a sociology of knowledge, that . . . Europe and Asia have tackled the possible tasks of human acquisition of knowledge from radically different directions. Europe was going from matter to the soul, Asia from the soul to matter." (Quoted by Paul Kecskemeti, in his Introduction to Karl Mannheim, *Essays on the Sociology of Knowledge*, London: Routledge and Kegan Paul, 1952, p. 17.)

p. 145: *Quotation from Freud.*

The Future of an Illusion, New York: Liveright Publishing Corporation, 1949, p. 93.

Chapter VIII

p. 148: "*Criticism . . . history . . . and science.*"

It should not be thought that criticism, history, and science are separate kinds of organized inquiry. They are aspects of all organized inquiry. Sensitivity to human values is indispensable to the study of history, the comparison of imagined alternatives is a regular part of systematic thinking, and the aesthetic affinity between mathematics and music has been noted since the time of Plato. Again, in any discipline, some acquaintance with its traditions is almost indispensable in understanding its ruling procedures and objectives; and knowledge of the historical circumstances in which a work of art or a scientific theory were developed stimulate critical awareness of the nature of the achievement involved. Finally, the framing of general principles is implicitly a part of criticism, which necessarily uses general terms and assesses the importance of things for one another, and of history, which must select significant events and indicate the connections among them.

p. 157: *". . . quantitative techniques permit us to make more minute and precise distinctions."*
Mathematics, however, is not exclusively quantitative. Topology, for example, though a branch of mathematics, is not quantitative.

Chapter IX

p. 171: *Toynbee: "The histories of . . . societies fall into successive chapters . . ."*
A Study of History, New York: Oxford University Press, 1951, 1954, Vol. I, p. 169.

p. 172: *Toynbee: "The real optimum challenge . . ."*
A Study of History, Vol. III, p. 119.

p. 173: *Toynbee: "The criterion of growth . . ."*
A Study of History, Vol. III, p. 216.

p. 173: *Toynbee: "Civilization is 'an audacious attempt to ascend from the level of Primitive Humanity . . .' "*
A Study of History, Vol. IV, p. 5.

p. 174: *Toynbee: "There is an overwhelming majority of ordinary people . . ."*
A Study of History, Vol. III, p. 243.

p. 179: *". . . its initiation into the communion of saints."*
When he comes to the higher religions, Mr. Toynbee writes:
" 'The relativity of historical thought' has now caught us out in our turn. . . . The single civilization, which . . . has worn the

appearance of a fully 'intelligible field of study', shrivels up, in its turn, into an unintelligible fragment of some far larger whole when we place ourselves at the standpoint, no longer of a national community, but of one of those churches in which the 'higher religions' embody themselves." (*A Study of History,* Vol. V, pp. 373-75.)

p. 179: *"Mr. Toynbee's ultimate message . . . the message of . . . Bishop Bossuet . . ."*

Mr. Toynbee writes, for example: "Instead of dealing with churches in terms of civilizations, as hitherto, we shall boldly make the new departure of dealing with civilizations in terms of churches. If we are looking for a social cancer, we shall find it, not in a church which supplants a civilization, but in a civilization which supplants a church."

(*A Study of History,* Vol. VII, p. 526.)

p. 180: *"Secular liberalism and democracy . . . revolts against 'the native genius' of the West."*

"From the modern West's own point of view," Mr. Toynbee writes, "its modernity had begun at the moment when Western Man had thanked, not God, but himself that he was as different a being from his 'medieval' predecessor as the Pharisee claimed to be from the publican in the parable." (*A Study of History,* Vol. VIII, p. 114.)

p. 182: *Toynbee: "The superlative physical challenges . . . to Venice and Holland . . ."*

A Study of History, Vol. II, pp. 263-64.

p. 183: *Quotation from Samuel Johnson.*

Quoted by Joseph Wood Krutch, *Samuel Johnson,* New York: Henry Holt and Company, 1944, pp. 23-24.

p. 184: *" 'Creation spells agony,' says Mr. Toynbee . . ."*

A Study of History, Vol. VII, p. 568.

p. 184: *". . . the conditions for making saints."*

"The goal of human endeavours," writes Mr. Toynbee, ". . . will only be attained when the whole of Society has come to consist of individuals of the new species which is represented by the Saints alone in human history up to date." (*A Study of History,* Vol. III, p. 373.)

p.186n.: *Toynbee: "The technique of iron-working . . ."*

A Study of History, Vol. III, p. 173.

p. 188: *"Renaissance architecture . . . an aesthetic failure . . ."*

According to Mr. Toynbee, Brunelleschi's Duomo—the Cathedral of Santa Maria del Fiore in Florence—is the first step in the growing "sterility with which the Western genius had been afflicted by the renaissance of Hellenism in the domain of Architecture. . . . At the time of writing, it looked as if, in all three visual arts, the sterilization of a native Western genius by an exotic Hellenizing renaissance might eventually be overcome; but the slowness and the difficulty of the cure showed how serious the damage had been." (*A Study of History,* Vol. IX, p. 85.)

p. 190: *". . . when we speak of a society 'as a whole' . . . we cannot possibly mean . . . that everything in it is connected to everything else."*

Mr. Toynbee in fact seems to hold a theory which in technical philosophical terms is called "the doctrine of internal relations." (See his discussion of the nature of "societies," for example, in Vol. III, pp. 223 ff.) In saying that a society is an "indivisible whole," he means, that is to say, that no single trait of a given society can be defined or understood apart from its relation to everything else in the society. Strictly speaking, this involves an ultimate logical absurdity which makes nonsense of any attempt to find general laws that apply to the rise and fall of all societies. For the making of a comparison or generalization between two or more things always involves the *selection* from these things of certain traits which they possess in common. But if, by hypothesis, the wholes from which these traits are abstracted are different, then, on Mr. Toynbee's logic, so must the traits be different: for they are "indivisible" from the whole, and are different from anything that is not part of the same whole. But then no comparison or generalization would be possible, and there are no general laws of the rise and fall of civilizations. This may seem to take Mr. Toynbee too literally; but there is at least some point in seeing that he is not to be taken literally.

p. 192: *"Mr. Toynbee has been looking for laws that lay down an inexorable direction . . ."*

I have not dwelt on the historical evidence which Mr. Toynbee adduces in support of his system because I have wanted to examine the basic logic of that system. Such an examination

231

suggests that no matter how voluminous his evidence, it would not support the conclusions he wishes to draw from it. But it should be said that while Mr. Toynbee's learning is immense, it is by no means infallible. And while he repeatedly claims that all his results are the products of "an empirical method of inquiry," his conception of such a method is an extraordinary one. I have space to give only one or two representative and important examples.

In explaining the rise of the modern West, Mr. Toynbee gives major credit to two "creative minorities"—the Italian cities of the *quattrocento,* and Great Britain during the seventeenth and eighteenth centuries. In accordance with the pattern of "Withdrawal-and-Return" through which, as Mr. Toynbee argues, all creative minorities must pass, he states that the creative contributions of these two groups of communities came out of periods during which they were isolated from the main body of Western civilization, the Italian cities behind their mountains, the British across their channel. But to take the case of Britain alone, "isolation" seems a very strange term to apply to a period during which the British contemplated forming a joint commonwealth with the Dutch, then engaged in commercial competition and naval warfare with that nation, seized Gibraltar, moved into Malta, and chose a King and Queen from the Continent to place on the throne of their own country. And did the centuries of *le roi soleil* and the *philosophes* in France, which by no stretch of the imagination can be called "isolated" or "withdrawn," make no creative contribution to the shape of Western civilization? Indeed, in Mr. Toynbee's own terms, it is difficult to see what he means by referring to the Italian city-states and the Britain of the Glorious Revolution as *creative* minorities. The contribution of the first, by Mr. Toynbee's own reckoning, is the sovereign-state system; the contribution of the second is parliamentary institutions and civil toleration on a secular basis. Both of these look like the efforts of dominant minorities to shore up a dying civilization. (For a fuller discussion of these and other points, and a general evaluation of Mr. Toynbee's performance as an empirical historian, see P. Geyl, "Toynbee's System of Civilizations," *Journal of the History of Ideas* [January, 1948], Vol. IX, No. 1.)

In appraising the historical evidence which Mr. Toynbee offers for his system, furthermore, attention must be paid to his remarkable use of language, including some of his own key terms. There are few books in history so rich in image and metaphor as Mr. Toynbee's. These images and metaphors bring a steady freshness and excitement to his study, are full of psychological and social insights, and frequently suggest connections between things that have been hitherto unsuspected. But Mr. Toynbee's words also stretch and bend unpredictably, and all his basic ideas are stated in a systematically vague way which makes it possible for him to prove almost anything he pleases. A notable example is found in Mr. Toynbee's attempt to prove the idea that all creative individuals go through a pattern of "Withdrawal-and-Return." To support this thesis, Mr. Toynbee offers an extraordinarily varied list of "creative individuals": Saint Paul, Saint Benedict, Saint Gregory the Great, Gautama Buddha, Kind David, Solon, Julius Caesar, Leo Syrus, Mohammed, Peter the Great, Lenin, Garibaldi, Hindenburg, Thucydides, Xenophon, Polybius, Josephus, ibn-Khaldun, Machiavelli, Clarendon, Émile Ollivier, Confucius, Kant, Dante, and Hamlet. But to begin with, despite the length of the list, there are certain conspicuous omissions: Garibaldi is there, but not Lincoln; Confucius is mentioned, but not Aristotle; Kant, but neither Newton nor Hume. And even forgetting the apparently negative instances that have not been mentioned, what has been included is curious. We have one fictional character, Hamlet, whose career has been given its shape by a dramatist for dramatic purposes. Here Mr. Toynbee admittedly employs a fictional figure merely for purposes of illustration. But this fades off imperceptibly into something else when he recounts the story of King David. For Mr. Toynbee treats David's career entirely in terms of the epic account of David contained in the Old Testament; and he presents this biography as though it rested on the same kind of materials as the biography of Peter the Great or Lenin. This method of writing history recurs again and again in Mr. Toynbee's *Study*. It is never plain whether Mr. Toynbee is using poetry and myth legitimately to *illustrate* his ideas or illegitimately to *prove* them. For whatever literature and myth may

233

prove, they certainly do not prove that the events they depict really took place. This is a simple idea. But it is not profundity to obscure it.

But consider Mr. Toynbee's list of "creative individuals" still more closely. He mentions eight historians—all of them men, as he sees it, who have "withdrawn" from the field of practical action to "return" on a higher spiritual level as historians. Mr. Toynbee summarizes their careers as follows: "On a comparative view, these eight lives fall into three groups. In five of them . . . the *motif* appears in a simple form. The break which cuts short the chapter of 'practical' action concludes it once and for all, and the chapter of literary activity fills the rest of the life to the end. In two other lives . . . the pattern is more complicated. Instead of there being only one break, there are two or three; and the periods of 'practical' and literary activity are interwoven in a series of alternate chapters. Finally, there is the life . . . in which a single short period of literary activity is followed, as well as preceded, by a long period of immersion in 'practical' affairs—the posterior period of 'practical' activity lasting . . . right down to . . . death." (Vol. III, p. 290.) In more direct terms, however, this merely seems to say that sometimes men withdraw on one level and return on a higher level; that sometimes they withdraw and then return to the same old low level; and that sometimes they just commute between jobs. But the mystery thickens when we compare Mr. Toynbee's stories of Peter the Great (who "withdrew" from Russia for an eighteen-month period of travel in Western Europe), Kant (who never left Königsberg, but whose thought "radiated . . . to the ends of the Earth"), Saint Paul (who had a spiritual conversion on the road to Damascus), and Hindenburg (who returned from retirement for old age to lead the German armies, and then returned from a second retirement to be President of the Weimer Republic). In the light of these and other biographies offered by Mr. Toynbee, his idea of Withdrawal-and-Return covers spiritual conversions and simple changes of occupation; forced exile and retirement for old age; men whose character and purposes have merely been intensified (Peter the Great), men whose character and purposes have been radically changed (Saint Paul), and men whose character and purposes have never substantially changed at all (Kant). What begins as a meaningful idea with a limited application ends as a meaningless idea with an unlimited application. Mr. Toynbee dilutes the idea of Wtihdrawal-and-Return—the genuine spiritual agony through which some of mankind's leaders have gone—into a turn of phrase that covers everything from the idea that travel is broadening to the workings of a pension system. In the end, there is only one trait which all the various figures whom Mr. Toynbee cites as exemplars of Withdrawal-and-Return have in common. This is that as reasonably active human beings, they have their ups and downs in life.

One final example will suggest that this effort by Mr. Toynbee to preserve the symmetry and all-inclusiveness of his system not only rests on using words with deliberate imprecision, but also leads to the failure to interpret historical events in appropriate terms. This example is offered by Mr. Toynbee's attempt to show that the idea of an "External Proletariat" applies even to the present situation of Western civilization. This is a peculiarly decisive question, because if there is no External Proletariat in the contemporary world it would indicate that some of the laws Mr. Toynbee finds in history are now outmoded, and that new elements can enter which change the character of historical processes. Mr. Toynbee's claim that all specimens of civilization, past and present, are "philosophically contemporaneous" would collapse.

Mr. Toynbee raises this question himself. And he answers with a rhetorical question. Who were the barbarians, he asks, in the Italian Fascist attack on Ethiopia? "If we are to pass beyond the baldly technical sense of the word 'barbarian', and to use it in its deeper moral connotation," he answers, then we must say it was the Fascists. And he goes on to quote Dean Inge: "Ancient civilizations were destroyed by imported barbarians; we breed our own." In short, as a proof that his system still holds, and that we have an *External* Proletariat today, Mr. Toynbee points to the birth, *within* Western society, of the Fascist Black Shirts and Nazi Storm Troopers. But "the baldly technical sense of the word 'barbarian'," which Mr. Toynbee so easily dismisses, is Mr. Toynbee's own technical use of the

235

term. What is the point of maintaining a category which, by its author's own admission, does not apply? The consequence is only to hide the novel character of a most significant modern phenomenon—the organization and recruitment of the lumpenproletariat and a déclassé bourgeoisie into an armed mob within a society.

In connection with Mr. Toynbee's specific historical interpretations, the reader should consult Herbert J. Muller's brilliant *The Uses of the Past* (New York: Oxford University Press, 1952), which gives alternative interpretations of some of the same materials as those covered by Mr. Toynbee.

p. 195: *Toynbee: "We have convinced ourselves that the destruction ..."*
A Study of History, Vol. V, p. 334.

Chapter X

p. 199: *"Gone are the days when madness was confined ..."*
Martyn Skinner, *Letters to Malaya,* I and II, London: Putnam, 1941, p. 34.

p. 205: *Liberalism's tendencies "to neglect the importance ... of secondary associations ... and to take a primarily legalistic and political view of power ..."*
For illuminating brief accounts of the historical origins of these tendencies, see R. R. Palmer's essay, "Man and Citizens: Applications of Individualism in the French Revolution," in *Essays in Political Theory,* edited by M. R. Konvitz and A. E. Murphy, Ithaca: Cornell University Press, 1948; and see also George H. Sabine's article, "The Two Democratic Traditions" cited above.

p. 206: *Quotation from Montaigne.*
Essays, Book I, Chapter 4, "That the soul discharges her passions upon false objects, where the true are wanting."

INDEX

Anomie, 83, 218
Aristotle, 161
Arnold, Matthew, 181
Authority, foundations of 30-33, 49-54, 60-66, 69-71, 78-84, 108-9

Barth, Karl, 220
Beard, Charles, 128 n.
Benda, Julien, 25
Bentham, Jeremy, 43, 221
Bergson, Henri, 193
Bossuet, J. B., 17, 179, 193, 230
Brunelleschi, 231
Bruno, 154
Burke, Edmund, 37 n., 43

Calvin, 87, 224
Cassirer, Ernst, 224, 225
"Challenge-and-Response," 169-74, 181-84
Chesterton, G. K., 47-48, 80, 82, 217
Communism, 27, 32, 39, 40-41, 53, 61, 92, 180
Comte, Auguste, 21, 111
Condorcet, 7, 36, 37, 102-6, 147, 221
Conservatives, New, 85, 220

Copernicus, 154
"Creative Minorities," 174-76, 232-35
Criticism, relation to history and science, 148-50, 162-63, 228-29

Darwin, 24, 132
Davenport, Russell, 220
Davis, Kingsley, 218
Descartes, 151, 155
Dewey, John, 36, 43, 71, 216
Diderot, 102
"Dominant Minorities," 174-76, 177-78, 232
Dostoevsky, 43, 85-86

Enlightenment, the
  Greek, 209
  in 18th century, 24, 43, 102, 106, 124, 141, 143, 159
Erasmus, 18
"Etherealization," 173
Existentialism, 218-19
"External Proletariat," 175, 178, 235

"Failure of nerve," 25 ff.
Fascism, 27, 32, 39, 53, 57 n., 92, 180, 235-36

237

Fiedler, Leslie, 215
Ford, Henry, 10
Freedom
  and determinism, 95-99
  and science, 153-58
  and secondary associations, 30-33, 205, 215-16
Freud, 55, 87, 119, 123, 129, 132, 144-45, 220, 228

Galbraith, J. K., 30
Geyl, P., 232
Gibbon, Edward, 8, 36, 165, 168, 193
Gilson, Etienne, 217-18
Godwin, William, 221
Grazia, S. de, 218

Hawthorne, Nathaniel, 38, 216
Hegel, 9, 118
Heidegger, J. J., 43, 219
Helvetius, 102, 107
Hemingway, Ernest, 113
Herodotus, 150
Historicism, 118-19, 146
History,
  accident in, 191-92, 194-95
  American attitude toward, 10-11, 214
  in the 18th century, 159
  in the 19th century, 20-22
  law in, 95-99, 131-33, 191-92
  objectivity in, 117-45
  philosophy of, 6-7, 9-22, 213-14
  role of theory in, 158-62
Hitler, 27, 120, 195
Hobbes, 25, 30, 101, 108, 221-23
Hobhouse, L. T., 39, 216

Hume, 55, 56, 108, 223-24
Huxley, Aldous, 139

Ibsen, 28, 215
Ideologists, the, 124-25
Ideology, 124-26, Chapter VII passim
Inge, W. R., 235
Intellectuals, role of, 128, 140-41
"Intelligible field of historical study," 166-69, 184-92
"Internal Proletariat," 175, 178

James, Henry, 41, 216
James, William, 94
Jefferson, 109
Jeremiah, 86
Jesuits, 111
Johnson, Samuel, 183

Kafka, 113
Kant, 156
Kierkegaard, 43, 87, 99 n.

Laski, Harold, 218
Liberals, New, 85, 101, 220
Lincoln, 195
Locke, 29, 30, 43, 101-2, 108, 216, 223
Lucretius, 72

Malthus, 132, 221
Mannheim, Karl, 5, 79 n., 117-45, 146, 153, 194, 217, 225-28
Maritain, Jacques, 5, 47-84, 91, 117, 146, 193, 217-18
Marx, 15, 21, 25, 29, 55, 87, 119, 125-26, 165

INDEX

Marxism, 11, 13, 119, 120, 121, 218

Mathematics, social role of, 157-58

Mauldin, Bill, 7

Mill, James, 30, 101

Mill, John Stuart, 7, 21, 25, 35, 43, 44, 94, 147, 216

Modernity, 1-2, 181, 197-209, 230

Molière, 129, 131-32

Montaigne, 206, 236

Moore, W. E., 218

Muller, H. J., 236

Mussolini, 57 n.

Napoleon, 125

Newton, 132

Niebuhr, Reinhold, 5, 16, 85-116, 117, 128 n., 138, 146, 193-94, 218-25

Nineteen Eighty-Four, 113

Northrop, F. S. C., 16, 142

Objectivity, scientific, 136-43

O'Connor, Frank, 81, 218

Orwell, George, 117, 225

Oxford Liberalism, 28

Paine, Tom, 111

Palmer, R. R., 236

Pascal, 224

Perfectibility of mankind, 102-6

Philosophic Radicals, 110

Philosophy, American attitude toward, 9-10

Plato, 63, 76, 78, 140, 155, 187 n.

"Platonism, natural," 75-77

Protagoras, 53

Quakers, 111

Rashomon, 123-24

Relativism,
 cultural, 16-19
 historical, 117-45
 philosophical, 54-56

Renaissance, 188, 231

Riesman, David, 221

Rochdale Pioneers, 28

Rousseau, 94, 102, 108, 224-25

Russell, Bertrand, 9, 30, 33, 36, 102, 216

Sabine, G. H., 215-16, 236

Saint Augustine, 15, 19, 25, 87, 94, 165, 193, 224

Saint Paul, 93-4

Saroyan, William, 113

Sartre, J.-P., 218

Scheler, Max, 120, 228

Schlesinger, Arthur, Jr., 109 n., 215, 220, 225

Science,
 and the liberal philosophy of history, 4, 34-37, 122, 142-44
 metaphysical foundations of, 135, 142-43, 226-27
 natural history of, 151, 153-58
 social origins of, 132-33

Secondary associations, 30-33, 205, 215-16

Shakespeare, 98

Shaw, G. B., 115-16

Sin, original, 85-116

Skinner, Martyn, 199, 236

"Social Contract," the, 31

Social Integration, 78-84, 188-92

239

Sociology of Knowledge, 117-45, 225-28
Socrates, 64
Sorokin, Pitirim, 16, 142
Spencer, Herbert, 15, 21
Spinoza, 66
Stalin, 21

Talmon, J. L., 225
Technics,
  and human progress, 186 n.-87 n.
Technology,
  and science, 151, 154, 156
  contemporary role of, 197-200
Thucydides, 20, 150
Tillich, Paul, 218
"Time of Troubles," 11, 176-77
Tocqueville, 214-15
Toynbee, Arnold, 5, 12, 16, 164-95, 229-36

"Treason of the clerks," 25
Trilling, Lionel, 215

"Universal Church," 178-79
"Universal State," 176-77

Veblen, Thorstein, 119
Voltaire, 7, 17-18, 29, 33, 36, 44, 102, 165, 193

Waste Land, The, 113
Weber, Max, 120, 121
Wellington, Duke of, 125 n.
Whitehead, A. N., 111, 225
"Withdrawal-and-Return," 232-35
Woodward, C. Vann, 215
Woolman, John, 111

Yeats, W. B., 26, 126, 215, 226
Young, G. M., 122, 160, 215, 225

Set in Linotype Times Roman
Format by Marguerite Swanton
Manufactured by The Haddon Craftsmen, Inc.
Published by HARPER & BROTHERS, *New York*